THE WORLD OF ASTROLOGY

AN ETHNOGRAPHY OF ASTROLOGY
IN CONTEMPORARY BRAZIL

THE WORLD OF ASTROLOGY

AN ETHNOGRAPHY OF ASTROLOGY
IN CONTEMPORARY BRAZIL

by

Luís Rodolfo Vilhena

Translated from the Portuguese by Graham Douglas

SCP

SOPHIA CENTRE PRESS

© Sophia Centre Press 2014

Originally published in Portuguese as *O Mundo da Astrologia*: *estudo antropologico*, by Jorge Zahar Editor, Rio de Janeiro, 1990.

First published in English in 2014.

Sophia Centre Press
University of Wales, Trinity Saint David
Ceredigion, Wales SA48 7AD, United Kingdom
www.sophiacentrepress.com

ISBN 978-1-907767-04-3

British Library Cataloguing in Publication Data.
A catalogue card for this book is available from the British Library.

Printed and bound by Lightning Source.

NATAL

A God is born. Others die. The truth
neither came nor went: Error changed.
We have now another Eternity,
And it was always better what happened.

Blind, Science works the useless field.
Mad, Faith lives the dream of its worship.
A new God is only a word.
Neither search nor believe: everything is occult.

FERNANDO PESSOA

For Sueli and Luiz Paulo, my parents,
Cleonice and Rodolfo my grandparents,
and Eduardo, my brother.
For Ana,
and in memory of Nilda, my grandmother.

ACKNOWLEDGEMENTS

This book, and likewise the master's dissertation which preceded it, would not have been possible without the presence of Gilberto Velho (1945–2012), who did me the honour of taking it on as my guide and, more importantly, as a friend. Maintaining a rare combination of rigour and tolerance, always respecting my independence, he had a decisive role in the research, from the choice of subject to the invitation to publish it. I am grateful for the opportunity to participate in the research project which he coordinated, during which I was also able to discuss aspects of my work with Hermano Vianna, Jr and Miriam Lins de Barros, who contributed greatly to the development of my ideas.

I thank the Postgraduate Programme in Social Anthropology, as represented by its coordinators, its teachers, secretarial staff and library. I also cannot forget the interest that various professors and colleagues showed in listening to my hypotheses and exchanging ideas.

I am grateful to all my informants who, besides obviously making the work possible, also made it more enjoyable.

I am grateful also for the indispensable financial resources of the CNPq and of CAPES, in the form of student grants, as much as FINEP and the Ford Foundation, in their support of the research described above.

I would also like to thank the three people close to me who formed a true 'team', without whom I would not have completed this work in the time allotted. Firstly, I was able to count on the infinite patience and companionship of Ana, in dealing with my 'scribbles' and support of my work during our living together. I also had the kind encouragement of my grandmother Cleonice, who reviewed and commented on the text, and the goodwill of Sandra Vilhaça, with her 'technical support' and her 'sayings' during the editing. To them all, [I give] my gratitude.

Finally, I am grateful for the attentive and generous comments of Professors Gilberto Velho, Luiz Fernando Dias Duarte and Otávio Velho, who examined the original version of this work. I have tried to take their comments into account as far as possible in the preparation of the present version.

TABLE OF CONTENTS

LIST OF FIGURES

TRANSLATOR'S PREFACE:
LUÍS VILHENA AND THE WORLD OF ASTROLOGY

by Graham Douglas

I came across this book *O Mundo da Astrologia* in a bookshop in Lisbon and was immediately impressed by its level of scholarship and the way it utilised anthropological thinking to address the practice of astrology in a modern context. At the time of its publication it was unique, although the *Radical Astrology Papers* (RAP) had been published in 1983, and sociologist Denise Newton had written about organised UK astrology in 1981.[1] But neither of them conducted the detailed sociological investigation which Vilhena completed for his MSc dissertation at the Universidad Federal de Rio de Janeiro, under the supervision of Gilberto Velho (1945–2012). Vilhena's study does have one thing in common with the RAP, which is the use of semiotics and structural anthropology, via the writings of Lévi-Strauss in particular.

Since 1990 there have been several PhD theses at European and US universities dealing with astrological practice, including those by Alie Bird, Kirsten Munk, Bridget Costello, Bernadette Brady, and Nicholas Campion.[2] Each of these studies adopts anthropological and cultural tools of analysis and considers the practices of western

---

[1] Martin Budd, Patrick Curry, Graham Douglas, and Bernie Jaye, eds., *Radical Astrology Papers*, (London: RAP Group, 1983); Denise Newton, 'A Sociologist examines Contemporary Organised Astrology', *Astrology Quarterly* 55, part 4, and 56, part 1 (1981).

[2] Alison Bird, 'Astrology in Education: an Ethnography' (PhD Thesis, University of Sussex, 2006); Kirsten Munk, 'Signs of the Times: Cosmology and Ritual Practice in Modern Western Astrology', (PhD Thesis, Dept. Of Philosophy, Education and Religion, University of Southern Denmark, (2006), available at http://bisboastrology.com/wp-content/uploads/2013/02/Signs-of-the-Times-Phd-Kirstine-Munk.pdf; Bridget Costello, 'Astrology in Action: Culture and Status in Unsettled Lives', PhD Thesis, University of Pennsylvania, 2006; Bernadette Brady, 'Theories of Fate among Present-Day Astrologers' (PhD Thesis, University of Wales, Trinity Saint David, 2011); Nicholas Campion, 'Prophecy, Cosmology and the New Age Movement: the extent and nature of contemporary belief in astrology' (PhD Thesis, Bath Spa University/University of the West of England, 2004), republished as *Astrology and Popular Religion in the Modern West* (Farnham: Ashgate, 2012).

astrology, based on interviews with astrologers and students of astrology. Lindsay Radermacher approaches the subject from a religious and psychological viewpoint.[3] Astrology is also considered as a cultural phenomenon by Willis and Curry.[4]

I will try to contextualise Vilhena's work by contrasting the way he and these later writers employ or avoid some key themes. Strict comparison is not possible because much has since been published which was not available to Vilhena, and of course the scope offered by an MSc dissertation is more limited than a PhD. It must also be recognised, as Costello does, that today we still have only a partial picture of who practices astrology and what they do with it;[5] there is plenty of ground left for investigation.

Vilhena places his work in relation to other studies of the urban middle classes in Brazil. He begins by asking 'to what extent does astrology contribute to the lifestyles and world views of these classes', but acknowledges a shift during the work. Thus his desire to 'identify experiences [of his interviewees] that were sufficiently meaningful to constitute symbolic boundaries' becomes more closely linked to his investigation of their lifestyles. He and Radermacher view their interviewees' experience of astrology as giving them a new vocabulary and a way of synthesising their life experiences. It is interesting to compare this with the question which Munk sets herself to answer: 'In which ways do people in the modern Western world experience astrology as a meaningful practice?'[6]

As Campion points out in his chapter dealing with the topic there are very few published interviews with astrologers.[7] The Radical Astrology Group recorded interviews with several UK astrologers and with Michel Gauquelin in 1988 but a publisher could not be found at that time and the recordings were donated to the Astrological Association library. A decade later, some of the same interviewees contributed to *Astrology in the Year Zero*, edited by Garry Phillipson, which remains a definitive sourcebook.[8] Vilhena's discussions with astrologers were less numerous than with students (four out of twenty-three), but revealed similar concerns; some were

---

[3] Lindsay Radermacher, 'The Role of Dialogue in Astrological Divination' (MPhil Thesis in Theology and Religious Studies, University of Kent, 2011).

[4] Roy Willis and Patrick Curry, *Astrology, Science and Culture: Drawing Down the Moon* (Oxford: Berg, 2004).

[5] Costello, 'Astrology in Action', p. 16.

[6] Munk, 'Signs of the Times', p. 3.

[7] Campion, *Astrology*, p. 186.

[8] Garry Phillipson, *Astrology in the Year Zero* (London: Flare, 2000).

self-taught others professionally trained. Like their students their affiliations to astrology, religion and eastern therapies were liable to fluctuate.

PENSÉE SAUVAGE

Vilhena, Bird and Munk draw on the work of the early authors Durkheim and Mauss, but in different ways. Bird and Munk refer to these authors for their theorising of magic, while Vilhena is unique in using their analysis developed in *Primitive Classification* as a tool for examining the structure of the symbolic language of planets, signs and houses.[9] This is an interest he shares with Martin Budd in his essay published in the *Radical Astrology Papers*.[10] Vilhena also follows Lévi-Strauss in refusing the idea that concrete thinking, or *Pensée Sauvage*, is in any way inferior or merely represents an early stage of human intellectual development. He uses Lévi-Strauss's contrast between scientific and pre-scientific thinking to theorise the working of astrological symbolism, and to show the eclecticism of astrology and astrologers. This acceptance of 'primitive' thought is common to all the subsequent writers, including Willis.[11] Interestingly Vilhena cites Lévy-Bruhl, whose work has for a long time been criticised by anthropologists for demeaning 'primitive thought', but which is recently becoming viewed more positively, as Willis points out.[12]

For Vilhena, *pensée sauvage* is a way of classifying the world through its concrete sense impressions, rather than abstract categories imposed from a pre-developed theory as in scientific thinking. In the introduction to RAP, Budd refers to Lévi-Strauss's concept of *bricolage* and points out that astrological systems have often developed historically through borrowing bits and pieces from different sources, pieces which can be assembled in different ways by different schools.[13] Budd writes as an astrologer, so his analytical approach is aimed at making astrological practice more self-critical. He observes a tendency among astrologers to always seek analogies, which he regards as 'careless thinking'. Vilhena gives the example of the attributes assigned to the outer planets by astrologers, after they were discovered, to illustrate the way that

---

[9] Émile Durkheim and Marcel Mauss, 'Algumas Formas Primitivas de Classificação', in *Ensaios de Sociologia*, ed. Marcel Mauss, (São Paulo: Perspectiva, 1981).

[10] Martin Budd, 'Introduction' to *Radical Astrology Papers*, eds. Budd, Curry, Douglas and Jaye.

[11] Willis and Curry, *Astrology, Science and Culture*.

[12] Willis and Curry, *Astrology, Science and Culture*, pp. 114–15.

[13] Budd, 'Introduction', p. 2.

the astrological symbol system is capable of retaining coherence while also being able to adapt to circumstances in an *ad hoc* manner. Since astrology does retain a 'grammatical' structure it might be better viewed as a symbolic *Creole,* rather than bricolage.

Vilhena notes five distinct structures relating the zodiac signs, including the sequence around the year, which is rarely treated in detail by astrologers (Sampson is an exception).[14] In using Lévi-Strauss's structural analysis and viewing the zodiac both synchronically and diachronically, he avoids the over-reliance on the four elements which seems to be characteristic of Jungian psychological astrology. It is worth mentioning that although Lévi-Strauss was often critical of Jung's approach to myth it is probable that he was also influenced by him (see d'Aquili and Gray for interesting discussions).[15] On the other hand Lévi-Strauss remarked in an interview that "astrology was Structuralist before the term was invented".[16] Citing this, Carvalho commented that it was 'an interesting way for the anthropologist from the *Musee de l'Homme* to place himself at the summit of the millennial evolution of human knowledge'![17]

HUMANISM

Martin Budd is interested in the possibilities offered by astrology to go beyond the naive Humanist view of the person as a conscious individual.[18] He refers to the tradition of Critical Theory which drew on both Marx and Freud to challenge the view that human beings are independent creative centres of action, as if there were neither unconscious psychological processes nor economic and political forces at work. Here he touches on what Vilhena's interviewees often saw in astrology: a means to escape the manipulations they attributed to modern behaviourist society, and a path of self-

---

[14] Walter Sampson, *The Zodiac: A Life Epitome* (London: The Blackfriars Press, 1928; re-published by Whitefish, MT: Kessinger Publishing, 2003).

[15] Eugene D'Aquili, 'The Influence of Jung on the Work of Levi-Strauss', *Journal of the History of Ideas* 11 (1975): pp. 41–46; Richard Gray, 'Jung and Levi-Strauss Revisited: An Analysis of Common Themes', *The Mankind Quarterly* 31, no. 3, (Spring 1991): available at: http://home.comcast.net/~richardmgray/jungandlevistrauss.htm

[16] Claude Lévi-Strauss, interviewed by astrologers André Barbault and Jean-Pierre Nicola in *L'Astrologue* 9 (1970): pp: 1–6.

[17] Olavo de Carvalho, *Astros e Símbolos* (São Paulo: Nova Stella, 1985), p. 25.

[18] Budd, 'Introduction', p. 5.

development free from the rigid practices of psychoanalysis. In this, however, they are probably closer in feeling to those like Curry who see a danger, in that critiques of humanism can lead to dehumanisation.[19] Again Vilhena's concerns are different: he is collecting data on the opinions and practices of astrologers and their students, not attempting to evaluate them as examples of good or bad astrological practice.

SCIENCE, SYMBOLS AND SIGNS

Budd and Bird both refer to Foucault's concept of *epistèmes* in order to examine the ways that the situation of astrology has changed since the sixteenth century, when it was accepted both by the ordinary people and the intellectual elite—if not always by the church.[20] According to Foucault the sixteenth-century epistème was based on a belief that knowledge was written into the fabric of the world and the problem was to decipher it. The principle of correspondence between the inner and stellar worlds was a given, and astrology was not separate from medicine, alchemy, or theology. In Vilhena's analysis he discusses these issues by referring to Bachelard, mainly to contrast the material sense of astrological symbols with the arbitrariness of conventional signs and the abstractness of theory in the physical sciences.[21] It is interesting that Vilhena quotes Bachelard's description of the four elements as 'the hormones of the imagination', because work by the psychologist Cloninger has identified at least three such brain chemicals which correlate with personality dimensions: serotonin, dopamine and oxytocin. The first two could be metaphorically expressed as Saturn and Jupiter, respectively, and are antagonistic even at the molecular level, while oxytocin, with its links to interpersonal bonding and the mother-child relation, could be happily symbolised by Venus.[22]

---

[19] Patrick Curry, 'An Aporia for Astrology', in *Radical Astrology Papers*, eds. Budd, Curry, Douglas and Jaye.

[20] Martin Budd, 'Astrology, History, Foucault', in *Radical Astrology Papers*, eds. Budd, Curry, Douglas and Jaye, Chapter 2, p. 5; Bird, 'Astrology in Education', p. 259.

[21] Gaston Bachelard, *La Poetique de l'Espace* (Paris: PUF, 1957); *La Poétique de la Rêverie* (Paris: PUF, 1961); *La Philosophie du Nom: Essai d'une philosophiew du nouvel Esprit Scientifique*, (Paris: PUF, 1960).

[22] Graham Douglas, 'Comment on Ertel (2007): hopeful findings unduly neglected'. *Australian Journal of Parapsychology* 7, no. 1 (2010): pp. 72–76; Robert C. Cloninger, 'The genetic structure of personality and learning: A phylogenetic model', *Clinical Genetics* 46 (1994): pp: 124–37.

Since the 1990s there has been a good deal of discussion among UK astrologers of the philosophical issues problematising chart interpretation; Budd and Geoffrey Cornelius, for example, both employ hermeneutics as an analytic approach. It is arguable that hermeneutic traditions existed in medieval times, especially in biblical interpretation, so this is an example of the way that interpretation in many disciplines draws on varied epistèmes.

The authors of RAP devote a lot of space to discussions of semiotics, as does Vilhena, an approach to astrology which none of the other theses have considered. Lévi-Strauss of course was influenced by Saussurean semiology as was the Structuralist movement as a whole. Vilhena also refers to the structuralist theorist Tzvetan Todorov who distinguished a variety of different traditions of interpretation in medieval times, including hermeneutics.[23] Cornelius has referred explicitly to the medieval theory of four levels of interpretation, as has Radermacher; I have drawn on the work of Northrop Frye—who identified a correspondence between the four seasons and the major styles of literature—to suggest how the circle of four elements is an enduring structure even in modern social science and management theory.[24]

Several thesis authors found astrologers to have ambiguous attitudes towards scientific thinking, which seems to offer them the possibility of gaining respectability but only at the price of applying statistical research to their work. Vilhena notes that the topic of statistical investigations did not emerge in conversations with his subjects.[25] Another facet of this ambiguity is revealed by Vilhena's informants. While some viewed astrology as a discipline which is free of the constraints of modern scientific thinking, others saw astrology as a 'New Age' science which will eventually be recognised as superior to what is accepted today.

Bird interacted with students and teachers of astrology in the UK during their courses and reported a tendency to avoid describing their work by the term 'divination', as they preferred to emphasise its scientific or rational basis. But she also noted that in different contexts these same astrologers emphasised the contingent, context-specific nature of their work. Differences like these draw attention to the way

---

[23] Tzvetan Todorov, *Theories of the Symbol* (Cornell: University Press, 1984).

[24] Geoffrey Cornelius, *The Moment of Astrology: Origins in Divination* (London: Arkana, 1994); Radermacher, 'Dialogue in Astrological Divination'; Northrop Frye, *Anatomy of Criticism: Four Essays* (Princeton NJ: Princeton University Press, 1957); Graham Douglas 'Catastrophes in Semantic Space: Signs of Universality', *Semiotica* 132, part 3/4 (2000): pp. 249–63.

[25] Luís Vilhena, *World of Astrology*, p.158, fn. 67.

that social environment, culture, history and also the self-image of the practitioner can affect the way they describe themselves. Vilhena's work therefore both provides useful data on the world of astrology in middle-class Rio de Janeiro, and also underlines the importance of considering a variety of sociological and cultural factors in research, as Munk has also done.

A negative view of modern science is also shared by some recent academic writers, who see an analogy between monotheistic religion and the totalising project of modern science. This is contrasted to astrology's natural connection with polytheism, and the world views of phenomenology and hermeneutics.[26] Curry says that cultural researchers must participate in what they study in order to understand it and acknowledge their own vulnerability as participating subjects, not pose as superior ambassadors of 'real science'.[27] Among the thesis authors, Radermacher has gone the furthest towards this, observing her own sessions as a professional astrologer, but without any consideration of social context.

DIVINATION

One area that has seen a lot of academic attention since Vilhena was writing is divination.[28] It figures extensively in Munk's and Radermacher's theses as well as in the books by Cornelius, and Curry and Willis.[29] Each of these subsequent authors focuses on astrological divination as a way for its practitioners and their clients to re-negotiate their reality and their future. This view is quite compatible with Vilhena's understanding derived from his interviews, although he did not have these sources to reference.

---

[26] Willis and Curry, *Astrology, Science and Culture*; Patrick Curry, 'Astrology: From Pagan to Postmodern?', *The Astrological Journal* 36, no. 1 (1994); Cornelius, *The Moment of Astrology*; see especially chapters 13 and 14.

[27] Patrick Curry, 'Epilogue: The Historiography of Astrology—a Diagnosis and a Prescription', in *Horoscopes and History*, eds. Kocku von Stuckrad, G. Oestmann and Darrel Rutkin (Berlin and New York: Walter de Gruyter, 2005), pp. 261–74.

[28] Philip M. Peek, ed., *African Divination Systems: Ways of Knowing* (Bloomington, IN: Indiana University Press, 1991); Patrick Curry, ed., *Divination: Perspectives for a New Millenium* (Farnham: Ashgate, 2010).

[29] Cornelius, *The Moment of Astrology*; Willis and Curry, *Astrology, Science and Culture*.

Divination is described by Munk as a process in which the astrologer and their client are imaginatively engaged in creating new meanings and identities.[30] She places divination in relation to literature and aesthetic appreciation, saying that the active participation of the 'reader' is required and notes, in common with Vilhena, that the process begun during a consultation often continues to incorporate itself into the narrative of the client's life.[31] Bird quotes Appadurai to point out that imagination is an essential part of postmodern society, 'a collective tool for the transformation of the real and for the creation of multiple horizons of possibility'.[32] All of this is consistent with Vilhena's account, but with the benefit of a foundation in more recent sociology. Vilhena, from his semiological perspective, contrasts the 'Classical' with the 'Romantic' aspects of the astrological system, the former a classification and the latter more expressive and improvised. The same contrast is echoed by Munk when she says that 'Astrologers are better understood as ritualists than as proto-scientists, and they aim not at describing the world in empirically falsifiable terms, but rather at creating a divinatory session conducive to empowerment and transformation'.[33] She goes on to say that divination of all kinds always articulates the existing cosmology of the society, which again is consistent with Vilhena's investigation of astrology's language and structure as used in practical interpretation.[34]

The concept of Fate is something that does not appear explicitly in Vilhena's book, although his interviewees are frequently concerned to say that they are not interested in prediction, or don't believe that it is possible. As discussed below, they value astrology as a route to personal liberation, whether from Catholicism, psychoanalysis or scientific determinism. Fate comes into the question of belief, to which Vilhena devotes more time. The fluidity of astrological thinking is illustrated by Vilhena, citing the way that his informants will refer to their own sun-sign characteristics to explain why they do or don't feel that astrology can offer predictions: using one kind of determinism to accept or reject another.[35]

---

[30] Munk, 'Signs of the Times', p. 287.

[31] Munk, 'Signs of the Times', p. 287; Munk, 'Signs of the Times', p. 16; Vilhena, *World of Astrology*, p. 141.

[32] Bird, 'Astrology in Education', p. 263; Arjun Appadurai, 'The Right to Participate in the Work of the Imagination', interview by Arjen Mulder in *Transurbanism*, eds. Joke Brouwer and Arjen Mulder (Rotterdam: NAi Publishers, 2002), p. 6.

[33] Munk, 'Signs of the Times', p. 284.

[34] Munk, 'Signs of the Times', pp. 7, 15.

[35] Vilhena, *World of Astrology*, p. 83.

Brady has devoted her whole PhD Thesis to the views of fate held by contemporary astrologers. She shows that fate and determinism are conceived among ordinary people more flexibly than by the various schools of philosophy, so that what is viewed deterministically in one context changes in another, especially when moral factors come into play that require free will and responsibility.[36] She finds that astrologers accept the reality revealed through knowledge of their birth charts as a framework within which they are free to make choices.[37] Vilhena uncovers an identical attitude in his informants who said that it was first necessary to 'take on' their birth chart in order to be free of deterministic constraints: self-knowledge leads to freedom, which is also a core assumption of most psychotherapy.[38] Brady uses the term *kairos* to indicate the importance of the quality of time which astrologers see represented by a planetary configuration, rather than an event predictable with clockwork accuracy.[39] The same point of view was frequently expressed by Vilhena's informants. Curry also draws attention to the moral dimension, when he says that the central question in all divination is not 'What will happen?', but 'What should I do?'[40]

THE SOCIOLOGY OF THE WORLD OF ASTROLOGY

Some thesis authors are concerned with different intellectual levels within modern astrology, so Bird distinguishes taught astrology in the UK as *real*, contrasting it with 'merely derivative' and 'uninformed' astrology 'adapted for mass consumption'.[41] Vilhena refers to a similar distinction by the French writer Edgar Morin, but rejects Morin's overall view of astrology as something pathological. Vilhena's sociological critique is unique in two ways. He attends to a difference between 'created' and 'consumed' astrology using concepts derived from sociological writings by Simmel and Gans, and also views the world of astrology as a network of social relations in which astrology is produced, distributed and consumed, as part of a circulation of 'symbolic

---

[36] Brady, 'Theories of Fate', p. 2.
[37] Brady, 'Theories of Fate', pp. 14, 289.
[38] Brady, 'Theories of Fate', pp. 113–14.
[39] Brady, 'Theories of Fate', p. 277.
[40] Willis and Curry, *Astrology, Science and Culture*, p. 57.
[41] Bird, 'Astrology in Education', p. 2.

goods'.[42] Here he borrows from Becker's study of the world of art and Bourdieu's analysis of cultural capital. The world of astrology creates sub-groups based on allegiance to different techniques and different authorities. In Vilhena's words:

> Being a classificatory structure which can be combined with different values, the zodiacal system and the language associated with it also play a part in organising the world of astrology. It is by the differential distribution of this language that I hope to explain the relations between the astrology of the masses and the erudite variety, without mechanically linking them to the structure of the surrounding society.[43]

It is worth noting here that Vilhena's interviewees were not simply of the average middle class but came from a privileged stratum, living in the rich Rio neighbourhoods of Ipanema and Leblon. Many of them had graduated from university but had chosen not to pursue a professional career. Brazil is one of the most unequal societies in the world, with tens of thousands in Rio living in crime-ridden *favelas* within sight of the most chic neighbourhoods. The interviewees' quests for personal liberation are often circumscribed by their economic privilege, and in fact Vilhena cites a study of the Brazilian 'counterculture' by Gilberto Velho, where the better-off rebels disparagingly referred to their less fortunate colleagues as 'museum hippies'.[44]

MODERNISM AND ITS DISCONTENTS

In the writings of Simmel and Gans modernity is characterised by fragmentation and crisis, so the practice of astrology can be viewed both as a feature of modernity and also as a resource through which Vilhena's informants seek to integrate and make sense of their life experiences, by resisting fragmentation. Somewhat similar conclusions were drawn by Campion.[45]

In discussing the symbolic language of astrology, Vilhena refers to an opposition between a particularising and a generalising pole. This contrasts two major functions

---

[42] Georg Simmel, *The Sociology of Georg Simmel* (New York: The Free Press, 1954); Herbert Gans, *Popular Culture and High Culture: an Analysis and Evaluation of Taste* (New York: Basic Books, 1974).

[43] Vilhena, *World of Astrology*, p. 104.

[44] Gilberto Velho, 'Nobres e Anjos: um estudia de toxicos e hierarquia' (PhD Thesis, University of Sao Paulo, 1975), pp. 143–48.

[45] Campion, *Astrology and Popular Religion*, pp. 215–16.

that he says astrology can fulfil: a way of delineating a unique individual character for the person, while at the same time situating them in relation to the super-terrestrial world represented by the planets and the zodiac. Campion comments similarly, referring to different sources.[46]

Vilhena's informants were from the middle class, those whom Simmel saw as most affected by the conflict and complexity of modern life, but astrology is not viewed simplistically as a 'safe haven' to which to retreat.[47] Instead, Vilhena sees astrology as offering a language of re-individuation, and re-creation of what society no longer offers them.[48] Through the richness of its psychological language, astrology overcomes the chaos in society by linking the inner processes of the individual to something larger than society: the cosmos.

He offers an interesting observation when he says that his informants frequently avoided talking about their belief in astrology, preferring instead to say that their approach was coloured by certain features in their own charts.[49] This is an example of the way that astrological language expands the practitioners' vocabulary for talking about their concerns. Likewise the polysemy of astrological symbols offers a way of integrating a life in which the individual takes part in multiple and often conflicting discourses and value systems. Thus for example, Mars combined with Saturn can signify determination, upset, or struggle in personal life, at work, or politically.

Munk concludes that the divinatory aspect of astrology meets peoples' need in postmodern society to keep re-adjusting their outlooks and even their identities, to a world of insecure work and intersecting and inconsistent value systems. In Denmark, she identifies the interest in astrology among educated, urban, middle-class people, mostly women—but increasingly men as well—as being consistent with their especially changing and fragmented social environment.[50]

The same topic is a focus for Costello who attends to astrology as a cosmology which is well adapted to people experiencing chronic social *unsettledness*, due to their inferior or marginal social roles.[51] This response to a lack of power applies especially to women, who also do more of the social and emotional work in society. Astrology can

---

[46] Campion, *Astrology and Popular Religion*, p. 212.
[47] Vilhena, *World of Astrology*, p. 183.
[48] Vilhena, *World of Astrology*, p. 73.
[49] Vilhena, *World of Astrology*, p. 84.
[50] Munk, 'Signs of the Times', pp. 284–88.
[51] Costello, 'Astrology in Action', pp. 170–93.

be used to negotiate their own futures, to counsel friends, and to interpret the behaviour of others. She also compares the different involvements of men and women, which Vilhena was not able to do from his data. Munk also noted a difference in astrological practice depending on class and education, so that an educated professional feels able to actively negotiate their future, while someone lower down the hierarchy experiences astrology more as a way of adapting, coping with, and understanding others.[52]

This leads to the central interest for Vilhena's informants, and probably for most astrologers and their clients: self-development, which concerns especially astrology's relationships with religion and psychotherapy.

ASTROLOGY AND PSYCHOTHERAPY

Vilhena's informants frequently distanced themselves from media astrology, which they saw as superficial and manipulative, a contrast also taken up in Bird's work.

Vilhena's interviewees were all aware of astrology as a means of self-development, but they distinguished it sharply from psychoanalysis, which they saw as constricting the client, through its imposition of a therapeutic model, and exploitative in demanding adherence to the person of the therapist for months or years. This contrast did not concern Campion's subjects, and probably reflects the fact that psychoanalysis became firmly rooted decades ago in affluent areas of both Brazil and Argentina. The same is true of New York and London, but Brazil only emerged from a military dictatorship in 1989, so a pluralist multi-cultural society was not allowed to flourish in Rio as it has in cities like New York or London. It also reflects the fact that Vilhena's informants came from wealthy middle-class backgrounds where psychoanalysis was part of their world.

Since Vilhena's work Radermacher, a professional astrologer, has considered the process of an astrological consultation in detail, in her thesis with a context of psychotherapy and religious studies.

Curry argues that astrological divination is a way of negotiating, not predicting the future.[53]

---

[52] Munk, 'Signs of the Times', p. 292.
[53] Curry, 'Pagan to Postmodern', and Curry, *Divination: Perspectives*, pp. 85–118.

ASTROLOGY AND RELIGION

Most of Vilhena's subjects saw a religious, or more accurately a spiritual, dimension to their use of astrology, while at the same time being attracted to it because it represented a freedom from the oppressive Catholicism they had experienced at home and at school. It is interesting to compare this with the findings reported by Campion when he questioned astrologers in many countries about their beliefs.[54] In common with the US and many European countries, except Serbia where Orthodox Christianity is stronger, astrologers reported that they had moved away from the religion of their upbringing; their adult affiliations were often 60% 'spiritual but non-aligned' (SNA), compared to under 20% conventional Christian. In Brazil and Argentina Campion also asked astrologers about their affiliations to SNA, both during their upbringing and as adults. The shift is very clear: from 9–14% in upbringing to over 60% as adults while the corresponding figures for Catholicism (which are much higher than in Europe or the US) fell from over 60% to 17–8% as adults. This quantifies what Vilhena found, but it is interesting that some of his interviewees espoused Orthodox Christianity after leaving Roman Catholicism because it offered *more traditional* rituals. Although Vilhena did not quantify his work with questionnaires his conversations allowed more freedom for his interviewees to bring up issues of their choice. This example shows how the attractions of astrology as an escape from modernity can lead people in different directions: either towards an eclectic modern astrology backed by Jungian psychology, or else towards loyalty to a Tradition in which religion is not felt to have been corrupted by modernity. As Campion also found, there was more reaction against institutional religion than against religion in general. Munk describes astrology as religion 'in terms of its content', but is careful to distinguish it from orthodoxy.[55] Costello too observed a dislike of conservative religion but not of religion in general among her informants in Pennsylvania.

For many of Vilhena's informants religion only became of interest as a result of their astrological studies, when they began to ponder deeper questions about the cosmos. In Brazil there are many more choices available to seekers of knowledge and meaning, due to the prominence of the African-derived cults of *Makumba* and *Umbanda*, and the Spiritism of Alain Kardec, as well as a huge variety of evangelical Christian churches.

---

[54] Campion, *Astrology and Popular Religion*, pp. 167–86.
[55] Munk, 'Signs of the Times', p. 5.

PURE AND PRAGMATIC ASTROLOGY

Vilhena's interviewees were often concerned with a contrast which seems to relate to the greater influence of esoteric astrologers in Brazil, especially the French occultist René Guénon. They were divided into the majority who saw astrology as a means of self-development and self-therapy, often quoting Jung and Jungian astrologers as their inspiration, and those who believed in a strict astrological discipline with faithful adherence to the *Tradition*. So within the field of astrological practices there are the majority who are comfortable with borrowing pragmatically from whatever tradition appeals to them in their quest for self-development, as well as being in opposition to science and psychoanalysis. The smaller group share the common distaste with the modern world, but adhere to a 'pure' tradition they see as providing a refuge from the modern 'marketplace' of therapies and self-development systems. Vilhena notes the claim that Theosophy became influential in Brazil due to German students of the subject who settled there after the Second World War.[56]

Vilhena and several other thesis authors point out that Alan Leo and Dane Rudhyar, who were responsible for the revival of astrology in the twentieth century were heavily influenced by occultism and esoteric doctrines. However, explicitly esoteric traditions are only followed by a minority of astrologers, while the popular person-centred astrology seems to rest on vaguer and less disciplined kinds of self-development linked to person-centred counselling.

BELIEF

Belief is an issue which comes up in every one of these theses and many other articles, because it sits astride two meanings: 'belief *in'*, or faith, and 'belief *that'* referring to objective facts. Vilhena and Campion both devote a good deal of space to the semantic range of the word in their different languages, while other writers describe the anxieties that astrologers feel about the question and the frequent conclusion that what works in astrology is what counts, it doesn't matter if you believe in it.

Bird refers to Wilfred Cantwell Smith's attempts to recover the Old English senses of the word, contending that belief was, in earlier times, rendered as what we would

---

[56] Vilhena, *World of Astrology*, pp. 164–65.

now call 'beloving', 'holding dear' or 'cherishing'.[57] She suggests that this interpretation fits naturally with the way that astrological thinking continues a tradition from the time when science and religion were not separated.

This is an area where practically everyone surveys the same ground and draws a similar map, so there is no need to discuss it further here.

FUTURE WORLDS OF ASTROLOGY

The multifaceted nature of astrological language, which both Bird and Vilhena identify, could serve as a cue to consider in more detail the existence of *multiple astrologies*, another theme which was discussed in detail in the *Radical Astrology Papers*, this time by Patrick Curry, and which he later took up in a different form.[58]

Since the title of Vilhena's book is The *World* of Astrology, it is only to be expected that there will be different cultures and practices within it. The factionalism which Vilhena and Bird noted suggests that many astrologers might usefully be viewed as belonging to what Mary Douglas identified as Small Group environments, in her Grid–Group Theory.[59] Small groups are described as high on social intimacy (Group +), and low on hierarchy and separation of roles (Grid -), and typically lack objective criteria to classify and structure their beliefs about the world; this leads to an uncritical tolerance (in theory) for all varieties of practice, but a ruthless rejection of those who deny a few basic truths. In practice the accompanying instability of interpretation frequently leads to emotional disputes.

There is now a significant amount of anthropological work relating cognitive styles, and importantly, cosmologies as well, to variations in social environments; this was systematised by Mary Douglas under the name Grid-Group theory and developed in a wide variety of settings in a later collection of essays.[60] More recently Fiske proposed

---

[57] Bird, 'Astrology in Education', p. 252; Wilfred Cantwell Smith, *Believing: an Historical Perspective* (Oxford: Oneworld Publications, 1998); first published as *Belief and History* (Charlottesville: University of Virginia Press, 1977).

[58] Curry, 'Aporia' and *Horoscopes and History*.

[59] Mary Douglas, *Natural Symbols* (Harmondsworth: Penguin, 1970); Mary Douglas, *Cultural Bias*, Occasional Paper, No. 35 (London: Royal Anthropological Institute, 1978).

[60] Mary Douglas, *Natural Symbols* and *Cultural Bias* and *Essays in the Sociology of Perception* (London: Routledge and Kegan Paul, 1982).

an alternative analysis more closely related to cognitive styles.[61] I have drawn on their work in several publications about astrology.[62]

Curry suggested five rough dimensions on which to contrast different varieties of astrology: radical/conservative; social marginality; elitist/populist; philosophically materialist/idealist; explicit/implicit rules of interpretation.[63]

The cosmological derivatives of Douglas's four types of social environments cover a wide dimensional range, of which the most relevant to astrological varieties are perhaps, Time, Space, Nature/Culture, medicine and health, and personal relations. Curry's suggestions regarding marginality, elitism, and radicality, can easily be found among the features of the four social environments, while the explicit/implicit social codes of Basil Bernstein were used by Mary Douglas in the development of the dimensions themselves.[64]

There is no space to discuss it here, but it also becomes apparent how the four social environments carry echoes of the traditional four elements of astrology, as I have developed elsewhere.[65] Olavo de Carvalho, a traditional esotericist, draws attention to the work of the French anthropologist Gilbert Durand, who has suggested that many analytical frameworks used in contemporary social sciences are fragments of a whole that can be found in traditional esoteric thought.[66] And Cloninger's work mentioned above suggests a new interpretation of Bachelard's 'Hormones of the Imagination'.

The ancient language comes full circle and re-appears in the dimensions of modern social and psychological classification: an adaptability which might explain its resilience across the centuries and imply the persistence of a World of Astrology into the future.

---

[61] Alan Fiske, *Structures of Social Life: the Four Elementary forms of Human Relations* (New York: Free Press, 1991).

[62] Graham Douglas, *Structuralism and the Four Humours*, (London: published by the author, 1981; revised as *Physics, Astrology and Semiotics*, 1983); Graham Douglas, 'Color-Term connotations, Planetary Personalities and Greimas's Semiotic Square', *Semiotica* 115, part 3/4 (1997): pp. 263–87.

[63] Curry, 'Aporia'.

[64] Mary Douglas, *Natural Symbols* and *Cultural Bias*.

[65] Graham Douglas, *Structuralism and the Four Humours* and 'Catastrophes in Semantic Space'.

[66] Carvalho, *Astros e Símbolos*, p. 86; Gilbert Durand, *Sciences de l'Homme et Tradition* (Paris: Tête de Feuilles–Sirac, 1979).

ABOUT LUÍS RODOLFO VILHENA

The author died in an accident in 1997 at the age of 33. *O Mundo da Astrologia* was based on his Master's thesis at the Federal University of Rio de Janeiro. An influential book describing the work of his Doctoral thesis on the history of the Brazilian Folklorist movement, *Projeto e Missao: O Movimento Folklorico Brasileiro 1947–64* was published posthumously and reviewed by Elizabeth Travassos in 1998. More biographical information can be found (in Portuguese) at: http://luisrodolfovilhena.googlepages.com/home

It is interesting that in this second book he was again focusing on the situation of a movement and a study (folklorism) which found itself excluded and dismissed by conventional science. In this case the sociologists, influenced by European and American traditions, rejected folklore studies as amateurish and unworthy of consideration as a science, at a crucial time in the intellectual history of Brazil and before the military coup of 1964. The folklorists insisted on the validity of data collected by amateurs engaged in the transmission, as well as study, of local folkloric traditions, and untrained in social-scientific methods.

TRANSLATOR'S ACKNOWLEDGEMENTS

We are grateful to Dona Cleonice Berardinelli, the author's grandmother and the copyright holder, for permission to translate Luís Vilhena's book and thus extend his legacy into the English-speaking world. I am grateful to Nick Campion for providing me with the opportunity to make this work available to an English audience. I also thank Sueli da Paixao Vilhena for arranging for the English language copyright to be transferred. Marcia Butchart has coped with my lack of editing skills with exemplary patience. This new edition of Vilhena's work has been completely re-set, with an index and an elegant cover design thanks to the skills of Jennifer Zahrt.

I am pleased to thank my Brazilian friends Abigail Sobral and Valeride de Jesus for help with understanding some words which cannot be found in any dictionary.

TRANSLATOR'S REFERENCES

D'Aquili, Eugene. 'The Influence of Jung on the Work of Levi-Strauss'. *Journal of the History of Ideas* 11 (1975): pp. 41–46.

Appadurai, Arjun. 'The Right to Participate in the Work of the Imagination'. Interview by Arjen Mulder. In *Transurbanism*, eds. Joke Brouwer and Arjen Mulder. Rotterdam: RAi Publishers, 2003. doi: 07/2006 http://www.appadurai.com/pdf/transurbanism.pdf.

Arroyo, Stephen. *Astrology, Karma and Transformation: the inner dimensions of the birthchart.* Davis CA: CRCS, 1978.

Bachelard, Gaston. *La Poetique de l'Espace.* Paris: PUF, 1957.

———. *La Poétique de la Rêverie.* Paris: PUF, 1961.

———. *The Psychoanalysis of Fire.* Translated by Alan C.M. Ross. Boston MA: Beacon Press, 1984.

———. *La Philosophie du Non: Essai d'une philosophie du nouvel Esprit Scientifique.* Paris: PUF, 1960.

Bird, Alison Gwendy. 'Astrology in Education: an Ethnography'. PhD Thesis, University of Sussex, 2006.

Brady, Bernadette. 'Theories of Fate among Present-Day Astrologers'. PhD Thesis, University of Wales, Trinity Saint David, 2011.

Budd, Martin. 'Introduction'. In *Radical Astrology Papers* , edited by Martin Budd, Patrick Curry, Graham Douglas and Bernie Jaye. London: RAP Group, 1983.

Budd, Martin, Patrick Curry, Graham J. Douglas and Bernie Jaye, eds. *Radical Astrology Papers.* London: RAP Group, 1983.

Campion, Nicholas. *Astrology and Popular Religion in the Modern West.* Farnham: Ashgate, 2012.

Cloninger, Robert C., 'The genetic structure of personality and learning: A phylogenetic model'. *Clinical Genetics* 46 (1994): pp. 124–37.

Cornelius, Geoffrey. *The Moment of Astrology: Origins in Divination.* London: Arkana, 1994.

Costello, Bridget McKenny. 'Astrology in Action: Culture and Status in Unsettled Lives'. PhD Thesis, University of Pennsylvania, 2006.

Curry, Patrick . *Astrology, Science and Society.* London: Boydell, 1977.

———. 'An Aporia for Astrology'. In *Radical Astrology Papers,* edited by Martin Budd, Patrick Curry, Graham Douglas and Bernie Jaye, Chapter 5. London: RAP Group, 1983.

———. 'Astrology: From Pagan to Postmodern?' *The Astrological Journal* 36, no. 1 (1994).

———. 'Epilogue: The Historiography of Astrology: A Diagnosis and a Prescription'. In *Horoscopes and History,* edited by Kocku von Stuckrad, G. Oestmann and David Rutkin, pp. 261–74. Berlin and New York: Walter de Gruyter, 2005.

———, ed. *Divination: Perspectives for the New Millenium.* Farnham: Ashgate, 2010.

Douglas, Graham. *Structuralism and the Four Humours.* London: published by the author, 1981. Revised as *Physics, Astrology and Semiotics,* 1983.

————. 'Meaning, Movement and Materials'. *Athanor* 1, part 1 (1990): pp. 59–64.

————. 'Greimas's Semiotic Square and Greek and Roman Astrology'. *Semiotica* 114, part 1/2 (1997): pp. 1–19.

————. 'Color-Term connotations, Planetary Personalities and Greimas's Semiotic Square.' *Semiotica* 115, part 3/4 (1997): pp. 263–87.

————. 'Catastrophes in Semantic Space: Signs of Universality'. *Semiotica* 132, part 3/4 (2000): pp. 179–280.

————. 'Comment on Ertel (2007): hopeful findings unduly neglected'. *Australian Journal of Parapsychology* 7, no. 1 (2010): pp. 72–76.

Douglas, Mary. *Natural Symbols*. Harmondsworth: Penguin, 1970.

————. *Cultural Bias*, Occasional Paper No. 35. London: Royal Antropological Institute, 1978.

————, ed. *Essays in the Sociology of Perception*. London: Routledge and Kegan Paul, 1982.

Fiske, Alan Page. *Structures of Social Life: the Four Elementary forms of Human Relations*. New York: Free Press, 1991.

Frye, Northrop. *Anatomy of Criticism: Four Essays*. Princeton NJ: Princeton University Press, 1957.

Gans, Herbert. *Popular Culture and High Culture: an Analysis and Evaluation of Taste*. New York: Basic Books, 1974.

Gray, Richard M. 'Jung and Lévi-Strauss Revisited: An Analysis of Common Themes'. *The Mankind Quarterly* 31(3) (Spring 1991). http://home.comcast.net/~richardmgray/jungandlevistrauss.htm

Lévi-Strauss, Claude. *La Pensée Sauvage*. Paris: Plon, 1962.

Munk, Kirsten. 'Signs of the Times: Cosmology and Ritual Practice in Modern Western Astrology'. PhD Thesis, Dept. Of Philosophy, Education and Religion, University of Southern Denmark, 2006. http://bisboastrology.com/wp-content/uploads/2013/02/Signs-of-the-Times-Phd-Kirstine-Munk.pdf

Newton, Denise. 'A Sociologist examines Contemporary Organised Astrology'. *Astrology Quarterly* 55, part 4, and 56, part 1 (1981).

Peek, Philip M., ed. *African Divination Systems: Ways of Knowing*. Bloomington, IN: Indiana University Press, 1991.

Phillipson, Gary. *Astrology in the year Zero*. London: Flare, 2000.

Radermacher, Lindsay. 'The Role of Dialogue in Astrological Divination'. MPhil Thesis in Theology and Religious Studies, University of Kent, 2011.

Sampson, Walter. *The Zodiac: A Life Epitome*. London: The Blackfriars Press, 1928. Re-published Whitefish, MT: Kessinger Publishing, 2003.

Simmel, Georg. *The Sociology of Georg Simmel*. New York: The Free Press, 1954.

————. *The Metropolis and Mental Life*. New York: Free Press, 1950. See also the website: www.gsz.hu-berlin.de/dokumente/georg_simmel-the_metropolis_and_mental_life.pdf

Smith, Wilfred Cantwell. *Believing: an Historical Perspective*. Oxford: Oneworld Publications, 1998. First published as *Belief and History*. Charlottesville: University of Virginia Press, 1977.

Tester, S.J. *A History of Western Astrology*. London: Boydell, 1987.

Todorov, Tzvetan. *Theories of the Symbol*. Cornell: University Press, 1984.

Travassos, Elizabeth. 'Review of *Projeto e Missao*'. *Mana* 4, part 1 (1993): pp. 186–88 (in Portuguese).

Velho, Gilberto. 'Nobres e Anjos: um estudia de toxicos e hierarquia'. PhD Thesis, University of Sao Paulo, 1975.

———. *Individualismo e Cultura: Notas para uma Antropologia da Sociedade Contemporânea*. 2nd Ed. Rio de Janeiro: Jorge Zahar Editora, 1987.

———. *Subjetividade e Sociedade: Uma Experience de Geracao*. Rio de Janeiro: Jorge Zahar Editora, 1986.

Vickers, Brian. 'Introduction, Analogy versus Identity: The Rejection of Occult Symbolism'. In *Occult and Scientific Mentalities in the Renaissance*. Cambridge: CUP, 1984.

Vilhena, Luís. *O Mundo da Astrologia*. Rio de Janeiro: Jorge Zahar Editora, 1990.

Willis, Roy and Patrick Curry. *Astrology, Science and Culture: Pulling Down the Moon*. Oxford: Berg, 2004.

INTRODUCTION

This book analyses the beliefs and cultural constructions of the world among a group of individuals who belong to the middle class in Rio de Janeiro and are involved with the practice of astrology.

Astrology is a divinatory system that postulates a correspondence between celestial movements and the character and life events of each individual. [In its modern form] it probably arose around the second century BCE, as a product of the association between Greek ideas and the beliefs of ancient Mesopotamian civilisations, then spread throughout the Roman world at the beginning of the Christian era. Its Greco-Roman heritage was preserved by the Islamic and Byzantine civilisations and introduced into medieval Europe and India. After its relative decline within European societies during the seventeenth century,[1] we have witnessed in the present (twentieth) century its return in large, modern, urban environments, where astrological consultancies flourish, and the daily press publish horoscope columns on a massive scale that contain forecasts for the natives of each sun sign.[2]

At the beginning of my research, I interviewed members of three groups who were studying astrology, which I will identify by the letters **a**, **b**, and **c**. The first two groups were led by an astrologer, Roberto and I regularly took part in group **a**.[3] Several members, including me, were part of a choir that practiced twice a week. This permitted me more frequent contact, and I came to know them better. A contrast to these groups, which were composed of people of 19–24 years of age, was provided by group **a**, which used to meet at the home of Alice, Roberto's mother. Group **a** was led by a different astrologer, and was composed of women of a range of ages, the youngest of whom was thirty-eight.

At this time I began my association with 'the world of astrology', initially through introductory courses which allowed me to begin to master the (symbolic) system shared by my informants. By the end of my research I had attended four courses, to

---

[1] It is worth consulting two books which cover an extensive period of the history of astrology: S. J. Tester, *A History of Western Astrology* (London: Boydell, 1987) and Patrick Curry, ed., *Astrology, Science and Society* (London: Boydell, 1977).

[2] A Glossary of astrological terms can be found in Appendix 2.

[3] All names are fictitious. In Appendix 1 the reader will find a list of 23 interviewees, with their basic data and their relationship to the world of astrology.

which can be added congresses and workshops, as well as discussion groups to which I belonged during my fieldwork, even after the other groups had dissolved.

Dealing with a world similar to that studied by recent work in urban anthropology, [which is] concerned with the life styles and worldviews prevalent among the urban middle classes,[4] I took as my hypothesis the following question: 'To what extent can we say that astrology contributed to the development of one of those worldviews?' Already, in that initial stage it was clear that many of the similarities present in the discussions with interviewees flowed from the manner in which they took part in the world of astrology as 'students'. It was this activity that permitted the formation of the networks that defined them as groups. I moved on to interview individuals outside this last group, members of those classes that regularly made use of astrology. I was then able to note definite differences in the vision of astrology on the part of informants who limited themselves to consulting an astrologer but had either no interest or no time to understand and become familiar with how the astrological system worked. Other students I interviewed preferred self-study and placed little value on courses and conferences. I also interviewed four [professional] astrologers.

The literature on astrology is composed of three segments, which are numerically very different: a vast literature produced by astrologers, a smaller historiographical bibliography, and a handful of sociological and anthropological works on the subject.

These writings brought me to the formulation of the hypothesis that, although each author, each historical period, and each social sector defined their own cosmological foundations and the specific use of specific types of astrology, their techniques and classifications present an extraordinary stability. This permanence exists in spite of— or because of—[astrology] having always appeared in syncretic environments, linked to other divinatory/curative systems and to beliefs of the most diverse origins: at times brought together under such headings as 'esotericism', 'the occult tradition', 'the counterculture', or 'the new gnosis'. As historian Brian Vickers reminds us, this 'resistance to change' is a trait of all occultism.[5] The same tension emerges in the

---

[4] This tradition is reviewed in part by Tania Salem. Although the author takes the theme of the family as the central line along which she compares the lifestyles which characterise them, she also includes other works where 'the analysis of the family or of kinship is, in principle treated as a subsidiary theme'. (Tania Salem, 'Família em Camadas Médias: uma revisão da Bibliografia', *Boletim do Museu Nacional*, no. 54 [Outubro 1985]: pp. 1–29.)

[5] Brian Vickers, 'Introduction: Analogy Versus Identity: The Rejection of Occult Symbolism', in *Occult and Scientific Mentalities in the Renaissance* (Cambridge: Cambridge University Press, 1984), p. 7.

discourses of several of my informants: at one and the same time they emphasise pluralism, affirming the need to compare different astrologers and different books, so that each person can adopt the type of astrology that appeals most to them; yet they still reaffirm the antiquity of the system, above and beyond the dates recognised by historiography, reinforcing the unity of the subject and its fidelity to its origins.

Thus, the present work, which is concerned with the diffusion of a millennial movement in an extremely restricted sector of Brazilian society, is marked by this tension between the general and the particular, and between abstract and concrete analyses. I begin in Chapter 1 with an analysis of the classifications on which astrological techniques are based; I attempt to show that, like the structure of myths analysed by Lévi-Strauss, their structure remains constant across various versions.

Chapter 4 is devoted to my conversations with informants, seeking to point out the specific details assumed by the theory and practice of astrology in segments of the urban middle class living in the south of Rio de Janeiro; I make a global interpretation based on the particular version of symbolism that has been developed in these groups.

These two chapters represent original contributions to the study of the urban middle classes—which already possesses a respectable tradition in Brazil—as well as of astrology as an example of 'alternative culture' in general, a sector until now little-studied by the social sciences.

The remaining chapters represent a transition within the continuum established between these two poles, developing progressive contextualisations of the astrological system. All of these [chapters] raise problems that require serious study in a larger work, but which here play only a subsidiary role. In Chapter 2, for example, I discuss the nature of modernity and the strategic role played by the middle classes in the articulation of those values in Brazilian society. Rather than comment on recent anthropological work on the subject, I will rely on the publications by Georg Simmel and Louis Dumont. I will try to show how they can help us understand the ambiguous relationship between modernity and astrology: although [re]emerging within modernity, astrology presents a discourse marked by a critique of modern values.

In the development of this work, my initial hypothesis underwent some modifications. The effort to 'identify experiences [that were] meaningful enough to create symbolic boundaries [for the participants]' remains, although it is no longer linked necessarily to the delimitation of 'lifestyles'.[6] We will see how the practice of

---

[6] Gilberto Velho, *Subjetividade e Sociedade: Uma Experiência de Geração* (Rio de Janeiro: Jorge Zahar Editora, 1986), p. 16.

astrology confers on each individual a specific vocabulary, a response mediated by the structure of astrology in his/her worldview that allows us to describe this practice as a 'synthesising experience' [of the type] with which [previous] studies of the middle classes have defined their objects. Although only some of the informants belong to definite groups, they all maintain the most diverse relations with the world of astrology, which can be described—as I will attempt to do in Chapter 3—as a large network, a category equally used in the literature on the middle classes, alongside that of 'ethos group', to delimit its objects.[7]

[7] Salem, 'Família'; Salem, 'A Trajetória do "Casal Grávido": Da Sua Constituição à Revisão do Seu Projeto', in *A Cultura da Psicanálise*, ed. Sérvulo A. Figueira (São Paulo: Brasiliense, 1985).

CHAPTER 1:
THE ASTROLOGICAL SYSTEM

Astrology can be defined as the divinatory art which postulates the existence of a relationship between celestial movements and everything that happens on earth, possessing a system of classifications which permits definite meanings to be attributed to each of these movements, as well as a group of techniques which establish the procedures suitable to interpret them. It will be within the terms of this definition that I will try to describe the system of astrology.

The analysis of astrological principles and classifications without reference to their application in any particular historical moment or social environment is important in the present work, and not just to clarify for the reader the combination of representations that provide the identity of the group [of users] being studied. Although, throughout its history astrology has been put to the most diverse uses, I will try to demonstrate that it can be seen as a system: it possesses its own consistent logic that must be analysed in conjunction with the investigation of its practice in any of the contexts in which it is found. It is important, however, before making this analysis, to make explicit the elements which serve as a basis for this approach, and which also reveal its limits.

So far I have used the word *astrology* without any qualification; however, it can be said in a fuller sense that there are several astrologies. This name with its two Greek roots has always been associated with the system that arose from the Hellenisation of a Babylonian 'astrology'. In this process, the original Mesopotamian form, which was just one of the various forms of divination monopolised by the priestly class, was submitted to various modifications, which both laicised and individualised it. I will be concerned only with the laicised form, which I will call zodiacal astrology, to distinguish it from other varieties.

The oldest astrological texts date from the third century BCE, written in Greek in occupied Egypt. From there it expanded throughout the Greco-Roman world, carried by the *matematici* or *chaldaei*, as the astrologers were called then. Although this science claimed to be a repository of ancestral wisdom from the Babylonians (and even the Egyptians, who we now know never developed an astrology of their own), it was already the product of the syncretism of the time, with the signs and planets given Latin names. Over time, a vast astrological literature arose, ranging from the relatively 'scientific' manual of Ptolemy—the *Tetrabiblos*, written in the second century CE—to the treatises attributed to the mythical Hermes Trismegistus, composed in reality in the first centuries of our era.[1] The dissemination of zodiacal astrology in the Roman world took place during the period of flourishing Oriental cultures, which marked the period of the empire before its Christianisation.[2]

The idea that Chinese, Mayan and Babylonian astrologies also existed, as well as the zodiacal form which was originally baptised with this name, is due, in the first two cases, to the presence of symbolic representations in those cultures which also featured homologies between the terrestrial and celestial worlds; in the third case, from the need to distinguish it from the syncretic [zodiacal] product which arose from it. However, from the theoretical point of view, I believe that it is an error similar to the 'totemic illusion' described by Lévi-Strauss, if the astrological classifications made by these societies along with their beliefs and practices, were to be isolated from the totality of classifications that marked the structure of their societies.[3] Totemism is more than an autonomous institution, but rather forms just one plane of the vast classificatory systems elaborated by these societies. In an essay which has justly become a classic for its pioneering approach, Durkheim and Mauss illustrated the Chinese classificatory system with a summarised description of its 'astrology'.[4] The reading by Michel Granet meanwhile shows us how complex this system is and the extent to which Chinese astrological beliefs overlapped with their cosmology.

On the other hand astrology—properly so-called, i.e., the zodiacal form—acquired, because it was a divinatory art, a relative autonomy that permits us to analyse it separately. The Greek and Latin literature on the subject was preserved by the Arab civilisations which introduced it into India, and permitted its rediscovery a little before the first millennium in medieval Europe. The survival of this large repository and its pagan origin allowed it to be researched and used, with more or less care, by philosophers, doctors, astronomers and the curious in general (as if there existed any such clear divisions of intellectual labour in medieval times). As Jack Goody pointed out, the coherence and homogeneity of the classification systems of the ancient civilisations to which I referred above can be linked to the existence of a restricted

---

[1] André-Jean Festugière, *La Révélation d'Hermès Trismegistre I: l'Astrologie et les Sciences Occultes* (Paris: Les Belles Lettres, 1981), pp. 67–68.
[2] Festugière, *La Révélation*, pp. 19–44; Franz Cumont, *Astrology and Religion Among the Greeks and Romans* (New York: Dover, 1960), pp. 50–56.
[3] Claude Lévi-Strauss, *La Pensée Sauvage* (Paris: Plon, 1962).
[4] Emile Durkheim and Marcel Mauss, 'Algumas Formas Primitivas de Classificação', *Ensaios de Sociologia*, ed. Marcel Mauss (São Paulo: Perspectiva, 1981), pp. 442–47.

domain of writing that kept what was considered legitimate, erudite knowledge in the monopoly of certain social strata.[5] Already however, at the end of the Middle Ages and during the Renaissance, we know that the exclusive dominion of the clergy over knowledge was not always complete, nor did it avoid the existence of serious dissent.[6] If we analyse the history of zodiacal astrology, we will understand that its moments of greatest expansion corresponded to those of the dissemination of education.[7]

These surveys already allow us a glimpse of some specific features of astrology as a form of divination. Its classifications are not necessarily the same as those of the culture in which it is practiced (although the two may tend to converge), and it is organised on the basis of the classification of the planets and their movements, whose meanings are interpreted according to techniques established in astrological literature. The use of the term 'technique' might be considered inadequate, keeping in mind the opposition that many anthropologists have established between technique and magic, and also taking into account that divination is classically seen as a magical procedure.[8] This opposition is also developed by Malinowski who recognised in primitive societies not only a 'sacred' wisdom, which corresponds with magic and religion, but also a 'profane' learning.[9] The latter would constitute 'primitive knowledge' in which we find the

[5] Jack Goody, 'Introduction', in *Literacy in Traditional Societies* (Cambridge: Cambridge University Press, 1968).

[6] This can be compared with Granet's description of classical China: 'The polemics between the *Schools* were the expression of conflicts of prestige. They don't imply any properly doctrinal opposition'. (Marcel Granet, *La Pensée Chinoise* [Paris: Albin Michel, 1981], pp. 11–12).

[7] As E.R. Dodds has shown, Hellenistic society in the third century BCE, when zodiacal astrology was born, 'was in several ways the closest approximation to an "open" society that had then been known, with its cosmopolitan culture and its institutions exposed to rational criticism'. (E.R. Dodds, *The Greeks and the Irrational* [Berkeley: University of California Press, 1951], p. 237). The expansion of the astrological system reached its apex during the first centuries of our era, when the Roman state was preoccupied with the founding of numerous centres of teaching through which the ancient scientific and philosophical knowledge was spread. It disappeared from the West during medieval times, to some extent due to the complex mathematical calculations that its practice required, only to reappear at the beginning of the Renaissance, when the intellectual panorama of the period was revolutionised by the rediscovery of Greco-Roman culture.

[8] Henri Hubert and Marcel Mauss, 'Esboço de uma Teoria General de Magia', in *Sociologia e Antropologia*, ed., Marcel Mauss, (São Paulo: EPU e Edusp, 1974), I: pp. 169–70.

[9] Bronislaw Malinowski, 'Magic, Science and Religion', in *Magic, Science and Religion and Other Essays* (Garden City: Anchor Books, 1954).

'rudiments of science'.[10] On the other hand, he relativises [the absolute terms of] this dichotomy, admitting that 'both science and magic develop special techniques'.[11] With this affirmation Malinowski shows that even in primitive societies, the practice of magic implies obedience to certain procedures and formulas, whose possession is at times a route to prestige, and access to which is restricted. What he seems to imply here is that, if these practices are distinguished from *techniques* (properly so-called—those of 'primitive knowledge') by their complete practical inefficacy, such is only the supposition of the researcher and not of the users, who evidently believe in the power of magic and attribute its failures to a failure to comply with the 'strict conditions' that should be observed in its practice. This formulation of Malinowski and the value judgements that it still contains reveal the delicate but strategic position occupied for him (at that time) by the transition of anthropology, through a process of self-criticism, away from [an earlier] evolutionist ethnocentricism.

This wide-ranging use of the term *technique* is extremely useful for describing certain essential aspects of a definition of astrology, once it has been characterised [as divination] by the important role of technique in its practice. Obtaining the raw materials for its interpretations—the astrological map or chart, a graph in which the positions of the planets are recorded at a given moment in time—demands complex astronomical and mathematical calculations. As Alexander Murray showed, the arithmetic operations required for the construction of charts during medieval times were the most advanced of the era.[12] Today of course, things are much simpler. Anyone who does not have access to a computer can make use of an ephemeris in book form, which records the positions of the planets at midnight or midday for each day of the year, and of a table of houses which allows the positions of the houses to be established for any latitude and any sidereal time. From the information obtained by consulting these publications, the construction of a chart requires only a few operations of addition and subtraction and the use of a table of logarithms, in order to determine the position of each planet at whatever hour and minute is desired.

Although it appears more complicated described in this way than it is in practice, not actually demanding great mathematical ability (if a user has access to a simple calculator), the ephemeris and the tables mentioned are generally imported [into Brazil]. In addition, the techniques and principles used in interpretation of a chart can

---

[10] Malinowski, *Magic, Science and Religion*, p. 19.
[11] Malinowski, *Magic, Science and Religion*, p. 89.
[12] Alexander Murray, *Reason and Society in the Middle Ages* (Oxford: Clarendon Press, 1978).

only be acquired by reading manuals, which are mostly in foreign languages, or by paying to join a class.

As we can see, even if zodiacal astrology had never been the monopoly of a priestly caste, the mastery of its knowledge demands the possession of a certain cultural capital. However it is *only* this that it demands. Using Weber's terminology, it can be affirmed that the authority of the astrologer has—in the last analysis—a rational basis, resting on the mastery of a specific, more-or-less defined knowledge accessible to open examination, not dependent on tradition or personal charisma for its legitimacy. In this way, the practice of astrology is not restricted by any professional body from which the user is obliged to obtain legitimacy as happens, for example, with psychoanalytical associations which, on the other hand, have greater scientific pretensions, despite their rituals of initiation, schisms and expulsions. Neither are any extraordinary abilities demanded from the astrologer: no falling into trance, nor possession of any state of spiritual grace are necessary in order to practice this type of divination. The astrologer relies only on his astronomical data and his knowledge and talent for interpretation. Clearly this is an 'ideal-typical' distinction, and the personal charisma of an astrologer today is a source of prestige which can be added to their rational legitimacy. We may also presume that astrologers in the past supported themselves as much by the authority of their tradition [as by their skill].

I know of only one apparent exception to this hypothesis. It concerns the astrology practised in the southeast of Madagascar, described by Maurice Bloch. In this region, Bloch tells us that the astrologer is required 'to possess a combination of complex knowledge as well as supernatural powers'.[13] I believe this is due to the peculiar form in which Islamic culture, the source of traditional Malagasy astrological knowledge, penetrated the island. Although this contact had ceased by the seventeenth century, it [was enough to] allow the adaptation of Arabic characters to local dialects, which gave rise to an extremely complex writing style in which its sacred texts were written.

Once the Malagasy astrological knowledge was discovered in these books, it was taken over by the literate aristocracy of the region. Thus, as Bloch shows, astrology became part of the 'traditional knowledge' of these societies, whose mastery is an important source of prestige. This means that the assimilation of this system in the island appears in a different form from those we find in other parts of the area of its

---

[13] Maurice Bloch, 'Astrology and Writing in Madagascar', in *Literacy in Traditional Societies*, ed. Jack Goody, pp. 278–97, (Cambridge: Cambridge University Press, 1968). [No exact page number was given for this quotation in the original.—Ed.]

diffusion: its origins—originally barbarian, then pagan—always made it difficult to integrate into the dominant traditional religion. Beyond this, Bloch's data does not allow us to exclude the possibility that, during its relative isolation from the rest of Islamic culture, Malagasy astrology underwent structural modifications, given that the sparse references supplied by Bloch are not sufficient for us to know how far it remains faithful to the original Hellenic postulates.

Defined in this way, astrology as a divinatory art is included in the more specific category of '-mancy'. This includes, for example, chiromancy and the various cartomancies (like the Tarot) that take, respectively, the hands or the cards as phenomena to be interpreted according to specific techniques. It is evident that the kinds of answers that these oracles will give and their application are intimately related to the nature of the phenomenon which they take as referent. Since only humans have hands, and as each one possesses absolutely individual lines (as the modern technique of fingerprinting has shown), the chiromancer claims to speak about the personality and individual destiny of the person whose hands are being analysed. In the same way, it follows that the application of conclusions taken from a 'reading' of a group of cards arranged at random on a table will be different. Thus the practice of Tarot reading is carried out by a process of question and answer.[14]

We can say that astrology, like all the different mantic arts, presents two classifications which we can call primary and secondary. In the first, through the qualities and stereotypes attributed to each planet and sign, certain finite combinations of species within distinct types can be classified. Thus, twelve parts of the human body are associated with the twelve signs of the zodiac (see fig. 1) in the same way that, in the past, each day of the week was associated with one of the seven visible planets, as is clear in many western European languages.[15]

---

[14] The techniques of cartomancers face this problem which implies that the same question may receive different answers on different occasions. I heard an interesting answer to this question from a Tarot reader I met during one of the courses I attended in my period of fieldwork. For him, the cards never respond to the same question. If someone continues asking the same question, they will move to supplying new facets, or unfoldings of the problem initially posed.

[15] Thus in English and German, Saturday/Samstag, Sunday/Sonntag, Monday/Montag were associated with Saturn, the Sun, and the Moon respectively. The lunar character of Monday is also indicated in French, Spanish and Italian (Lundi/Lunes/Lunedi), which record the other planetary classifications as well: respectively, Mars, Mercury, Jupiter, and Venus with Mardi/Martes/Martedi; Mercredi/Miercoles/Mercoledi; Jeudi/Jueves/Giovedi; Vendredi/Viernes/Venerdi.

Temperament	Humour	Element	Colour	Condition	Quality	Age	Season	Wind	Zodiac Sign	Body Part
Sanguine	Blood	Air	Red	Liquid	Hot-Wet	Infancy	Spring	South	Aries	Head
									Taurus	Neck
									Gemini	Shoulders
Choleric	Yellow Bile	Fire	Yellow	Gaseous	Hot-Dry	Youth	Summer	East	Cancer	Breast
									Leo	Heart
									Virgo	Stomach
Melancholic	Black Bile	Earth	Black	Dense	Cold-Dry	Maturity	Autumn	North	Libra	Waist
									Scorpio	Genitals
									Sagittarius	Thighs
Phlegmatic	Phlegm	Water	White	Solid	Cold-Wet	Old Age	Winter	West	Capricorn	Shins
									Aquarius	Ankles
									Pisces	[Feet]

Fig. 1: [Table of zodiacal symbolic correspondences], taken from *The Domestication of the Savage Mind*.[16] I took the liberty of completing the list of parts of the body, which originally only attributed specific parts to the first three and last three zodiac signs.

It is important to emphasise the limited extent of this classification which, although primary, stops at the level of species; in other words, it classifies *the* head and *the day in general*, but not the head of a particular person or one particular Sunday.

Correspondingly, the secondary classifications of astrology require the mediation of time which allows them, in contrast, a practically unlimited capacity for making particular distinctions. The most common form of this process is the connection of the destiny of an individual to their natal astrological chart, in which the planetary positions are precisely indicated in relation to the latitude and longitude of the person's place of birth. The interpretation of this chart is developed in relation to the planetary standards and qualities already mentioned: the same ones used in the primary classifications. Such standards are defined in accordance with the position each planet and sign occupies in the total system of astrology. It is thus the structure of this system which presides over the classifications and interpretations used in astrology.

---

[16] Jack Goody, *The Domestication of the Savage Mind* (Cambridge: Cambridge University Press, 1977) p. 69. In Goody's figure caption, he thanks 'Diana Burfield, for pointing out that there could be alternative versions to the scheme above, especially in terms of the grouping of the signs'.

Some may point out the contradiction which exists between the divinatory character that I attribute to astrology and the scientific nature that some astrologers associate with their subject. The present work starts from the assumption that the model of science, which emerged around the seventeenth century—and which to a large extent still remains dominant—possesses a value which must be contextualised historically and culturally; thus we are not authorised to make absolute judgements about astrology. However, most of the time when astrologers claim that the system they use is a science they are seeking to defend themselves from the disqualification that they have suffered since that period, when the paradigm on which astrology was based began to decline. In doing so they are adopting an ethnocentric judgement common in modern culture: that of equating science with truth. I maintain the need to contextualise this judgement, and if I try to demonstrate how astrology is distant from the modern model of science, this does not imply a condemnation.

On the other hand, it is important to note that many arguments of this type affirm, not only the [supposed] scientific character of the astrological system, but that it also has the capacity to go beyond modern science. The radical nature of this argument may lead to a second type of criticism of my approach. I refer to the condemnation of modern, scientific thinking by some astrologers who view it as a source of empty and manipulative technique, while [in their view] astrology, in common with other '-mancies' or 'traditional sciences' would also contain, besides its efficacy, an implicit wisdom. Although this is a very common idea, it is necessary to recognise that there exist the most diverse interpretations of the true nature of such wisdom, constituting a bone of contention in the debates which run through the field of intellectual esotericism, as we shall see in the last chapter. Apart from this, several interpreters recognise with regret that the great majority of users are not interested in such questions, just taking advantage of the benefits that each system offers.

Thus, to define the system of astrology, I follow the Weberian principle, by which in the sciences of [a] culture, analysis must be done in relation to values without, however, seeking legitimacy for any one of them. My objective was the construction of a model which can be applied to all the uses and interpretations of astrology, in order for us to understand them. My hypothesis is that there is an underlying structure that confers unity on these uses, and gives astrology its systematic character.

One question that must be answered, at least in part, concerns the extent of this unity. If I choose to follow the hypothesis that it [this unity] exists, I am following the dominant way of thinking in the group that I am studying, privileging the 'native point of view' so dear to the anthropologist. The 'antiquity' of astrology is one of its fundamental values and, although in different forms, its users construct its legitimacy by claiming faithfulness to its origins, which doesn't necessarily need to be literal; it can be expressed in more indirect ways. Certain authors, for example, defend the need to understand astrology 'in present-day terms' and the elucidation of 'both the structure and the application of this science in relation to contemporary psychology, psychotherapy and concepts of energy'.[17] This is the position of Stephen Arroyo, a representative of the current, self-named [genre of] Humanistic Astrology.[18] However, establishing that the modernisation of astrology is inevitable has a complementary side: its adoption of modern ideology will imply the possibility of a return to the valuing of traditional knowledge. For Arroyo, this ideology:

> ...has gone too far in its effort to free itself from limitations and traditions. It has lost contact with the archetypal bases of its essence and with its source of support and the psychological and spiritual nourishment which these bases provide. Astrology can be used as a resource for re-uniting human beings with their interior selves, with nature, and with the process of the evolution of the universe.[19]

As we see, independently of the anti-traditional character that modern culture may have, the valuing of tradition is always an ingredient of the practice of astrological beliefs. However, other astrologers do not agree with the compromise suggested by Arroyo. Authors who defend so-called traditional astrology, inspired by the French thinker René Guénon,[20] believe that, detached from its traditional context as it is today, (astrology) 'can only survive as a pale caricature of itself'.[21] Its practice thus becomes marked by an impasse between the affirmation of the need to contextualise it in its

---

[17] Stephen Arroyo, *Astrologia, Psicologia e os Quatro Elementos; uma abordagem astrologica ao nível de energia e seu uso nas artes de aconselhar e orientar* (São Paulo: Pensamento, 1985), p. 20.

[18] Arroyo, *Astrologia*, p. 14.

[19] Arroyo, *Astrologia*, p. 45.

[20] The meaning of the adjective 'traditional' may be too vague to define a current of thought which is as jealous of its orthodoxy as this one. Some of its connotations are even rejected by Guénon himself (René Guénon, *A Crise do Mundo Moderno* [Lisboa: Vega 1977], p. 53). However, the term 'traditional astrology' is generally used here to refer to astrologers who follow this author. The theme of tradition is important, not just for astrology but also, as we shall see, for esotericism as a whole. However this is the sector of esotericism which treats it in the most radical way.

[21] Olavo de Carvalho, *Astros e Símbolos* (São Paulo: Nova Stella, 1985), p. 19.

originating doctrines, and the recognition that 'astrology, as practiced today in the west, is only the vestige of an ancient form of science'.[22]

This small example illustrates, nevertheless, how contrasting visions of the world can be appropriated by astrology and, in doing so have to confront certain common questions. The analysis of the history of astrology that will be shortly undertaken is also capable of furnishing a myriad of examples of the dialectic between continuity and discontinuity which characterise astrology. Astrology merely postulates the relationship between the earth and the movements of the planets according to certain secondary classifications. Nothing in it expressly determines a particular use nor supplies its metaphysical or epistemological presuppositions, on which there is no consensus.[23]

My hypothesis is that astrology's plasticity is limited and that those limits can be determined through understanding the structure that organises its classifications and the principles which form the foundation of its techniques. I will then try to carry out this task, at least partially, at the end of which certain empirically identified constancies, such as the importance of valuing tradition, can be established on the basis of a theoretical analysis.

The following description presents the understandings shared by all those who have [learned] the rudiments necessary to the construction and interpretation of astrological charts. It will be succinct, given that its purpose is not to teach anyone to use this knowledge, but to determine the common features of the practice of astrology and to analyse them, guided by anthropological theory. I will try, as far as possible to remain at a distance from doctrinal polemics, and the bibliography I used was chosen without any attempt to make a selection based on merit within the genre. These are books with which I had contact during the research, led by curiosity or the suggestions of my informants, and will be cited only as examples of what is being referenced.

---

[22] Cid de Oliveira, 'Plotino e as Funçôes Fundamentais da Astrologia', in *Astrología Hoje: Métodos e Propostas*, Ana Maria Costa Ribeiro et al., (Rio de Janeiro: Massao Ohno, 1985), p. 47.

[23] I refer here to what Kemper called the '"partial" quality of astrology' in an article on Singhalese astrology. For this author, by itself, it [astrology] is not capable of creating a cosmology (Steven Kemper, 'Time, Person, and Gender in Sinhalese Astrology', *American Ethnologist*, Vol. 7, no. 4 [Nov 1980]: p. 755).

COSMOLOGY

The word *cosmology*, besides defining a branch of astronomical knowledge, is also used in two other senses. In an inclusive usage, it defines a vision of the world, the ideology of a group, a culture, or a society. In this sense, astrology does not possess a unique cosmology. If my hypothesis is correct, each school of astrology or each historical period assembles its own vision of the world into a system which forms the foundation and the limits of its employment and supplies the explanation of its efficacy.

Again, in a more restricted sense, cosmology signifies a definition of the composition and organisation of the cosmos. It is this sense that I use to define the way in which the system of astrology conceives the positions and movements of the planets which it takes as the reference points for the construction of its charts. That technical necessity determines the geocentrism of its cosmology; a chart represents the positions of the planets in relation to that to which it refers. Now, the objects and individuals over which astrology establishes its interpretations are all found on the earth.

For modern relativistic physics it is irrelevant to know whether the earth or the sun are situated at the centre of the universe given that, according to relativity, motion can only be defined in relation to an arbitrary reference point. Today it is simpler to suppose that our planet revolves around the sun than to believe, with the [pre-Copernican] ancients (who, however, did not work from a relativistic viewpoint), that the whole universe revolves around the earth. In antiquity, the dimensions of the cosmos were much smaller. Seen without the aid of sophisticated instruments which were developed later, the sky appears to present two kinds of stars.[24] The first, most numerous, are the *fixed stars*, which move while maintaining a fixed arrangement and distance between each other, as if they formed a sphere surrounding the earth which completes one revolution around our planet every twenty-four hours. The other type is composed of stars that make circular motions which are slightly slower than the stars, seeming to move through the sphere of which they are part. They are called *planets* by virtue of their 'wandering' character (this is the meaning of the Greek word 'planet').

---

[24] The postulation of the finiteness or infinity of the universe does not depend on the presence or absence of the observer. Johannes Kepler, even after the telescopic observations of Galileo which revealed new stars invisible to the naked eye, still believed in the finiteness of the universe and the equidistance of the stars in relation to the earth, due to his religious convictions (Alexandre Koyré, *Do Mundo Fechado ao Universo Infinito* [Rio de Janeiro: Forense Universitária, 1986], pp. 63–89).

The sun and moon also show this type of motion, making a complete revolution within the sphere of the fixed stars every 365 and twenty-eight days, respectively.

The line which runs through the celestial sphere on which the sun executes its movement is known as the *ecliptic*. The rest of the planets never move more than five degrees from this line, thus marking out a strip of the ecliptic called the *zodiac*, which represents the region of the sky where they may be found. The zodiacal strip is divided into twelve signs of thirty degrees each whose Latin names were taken from the twelve constellations which are found more or less on the strip: *Aries, Taurus, Gemini, Cancer, Leo, Virgo, Libra, Scorpio, Sagittarius, Capricorn, Aquarius and Pisces.*[25] But the zodiac's true localisation is determined by the positions which the sun occupies during the cycle of seasons, in such a way that, for each season it crosses three signs. Due to the phenomenon of the 'precession of the equinoxes', the correspondence between the signs and the constellations no longer exists. This phenomenon consists of the shifting of the vernal point—where the ecliptic begins and the sun is found on the first day of spring—in relation to the constellations. This point lies today between the constellations of Pisces and Aquarius. The relationship between the solar movement around the ecliptic, the positions of the signs within the zodiac, and the cycle of seasons in the northern hemisphere (which is also used as a reference in astrology practiced south of the equator), can be seen in Figure 2.

---

[25] Although the Latin terms have remained as a fundamental reference some languages, like Portuguese, have translated the majority of the names but adapted others which are untranslatable, such as Aries, Cancer and Libra. It is very common to use the latter with the appropriate accents to match Portuguese orthography; this is the nomenclature I shall use.

AR	Spring			Summer		LI	Autumn			Winter	
AR	TA	GE	CN	LE	VI	LI	SC	SG	CP	AQ	PI

Summer Solstice

Tropic of Cancer

Vernal Point

New Spring Equinox

Libra Equinox

Spring Equinox

Equator

Equator

Tropic of Capricorn

Winter Solstice

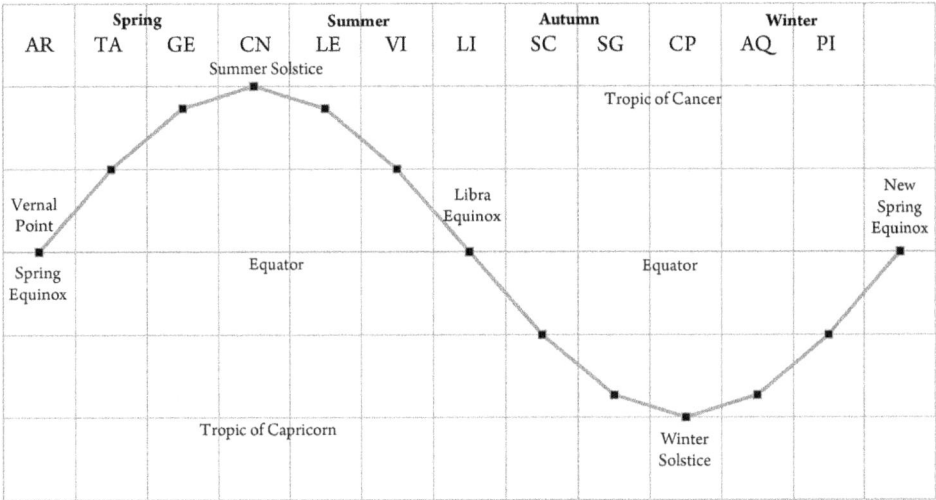

Fig. 2: The planar projection of the [apparent] movement of the sun around the celestial sphere (seasons correspond to the northern hemisphere).

Although they show, during their journey around the zodiac, regular small variations in velocity, the two 'Lights' move always in the opposite direction to the vault of stars, from west to east or, taking the graphical representation of the zodiac as reference, in a counter-clockwise direction. The planets, as well as displaying sharper accelerations and decelerations during their revolutions in the same direction, also change direction at certain times. This is known as retrograde motion in astrology. However, even these motions take place with regularity, which permitted the Babylonian mathematicians, from the fifth century BCE onwards, to begin predicting planetary positions by the use of mathematical formulas.[26]

We can understand that astrological cosmology is made up of a number of cycles, during which each planet makes a complete orbit of the zodiac; each chart is a record of a particular instant of each one of these cycles. Before describing them and showing their representation in astrological charts, I would like to mention one cycle which, due to its duration, is not represented graphically. Astrology considers that the shifting of

---

[26] Cf. Otto Neugebauer, *The Exact Sciences in Antiquity* (New York: Harper Torchbooks, 1962), pp. 97–138.

the vernal point constitutes a cycle, the Great Year. Every 28,500 solar years the vernal point makes one complete revolution around the equator and returns to its initial position. In accord with the constellation that the vernal point occupies, the astrological era in which we find ourselves is determined. From this description it can be understood why it is said that we are living through the passage from the Age of Pisces to that of Aquarius. For astrology, the consequences of this passage are felt across the whole planet, so that it has no meaning to include it in astrological charts. On the other hand, it is just this inclusivity that makes the astrological ages the best known topic in astrology.

There are ten planetary cycles.[27] That of the sun corresponds with the passage of the year and that of the moon with the months. The remaining planetary cycles have different durations. In each chart are represented the sign and degree in which each one of these is found at that moment.

There are also other points marked in a chart which have less importance than the planets for interpretation. These are the lunar nodes (points at which the orbit of the moon crosses that of the earth), Lilith (the diameter which joins the apogee and perigee of the moon), associated with a mythical character in the Judaic tradition, and the so-called Arabic Parts.

Finally, there is a representation of the diurnal cycle in every chart, caused by the rotation of the earth, and which is illustrated by the twelve astrological houses. As I affirmed, the planetary cycles do not revolve around the earth, but around the zodiac. The latter, like the whole celestial vault, appear to revolve around the earth, producing the sequence of days and nights. So in the chart an axis is drawn to represent the line of the horizon. The point of the zodiac intercepted by the left-hand side of this axis (representing the east) is the Ascendant, while the opposite side is the Descendant. This line divides the map into two equal hemispheres: those signs which are visible and those which remain invisible. A second axis is traced joining the two points in which the meridian which runs through the zenith and the celestial poles intercept the ecliptic. The point of the zodiac intercepted in the nocturnal half is called the base of heaven (or IC, *Imum Coeli*); the other is the Midheaven (or MC, *Medium Coeli*), the culminating point of the daily solar movement at the place for which the chart is drawn. The resulting division into four parts is not symmetrical, since the angle formed by the axis of the Ascendant is not perpendicular to that of the MC. This distortion is

---

[27] Ancient and medieval astrology evidently used only the Sun, Moon and five planets. Uranus, Neptune and Pluto were only incorporated into the astrological system later.

due to the obliquity of the ecliptic in relation to the equator. Each of these four quadrants is subdivided into three unequal parts because of this distortion. So, the division into twelve houses is superimposed on that of the zodiac without ever conflating the two, not only due to the different sizes that the former possess, but also because of the small probability that the axes [house cusps] intercept the zodiac at exactly zero degrees of a *sign*.[28] Each of the radii running out from the centre of the chart, dividing it into twelve sectors, is called a [House] Cusp. A cusp represents the beginning of each house in numbered order, starting from the Ascendant, in Roman numerals.[29] Thus the cusp of the 1st house is the Ascendant, the 10th the MC, the 7th is the Descendant, and the 4th the IC (see fig. 3).

Key to Symbols for Zodiac Signs and Planets

♈ Aries	♉ Taurus	♊ Gemini	♋ Cancer
♌ Leo	♍ Virgo	♎ Libra	♏ Scorpio
♐ Sagittarius	♑ Capricorn	♒ Aquarius	♓ Pisces

☉ Sun	☾ Moon	☿ Mercury	♀ Venus
♂ Mars	♃ Jupiter	♄ Saturn	♅ Uranus
♆ Neptune	♇ Pluto	⊕ Part of Fortune	

---

[28] The more precise astronomical explanation for this distortion and the determination of the dimensions of the houses can be found in Paul Courdec, *L'Astrologie* (Paris: PUF, 1978), pp. 20–21, 39–40. All my descriptions are based on the Placidus method, used by the majority of Brazilian astrologers and by all those I contacted. There is another method, widely used in England, in which, starting from the Ascendant, twelve equal houses of exactly 30 degrees each are marked out, with the MC not corresponding to the cusp of the 10th house.
[29] Modern convention employs Arabic numerals, rather than Roman, to designate the astrological houses; this is the convention that will be followed in the text.—Trans.

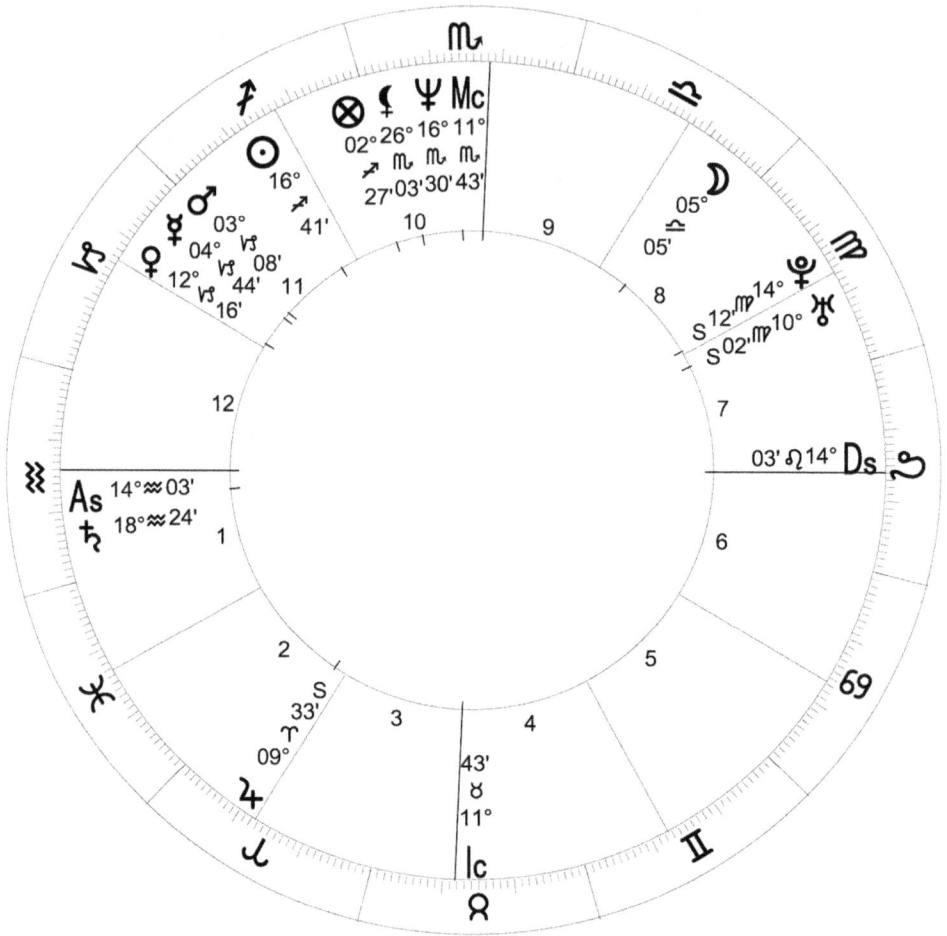

Fig. 3: An example of a simplified astrological chart for someone born on 9 December 1963 at 10:20 AM in Rio de Janeiro. Each sign occupies 30 degrees, so the positions of the planets, house cusps and other points are shown in relation to [degrees of] each sign. As the chart shows, the subject has a Sagittarius sun sign and ascendant in Aquarius.

Starting from the record in a natal chart of the planetary positions and the houses in relation to the zodiac, the astrologer has available a large amount of information with which to interpret the personality and destiny of the person who was born at the place and time for which he drew the chart. Using the symbolism of these elements, given by the astrological classification system, the interpreter is able to formulate judgements based on the combinations of planets and houses within the signs which they occupy and of the relations between the planets. The best known of these combinations is the determination of the Sun sign (the (zodiac) sign occupied by the Sun in the chart) and the Ascendant sign (the sign intercepted by the first house cusp). These are certainly the most important elements in reading a chart according to astrology. However there are several other supplementary factors which don't refer just to other planets and houses. The information obtained about the Sun sign can be enriched if the house it occupies is determined. The implications of having a particular sign on the Ascendant can also be modified, depending on the presence of planets in the first house. There is still a fourth factor in reading a chart which, contrary to the first three, does not belong to the classificatory system as it does not possess an autonomous symbolism: the aspects. These allow the symbolism of the planets to be combined when certain angles exist between them. Each aspect determines a certain relationship between two planets. The most commonly used are the Conjunction (0°), the Opposition (180°), the Square (90°), the Trine (120°), and the Sextile (60°). The angles do not have to be exact and can have a margin of up to about 8° from these values. This margin is called the Orb. The only exception is the Sextile, which has an orb of 5°. In Figure 3 for example, there are—among other aspects—a conjunction between Mercury and Mars in Capricorn; similarly, a line should be drawn between the Moon and Jupiter, which are in opposition. I will characterise the aspects in the following section devoted to the analysis of the planets.

In conclusion, we see that, through the natal chart, the astrologer analyses and at the same time synthesises each moment that he tries to record; each chart is the unique intersection of particular moments of different cycles which always repeat separately. The separate systems which make up the three components of astrological signification—planets, signs and houses—are found in a unique combination in the chart. Such combinations constitute the raw material from which astrological divination is carried out; that is the reading of the chart. However, before commenting on the procedures used, it is necessary to understand the meaning of each of these elements.

CLASSIFICATION

In studying the bibliography within the social sciences which refers to astrology, it is evident that the hypothesis put forward by Durkheim and Mauss—according to which such systems (in their case, the Chinese) can be analysed as a form of classification—has not been much followed since then. However this is not due to the weakness of the hypothesis but is a consequence of academic specialisation. The inclusive sociological project formulated by Durkheim was unable to prevent the process of specialisation of the social sciences, in which the privilege of studying 'primitive' societies fell to anthropology. Although this exclusivity has been weakening in recent decades in favour of a larger investigation of socio-cultural phenomena, traditional historical societies—accessible only through written sources and in which the initial flowering of astrology occurred—were little affected by this movement. Astrology remained an object of study only for historians.

In Lévi-Strauss—probably the author who tried most systematically to develop the implications of Durkheim's and Mauss's article—the privilege of studying primitive societies is articulated in a more complex form, which attempts to determine the properties of the 'human mind'. As he himself makes clear, this is not due to any intrinsic property of these groups, but to the relations we have with them, or rather the opportunity to take a '"distanced view" which allows us to grasp the "facts of general functioning" (…) that have the possibility of being "more general" and "more universal"'.[30] In affirming this we see that Lévi-Strauss deliberately adopts a *demarche* which emphasises the differences between primitive societies and our own, in order to reach conclusions which, among other things, aim to demonstrate the unity of the human species.

However, these theories have recently received several criticisms from Jack Goody, the anthropologist responsible for the re-inclusion of astrology in the spectrum of interests of the social sciences. Unfortunately, he only invokes the subject in his books as an example used in directing criticism at Lévi-Strauss. Goody tries to show by means of astrology how—as in other similar classification systems—the activity of classification would be a product of the emergence of writing, thus not being typical of primitive societies once they experienced rapid expansion with periods of rapid growth in literacy.[31] Beyond this, he believes that the greater or lesser dissemination of writing would be the causal factor explaining the difference between the type of thought which characterises primitive societies, described by Lévi-Strauss as 'savage' or 'wild', and that

---

[30] Claude Lévi-Strauss, *Antropologia Estrutural*, Vol. 2 (Rio de Janeiro: Tempo Brasileiro, 1976), p. 35.
[31] Cf. Jack Goody, *The Domestication of the Savage Mind* (Cambridge: Cambridge University Press, 1977), pp. 70–73.

of complex societies which he called 'domesticated'.[32] For Goody, this distinction as formulated by his French colleague offers only an impoverished binarism; on the one hand, it does not explain the causes of the phenomenon it describes and, on the other, is unable to comprehend the intermediate shades—illustrated, for example, by astrology—between the extreme types with which he [Lévi-Strauss] was concerned. A good deal of Goody's recent work is made up of a reiteration of his theory about this supposed causal factor—writing—whose long-term dissemination would condemn 'savage thought' and its corollaries, such as the belief in magic, to disappearance.[33]

If my hypotheses about astrology are correct, the present work constitutes a refutation of these theories, given that I have tried to demonstrate how astrology presents a [system of] logic relatively similar to those of the magical systems found in primitive societies which were analysed by Lévi-Strauss in *La Pensée Sauvage*. In spite of this, we find the practice of these systems in sectors of Brazilian society with a relatively high level of education, which demonstrates that the influence of writing is not as radical as Goody believes.

Nevertheless, before analysing astrology using the theoretical apparatus developed by Lévi-Strauss it is necessary to examine the second criticism put forward by Goody, according to which this scheme only amounts to a simplistic binarism. This is particularly important, from the present point of view, given that it implies the idea that Lévi-Strauss would not admit the presence of 'savage thought' in literate societies, exactly those in which we find the different 'astrological systems' which demand a complex numerical calculation of planetary motions.

Now, Lévi-Strauss states explicitly that there is not necessarily either a logical or a chronological succession between the two types of thought which he distinguishes, since he also does not claim the existence of two varieties of society, marked by one or the other of the two types of thought. Such a model might be present in an evolutionary perspective accodring to which there is an ineluctable tendency in human societies towards the development of the means of communication, thus producing a more and more 'domesticated' kind of thought.[34] But Lévi-Strauss considers that:

---

[32] Lévi-Strauss, *La Pensée Sauvage*.

[33] Goody, *The Domestication of the Savage Mind*, p. 149.

[34] At times, this appears to be Goody's perspective when, for example, he claims to believe that human history has a direction 'especially in areas that can be called "control over nature" and "growth of knowledge"'. (Goody, *The Domestication of the Savage Mind*, p. 151).

There exist two distinct modes of scientific thought, each of which do not function like unequal stages in the development of human thought, but rather as two strategic levels in which nature is engaged by scientific knowledge; one closely related to sensation and imagination and the other detached from them, as if the necessary relations that constitute the object of all science (...) could be reached by two different routes: one very close to sensory intuition, the other very distant from it.[35]

For Lévi-Strauss, instead of constituting pre-scientific systems, magical-classificatory schemas would be the expression of a 'science of the concrete' that still survives in the arts, and was also present in the speculations of the naturalists and hermeticists of the Middle Ages.[36] In this analysis, we enter into those sectors of social life 'not yet deciphered and where, by indifference or inability, and more often without us knowing why, savage thought continues to prosper'.[37]

Anthropological consideration of astrology was born under the influence of evolutionism. When a system of astrology such as the Chinese was described for the first time as a classificatory system, Durkheim and Mauss attributed to it an intermediate position on a scale which had totemic Australian societies at its lower end and modern scientific classifications at its upper end. The form of the Chinese system would not have been derived anymore from the social morphology as it existed in those societies, but its elements were still grouped in classes and species based on 'social affinities'.[38] Thus, although we must credit their pioneering effort in recognising in astrology an autonomous logic this was, for them, only appropriate for a stage in the development of the human mind. According to this view, the presence of astrology in modern society could only be seen as a survival or an irrational residue. The hypothesis of Lévi-Strauss, by which either so-called 'savage thought' or 'scientific thought' carry out distinct operations which do not evolve from the former to the latter, either logically or chronologically, is nevertheless strategically important for the present work:

---

[35] Lévi-Strauss, *La Pensée Sauvage*, p. 24.

[36] After making this last reference, Lévi-Strauss makes some rapid observations about the astrological, botanical classifications of antiquity. For more on these classifications see Festugière, *La Révélation*, pp. 123–82.

[37] Lévi-Strauss, *La Pensée Sauvage*, p. 290.

[38] Cf. Durkheim and Mauss, 'Algumas Formas Primitivas de Classificação', p. 453.

Magical thought is not an origin, a beginning nor a sketch, apart from a whole still to be realised; it forms a well-articulated system, independent in this viewpoint, from the other system constituted by science (…). Instead, however of opposing magic and science, it would be better to place them side by side, as two modes of knowing, unequal in their theoretical and practical results (…), but not in terms of the mental operations which each imply, and they differ less in function than in the types of phenomena to which they are applied.[39]

In this way I will explore, in parallel, the classification principles of astrology and the theory of Lévi-Strauss, interpreting the first through the second, and attempting to demonstrate my hypotheses on the systematic and structural character of zodiacal astrology.

A: Signs: Synchronic Classification

Among the four classificatory elements which constitute astrological interpretation only the aspects do not play a role in the primary classification.

The classification of signs is obtained through two complementary criteria: one synchronic and the other diachronic.[40] In the first, the signs are arranged according to their different characteristics, without any reference to temporality. In the second, each is defined as a stage in a closed cycle.

The synchronic classification divides them into two categories that can be associated with certain analogous binary oppositions: positive/negative, masculine/feminine, active/passive, etc. This division, in turn, is repeated in another quaternary, that of the elements, with the first two linked to the first pole of the previous binary oppositions: fire, air, water and earth. The zodiac signs are distributed among these elements according to their sequence: the first is fire, followed by earth, then air and finally water; the sequence then repeats for the next [two sets of] four signs. Superimposed on this is a ternary classification, by which each sign receives, also in order, one of three modalities: cardinal, fixed or mutable. Thus the zodiac is made up of a combination of elements and modalities as follows:

---

[39] Lévi-Strauss, *La Pensée Sauvage*, p. 21.
[40] This definition was made for descriptive reasons and will not be found in any manual or course on astrology.

ARIES: fire and cardinal

GEMINI: air and mutable

LEO: fire and fixed

LIBRA: air and cardinal

SAGITTARIUS: fire and mutable

AQUARIUS: air and fixed

TAURUS: earth and fixed

CANCER: water and cardinal

VIRGO: earth and mutable

SCORPIO: water and fixed

CAPRICORN: earth and cardinal

PISCES: water and mutable

To determine the symbolism of each sign, the properties of each element and each modality must be combined, together with their position in the diachronic classification. I would like to comment first on the form in which the elements are used. In the groups of users among which I did my fieldwork, this latter criterion seemed to me to be the privileged one in the characterisation of each sign. So while on the one hand it was quite common to comment that the sign of a particular person was, for example, fire or water, I never observed, except in cases when it was explicitly requested, any reference to the modality of the person's sign.

The four elements were originally established in antiquity by Empedocles, and received their characteristic definitions in the physics of Aristotle. They were defined as the four basic components of the sublunar world, out of which were created all of the material the world contained. Initially, their definitions were a product of the four sensory qualities which refer to temperature and humidity.

	DRY	HUMID
COLD	Earth	Water
HOT	Fire	Air

On the other hand, they can also be organised in a repeat of the opposition between high and low, which is related as positive/negative. Aristotelian physics attributed to each element a natural place to which each of them tended to move in the absence of any applied force. The two dry elements occupied the extreme ends of this division:

HIGH   Fire

∧   Air

∨   Water

LOW   Earth

Humidity would then be a subordinate factor; its function would be to moderate the temperature either of heat or cold, characterising the intermediate elements (of air/water), in contrast to the extremes of fire/earth.

It is not useful to attempt to show how much the physics of Aristotle, on which astrology is based, has been overtaken by modern science. Today modern chemistry has established that the smallest constituent of matter is the atom. However, although I believe that the vast majority of astrologers are informed about this transformation in the field of science, only one or two mentioned this apparent contradiction: not to point it out, but to condemn those astrologers who, because of it, had abandoned the four elements, not understanding that they 'are in fact, the basis of the zodiac, and consequently of all of astrology'.[41]

The little enthusiasm demonstrated for these discoveries of modern chemistry can perhaps be explained if we follow Lévi-Strauss and recognise that scientific thought and the classification system, working 'by two different routes', are heterogeneous. In reality, the classification systems are seeking 'systematisation at the level of sensory data', on which science has long ago turned its back.[42] The high level of abstraction at which modern chemistry works makes it inappropriate for a science of the concrete.

The difference between the modern chemical elements and the four traditional astrological elements resides in the fact that, in the first case, they are concerned with concepts, and in the second with signs, following the characterisation that Lévi-Strauss gives us. The first type aims to be wholly transparent to reality and attempts to free itself of any reference to the concrete contexts in which it appears, whether they be linguistic, historical or practical. It is evident that all science takes place in a historical-cultural context; but the concept, as in the case of the engineer in Lévi-Strauss's analogy, 'always attempts to open a path and situate itself at a distance'.[43] Hence, the

---

[41] Arroyo, *Astrologia*, p. 100.

[42] Lévi-Strauss, *La Pensée Sauvage*, p. 19. He ends this sentence saying: '(…) that it (science) is just beginning to re-incorporate this perspective'. Frequently, besides the distinctions between scientific and magical classification, Lévi-Strauss makes a nod towards a newly emerging scientific paradigm, of which structuralism is certainly intended to be part, that would have the aim of reconciling them. This question about the ultimate aims of anthropological structuralism will not be developed here, given that they do not impede the analysis proper of 'savage thought', which is more programmatic than analytical. On the other hand, it is this that justifies the use by Lévi-Strauss of the term *science* for both types of knowledge, as much for the concrete as for science proper: a terminology that I do not use, so as not to obscure their differences.

[43] Lévi-Strauss, *La Pensée Sauvage*, p. 30.

recourse to the language of mathematics, which installed itself definitively with Galileo. The sign, also having a referential power which allows it to realise classifications, is contrary to the concept, 'a concrete existent',[44] maintaining mythical and magical thought 'incrusted with images'.[45]

To show how this thesis applies to the distinction between the four elements of Empedocles and those of modern chemistry, I would like to make a quick reference to the work of Gaston Bachelard. His commentators are in the habit of distinguishing two apparently contradictory scales in his work: epistemology, and the study of aesthetics and the imagination (sometimes grouped under the concept of daydream (*reverie*)). Although the true nature of the relation between these two segments of his work remains under discussion by critics—due to the changes of position he took—the one thing that seems clear is their reciprocal exclusion.[46]

In Bachelard's work daydreaming appears initially as the enemy of scientific work. In *La Formation de l'Ésprit Scientifique*, it arises through the analysis of symbolic evocations, from metaphors and analogies, from which the 'new scientific spirit' must escape: characterised (according to Bachelard) by an abstraction and a mathematisation even more radical than those found in Newtonian science. However, in his book published three years later, *Lautréamont*, he begins to analyse literature and to understand that 'images' and 'complexes', that were previously taken as obstacles to the development of science, determine the dynamic creativity of the poetic activity.

Within this second scale, dedicated to imagery, an important place is occupied by the books he devoted to the four elements of Empedocles,[47] which he came to call 'the hormones of the imagination'.[48] Although he recognised in a later work (1947)[49] that

---

[44] Lévi-Strauss, *La Pensée Sauvage*, p. 28.

[45] Lévi-Strauss, *La Pensée Sauvage*, p. 31.

[46] 'It is necessary however, to oppose to the expansive poetic spirit, the taciturn scientific spirit for which an initial antipathy is a healthy precaution…'. (Gaston Bachelard, *La Psychanalyse du Feu* [Paris: Gallimard, 1985], p. 10). And, in an earlier book, commenting on his own work, he affirms: 'If I had to summarise an irregular and laborious career, marked out by different books, the best would be to place it under two contradictory signs, masculine and feminine, of *concept* and of *image*. Between the concept and the image, there is no synthesis'. (Gaston Bachelard, *La Poétique de la Rêverie* [Paris: PUF, 1961], p. 45).

[47] The books are: *The Psychoanalysis of Fire* (1938), *Water and Reverie* (1942), *Air and Dreams* (1943), *Earth and the Reveries of the Will* and *Earth and Reveries of Rest* (both in 1948).

[48] Bachelard, *La Poétique de la Rêverie*, p. 19.

[49] No further information is given on this work by Bachelard.—Ed.

the privilege allowed to these four images had not been shown to be scientifically correct, this first choice was no less revealing of the power of their symbolism in Western culture. This influence is felt principally in the 'pre-scientific' literature studied by Bachelard in his search for epistemological obstacles, among which are included works by the alchemists, who frequently studied astrology.

Meanwhile, the choice of the four elements as a starting point for the scientific analysis of matter is shown to be entirely inadequate from the epistemological point of view. As we have already seen, their definition is made through sense impressions like heat and humidity, which are inappropriate for the language of modern science. In the first stage of the evolution of the latter, precision instruments are placed between the observer and his objects. Such instruments allow the introduction of mathematical references in the research process. However, this instrumentalised empiricism that can be illustrated by an aphorism of Lord Kelvin (to weigh is to think, to think is to weigh), is still excessively realist for Bachelard.[50] In the rationalism of the new chemistry, theory is superimposed on practice, not receiving its information passively from the latter, but creating its own reality: 'There is more chance of knowing sugar by making sugars than by analysing one particular sugar'.[51] The same happens with Mendeléev's Periodic Table of chemical elements. In this, 'the law precedes the fact (…), the order of substances is imposed like a rationality'.[52] Thus, establishing a sequence of elements on the basis of increasing atomic numbers allows the properties of elements then unknown (but which already had their defined place in the table) to be predicted. This tendency reaches its maximum expression with the synthesis of artificial transuranic elements, in which theory creates the fact.

We have already given examples of the open character of the concept as defined by Lévi-Strauss:[53] if the linguistic sign is, by contrast closed, this is due to its limited decontextualisation. However, it is exactly its 'pre-constraint' that confers on it the possibility of being deployed in a multiplicity of significations.[54] The affirmation that Bachelard made in relation to the poetic image is also valid for the sign; it is

[50] Gaston Bachelard, *La Philosophie du non: essai d'une philosophie du nouvel esprit scientifique* (Paris: PUF, 1960), pp. 26–27.
[51] Bachelard, *La Philosophie du non*, p. 56.
[52] Bachelard, *La Philosophie du non*, p. 57.
[53] 'The concept thus appears as the operator opening the combination on which it works'. (Lévi-Strauss, *La Pensée Sauvage*, p. 30).
[54] Lévi-Strauss, *La Pensée Sauvage*, p. 29.

contextually variable, 'it is not like the concept, constitutive'.[55] Bachelard recognises therefore, its efficacy in poetic discourse. If he is unable to do this when dealing with pre-scientific knowledge, this is due to the fact that his epistemology is intended to follow the trajectory of science and this, in his opinion, turns more and more towards the concrete [rather than towards the poetic].[56]

I will now illustrate how the four elements—which will be progressively shown to be inadequate for an abstract scientific analysis, whether taken as signs or images— manage to become, via the sensory impressions that they can evoke, a powerful classificatory matrix.

Freed from the substantialist relation that they possessed through belonging to Aristotelian physics, they became defined in more diverse and always inclusive forms. This can be understood when we read the formulation of Charles Carter, one of the most respected English astrologers of this century, who claimed that they are the 'basic principles of astrology'.[57] Arroyo relates the difficulties of Carter's position, reproducing extracts from his Encyclopaedia of Psychological Astrology:

> The elements can be described from different points of view and with an abundance of details, but as is obvious, this is far from making it easy to describe, exemplify and explain something which is, neither more nor less than, the basic laws of the solar system, if not of the universe.[58]

Also using a para-scientific language, Arroyo tries to escape from these difficulties by defining the elements as 'vital forces' or 'energy fields'.[59] Not all astrologers are so concerned to make their epistemological premises explicit. The majority limit themselves to defining each symbol in terms of its classificatory capacity. Even when alternative definitions of the elements are proposed which don't treat them simply as 'symbols or abstract concepts' (as Arroyo complains), they are so all-embracing that little or no clarity is introduced into the debate. In practice the use of the elements is nearly always symbolic.

---

[55] Gaston Bachelard, La Poetique de l'Espace (Paris: PUF, 1957), p. 3.
[56] We see here that he disagrees with Lévi-Strauss; cf. Goody, The Domestication of Savage Thought.
[57] Cited in Arroyo, Astrologia, p. 100.
[58] Cited in Arroyo, Astrologia, p. 100.
[59] Arroyo, Astrologia, p. 140.

They can be linked to other quaternary classifications, such as those mentioned by Goody, where they are found related to the traditional associations of the elements with the four Galenic temperaments and to the four seasons (see fig. 1). The sensory qualities such as temperature and humidity (which I mentioned earlier) are the basis of this association. In the table however, the elements function as mediators between the two extremes of temperaments and seasons which, in their turn, are related in accordance with the solar cycle, to the twelve signs. With such a superimposition of classifications, a correlation between signs and elements is arrived at which differs from the traditional one, as Goody appears to have noticed, judging by the commentary that is attached to the table.

The most frequent use of the elements concerns, however, the determination of individual personality. Here we already have a play of secondary classifications given that, from their frequency in each chart, individuals can be related to each of them. The element of the Sun and Ascendant signs are most important. Thus astrological manuals offer us characteristic typologies for each one, so as to define the framework by which each chart is structured. It is not necessary to repeat that the typology of the elements is intimately linked to that of the signs associated with them.

This typology is constructed basically from the high/low axis. The positive elements produce active, expansive personalities, while the negative elements produce receptive, introverted people. Fire, occupying one of the extremes of this axis is, more than any other element, characterised by initiative and enterprise. Arroyo affirms that its signs 'exemplify decisiveness, great self-confidence, enthusiasm, limitless force and direct honesty'.[60] Likewise, the self-expression of individuals marked by Air is less ardent, more intellectual, showing a 'desire to be communicative, projecting an energy which is basically mental'.[61] Among the receptive elements the most humid, Water, is more flexible and unstable. Its passivity does not exclude a reaction which, however, remains internal and emotional. The signs of this element are characterised by 'sensitivity and susceptibility'.[62] By contrast, those of Earth are defined by their great stability, which can sometimes lead to 'a narrowness of viewpoint, an attachment to routine and order'.[63]

---

[60] Arroyo, *Astrologia*, pp. 107–08.
[61] Martin Freeman, *How to Interpret a Birth Chart: Guide to the Analysis and Synthesis of Astrological Charts* (Wellingborough: The Aquarian Press, 1981), p. 35.
[62] Freeman, *How to Interpret a Birth Chart*, p. 36.
[63] Arroyo, *Astrologia*, p. 112.

But what makes the elements a richer starting point for a typology is the imagery associated with each of them. We have here a rich illustration of the way in which the signs, classificatory in two senses, remain at the concrete and sensory level, thus offering an extremely strong evocative power.

On the impetuous Fire [signs]:

Fiery types, in fact, (the fire signs) provide energy, heat, and that creative vision which sometimes can be seen in burning flames or hot coals in a fireplace. But fire can also consume itself and be reduced to ashes if it is not controlled. Excitement and grandness of vision which are open to all possibilities can have a certain glamour, but the fire signs constantly frustrate themselves, since they are not able to translate their visionary ideas into reality.[64]

On the intellectual Air [signs]:

Air is the medium through which living beings breathe, it is the medium of sound transmission, no speaking can happen without it, it connects everything (...). So, those charts in which one or more of these air signs are prominent tend pre-eminently to emphasise communication. They are inclined towards rationality, intellectual investigations, and work in the field of ideas. They enjoy making contacts with thoughts, people or places.[65]

On the emotional Water [signs]:

Water reflects, dissolves, washes, assists growth. The sea possesses unknown depths and carries many cargoes. It may have a calm surface that is illusory, given that sudden storms can arise and hidden currents can pull (...). Their (those who have water signs prominent in their charts) defects are derived from being 'unstable like water', very easily turning into a reflection of the last person they were with, and very prone to emotional outbursts.[66]

This logic also appears in the relationship between people of different signs, as we can see from the following description of the relationship between pragmatic Earth types and those of other elements; they:

---

[64] Freeman, *How to Interpret a Birth Chart*, p. 34.
[65] Margaret Hone, *The Modern Textbook of Astrology* (Essex: L. N. Fowler, 1980), p. 39.
[66] Hone, *The Modern Textbook*, pp. 39–40.

...feel that the air signs are above them, in the clouds, childishly playing with impossible plans and with no practical value. They also think that the fire signs will scorch the earth, passing tempestuously through life too fast. (...) The water signs, on the other hand, share qualities of acquisition, retention and self-protection. Thus, earth thinks that water will refresh it and make it become still more productive.[67]

In this last passage we can see the theory of Arroyo, according to which signs of the same polarity, either negative or positive, combine more harmoniously than signs of the opposite polarity.

My objective through these rather extended examples is to illustrate how, in the elaboration of a typology of the elements, the familiar images evoked permit the construction of rich metaphors that express that typology. As it is not a case of an exhaustive exposition of astrological classifications, those already familiar with them will consider this exposition rather sketchy, given that I have focused only on a few lines within the rich characterisation of each element. Thus, for example, I may have left an exaggerated impression of the rigidity of [individuals of the] Earth signs; but this attitude can be healthy given that, as Freeman affirms, 'all physical growth requires roots (...). The adventure of a seed under the earth beginning to germinate is one of the most stimulating and creative acts of nature'.[68]

The elements, staying on this concrete sensory level, play a synthetic, encompassing role that is demanded by the classificatory procedure. It is important to make clear, however, as I do more systematically later, that this symbolic power is not simply an intrinsic property of each which would unequivocally determine each of their uses.

The three modalities do not possess such strong evocative power; even so, they must be taken into account in the characterisation of each sign. The cardinal, fixed and mutable signs are defined by representing, respectively, the beginning, middle, and end of each season. Thus, the behaviour of the signs of each of these modalities is that of (in order): beginning an action, consolidating what was begun, and adapting what was established; in other words, what their own names already suggest.[69] Because of their logical sequence, the classification of modalities is linked more closely to diachrony.

---

[67] Arroyo, *Astrologia*, p. 112.
[68] Freeman, *How to Interpret a Birth Chart*, p. 35.
[69] Ana Maria Costa Ribeiro, *O Conhecimento da Astrologia* (Rio de Janeiro: Hipocampo, 1986), p. 44.

B: Signs: Diachronic Classification

The contribution of Lévi-Strauss on the question of primitive classificatory systems was preceded by a volume in which he returned to the old question of totemism. There is no need to relate the arguments of *Totemism Today* where, in reviewing the classical literature on the subject, he tries to dissolve the so-called 'totemic illusion' that takes a particular case of the phenomenon of classification as if it were an autonomous institution and, in doing so, finds itself in terrible difficulties trying to define it in a precise form.[70] However, this dissolution leaves behind, as he himself recognises, a residue: what is the motive for the manifest preference of primitive societies to take natural species as the basis for their classifications? It is the response to this question which will allow us to make clear the originality of his new answers.

After criticising functionalist explanations, which suppose an affective relationship between totems and their groups, Lévi-Strauss makes clear his belief that the interpretation of totemism can only be obtained through the primitive intellect. As he has already made clear in his introduction, the preference for the animal and vegetable worlds in the construction of classificatory systems is due to the fact that they 'offer to man a mode of thinking'.[71] They offer a paradigm from which humans can symbolise their social relationships. It is fundamental to clarify that, before formulating this hypothesis, it was necessary for him to discard Durkheim's theory which sought in social morphology the origin for the forms assumed by classification systems. The ability to establish oppositions and metaphorical and metonymic relationships defines the human spirit and its faculty for symbolisation. Faced with the project of the French Sociology School to seek a sociological theory of symbolism, Lévi-Strauss affirmed the need to do the opposite: to seek a symbolic origin of society.[72]

However, it is important to know that the metaphorical model offered by natural species does not necessarily make them the unique starting point for the classification

---

[70] In *La Pensée Sauvage*, Lévi-Strauss summarises his conclusions about the supposed institution of totemism, affirming that 'we are not dealing with an autonomous institution which can be defined by distictive properties typical of certain regions of the world and certain forms of civilisation, but with a *modus operandi* which can be found even beneath traditionally-defined social structures in diametrical opposition to totemism'. (p. 172).

[71] Claude Lévi-Strauss, *A Noção de Estrutura em Etnologia: Raça e História; Totemismo Hoje* (São Paulo: Abril Cultural, 1980), p. 104.

[72] Claude Lévi-Strauss, *Antropologia Estrutural*, Vol. 1 (Rio de Janeiro: Tempo Brasileiro, 1974), p. 12.

systems to which they belong. Between groups and concrete individuals and more all-encompassing general principles they can occupy a mediating role, given that each species is distinctive in relation to the others, and to a generality that includes all their concrete manifestations.[73]

I referred earlier to the three ancient civilisations that constructed astrological symbolism in a complex form with their classification systems. They were the only ones to develop an original astronomy. The separate analysis that I made of the zodiacal system is because of its historical autonomisation, proceeding from its absorption by Hellenism. Thus we can repeat a similar question put by Lévi-Strauss: what particular characteristics of celestial movements make them 'good for thinking'? If I may be allowed to formulate a hypothesis based on data taken from the bibliography referring to Mesopotamia and Hellenism, I would postulate that an important reason was the discovery of the great regularity presented by their motions, and their relative synchrony with natural cycles. As historian Franz Cumont showed, Chaldean theology established that these motions were a palpable representation of 'necessity', the principle which governed the gods themselves, identified with the planets.[74] The latter were called 'the interpreters' since, through their motion, 'above all its order, they made manifest to man the intentions of the gods'.[75] In a Latin poem composed in the first century CE, expounding the astrological principles of the time, one can also see the emphasis on celestial regularity and its ability to reveal divinity and its purposes to us:

> In this vast universe nothing is as surprising as its uniformity and constant order that regulates all the activities there; the number of regions does not cause any confusion, nor do they move from their places, the motions never speed up nor slow down, they never change direction. Could a machine be conceived that was more perfect in its actions, more uniform in its effects? In my opinion, I don't think it is possible to

---

[73] 'All things considered, if zoological and botanical typologies are used more frequently and habitually than others, this only happens because of their intermediary position, at an equal logical distance between the extreme forms of classification, categories and particulars'. (Lévi-Strauss, *La Pensée Sauvage*, pp. 179–80).

[74] Cumont, *Astrology and Religion*, p. 17.

[75] Cumont, *Astrology and Religion*, p. 20.

demonstrate with greater evidence, that the world is governed by a divine power, which is God himself.[76]

When I described astrological cosmology, I tried to show how each sign represents a stage of the annual cycle. The other astrological cycles are defined, in a diachronic classification, through this homology. In it, the meaning of signs is given by their sequential positions in a closed cycle, hence irreversible: or, in other words, which always moves in the same direction.

Each sign may represent, for example, each of the stages in a cycle of germination, growth, harvest and planting of vegetables.[77] However, the meaningful power of the diachronic classification is more easily expressed in the determination of the cycle of an individual life. In Figure 1 we can understand how a group of three signs, related to the four seasons, could express the stages of growth of an individual. Besides this, it is very common to use the unfolding of this division into twelve, so as to represent the phases of a process of self-development, whether on a spiritual level, or as is becoming more common these days, psychologically.

I will now give a simplified characterisation of each sign, showing how the convergence of the two classifications tends to produce a coherent picture; although it applies to a wide range of things, it seeks basically a typology of personality. As will become clear in Section C, the traits attributed to each of the signs represent tendencies that are almost always present in natives of their type, but which can be used 'positively' or not. Thus each stereotype contains within it a possible defect which can be found in each sign. Starting from the seventh sign, I will try to show how astrology analogically opposes characteristics to signs which occupy opposite positions in the zodiac circle.

ARIES: The first sign marks the initial impulse which, added to the element fire and its cardinal modality, favours an aggressive, impulsive personality. It is usually said that Arians are those who initiate things, often without thinking of the consequences.

TAURUS: The first earth sign and of fixed modality represents the consolidation of the creative force of the previous sign. If Aries were pure

---

[76] Marcus Manilius, *Os Astrológicos: Ou a Ciência Sagrada do Céu* (Rio de Janeiro: Artenova, 1974), p. 49.
[77] Arroyo, *Astrologia*, pp. 54–55.

impulse, Taurus would be pure accumulation. Taureans are comfort-seekers and their desire to accumulate manifests in different forms, such as putting on weight, building collections [of possessions], etc.

GEMINI: The second outgoing impulse no longer seeks affirmation, but communication, through being an air sign. The Gemini person is described as being very curious and talkative, but finds difficulty in concentrating on one thing, as its mutable modality shows.

CANCER: Its cardinality gives it initiative which, however, remains internal due to its negative polarity. Marked by water, it is the sign of a very rich emotional life, connected with the primary emotions, linked to maternity. Cancerians would therefore be maternal, even being exaggerated in this trait.

LEO: The self-expression of fire gains a fixed character, i.e., it becomes centred on itself. After the first contact with its surroundings, whether intellectual or emotional, expressed in the previous signs, self-affirmation of the individual is realised in Leo. Typical Leos will be generous and proud and thus, at times, egocentric.

VIRGO: After the definition of the ego comes the phase of setting limits and organising the surrounding world. It is the Virgo person who carries out this task. Its earthy practicality works with a great variety of things since it is a mutable sign. These people are methodical, critical and very often sceptics.

LIBRA: In this air sign, the *I* now comes in contact with the *Other* and this initiative is the expression of its cardinality. It is the sign of intersubjectivity, balance, and consensus. In this way, its qualities may degenerate into an inability to affirm one's self in the presence of others with whom, as a typical air sign, the Libran is always concerned about keeping in contact. It thus faces the opposite problem to the sign on the other side of the zodiac, Aries.

SCORPIO: [This is] where the emotions of water, due to its fixed modality, are found more under control. They are not diminished, but the Scorpio person acquires a great capacity to understand the interior states of others and to identify with them. In the sequence of signs, it is the stage of profound internal transformation. Scorpios will be extremely ingratiating but this power, in contrast to Taureans, who are nearly always peaceful, may become dangerous.

SAGITTARIUS: The impulse of fire takes a larger range of action due to its mutable modality. In this sign there will be a desire for expansion in the direction of larger spaces, ideas, religion, and knowledge. This expansion is made possible by the internal changes favoured by the previous sign and would give direction to the dispersed interests of the Gemini person. Sagittarians are characterised by optimism and intellectual curiosity, which doesn't always stop them from becoming fanatical about the values they prize so much.

CAPRICORN: Earth becomes cardinal, practicality gains an entrpreneurial sense; having the force to make the ideals of the previous stage concrete, the Capricornian is oriented towards the future. He is seen to be responsible and ambitious, but may show some rigidity and become authoritarian and inflexible.

AQUARIUS: The last air sign, this time fixed, its desire for understanding and contact is more concentrated, allowing it to include a wider world. The Aquarian is concerned with humanity and its future, unlike the Leo who is self-centred. But the search for novelty and freedom can become eccentric and anti-social.

PISCES: After its initial individualising impulse, the cycle closes with a mutable water sign; two traits are imprecision and dispersion. The Piscean will be the one who seeks totality, in contrast with the Virgoan who is concerned with details. This can carry them towards religion and mysticism, but their difficulty in perceiving the limits of things can amount to an escape from reality.

This then is the schematically [presented] diachronic classification in its articulation with the synchronic. I have presented a very condensed typification of each sign, attempting to demonstrate its relationship with each of the others. Such a conjugation of classificatory principles however, makes possible a richer characterisation. This can be verified from reading any astrology manual where the primary classifications of metals, colours, and parts of the body, etc., associated with each zodiac sign are also sometimes provided. Illustrating this with some examples in Figure 1, it can be shown how the standards of personality are related to these classifications; thus the neck has the purpose of maintaining stability, a trait characteristic of Taureans while, since the feet support the weight of the body, they symbolise the spirit of self-sacrifice which is typical of many Pisceans.[78] To this must be added the fact that, for astrology, no one is framed exclusively by any one of these types, since the natal chart contains traces of them all.

---

[78] Hone, *The Modern Textbook*, pp. 51, 84.

C: *The Astrological Houses*

Given that the twelve houses represent a cycle of the day, derived from the zodiacal signs, their symbology is derived from the latter. This confers on them a hierarchically inferior position in the interpretation of a chart.

While the zodiac constructs an inclusive symbolic matrix, from which all the signs can be interpreted, the houses refer specifically to the different areas of the practical life of the individual. The attribution of these areas to each house is defined by an analogy with the corresponding sign. Thus the 2nd House is related to the symbology of Taurus, the second sign. It refers to material goods, an area in which accumulation, a Taurean property, can be manifested in the individual. However, in a particular chart, the cusp of the 2nd House could be in Gemini. This would mean that the person who has this chart would work with goods and values in a Geminian, i.e., in an uncertain and dispersive, way.

Thus, the *horoscope* or ascending sign was one of the most important in the interpretation of this system. Today, not only its cusp, but the whole of the first house occupies a prominent place in the chart reading, as is also the case with the [other] so-called angular houses (4, 7, 10). In old manuals there was a tendency to say that any planets occupying succedent (2, 5, 8, 11) and cadent houses (3, 6, 9, 12) had less 'force'. More modern manuals try to link the three types of houses to the three modalities, seeking to show that a privileged place should not be reserved for the angular houses; this is really linked to the initiative which characterises the cardinal signs with which they are analogous. The Ascendant is the only house that continues to play a clearly superior rôle to the others, joining with the Sun to determine the two signs that define the principal character traits of the person. This importance can also be attributed to its analogy with Aries, the sign of individuality and self-expression.

Below I present the areas 'ruled' by each of the other houses and their relationship to the homologous zodiac sign:

2nd House: material goods and values—Taurus is linked to accumulation.
3rd House: siblings, neighbours, primary education—Gemini is the moment of first contact with the surroundings.
4th House: mother, the home, roots—Cancer is linked to origins and the past.
5th House: pleasures and children—Leo is related to individual wellbeing and its perpetuation.

6th House: health, work—if health seems to have a more obvious relationship to Virgo, it is through work, basically, that it is maintained and practical relations with others are realised.

7th House: marriage and unions—Libra expresses contact with the Other when it is invested with a spirit of equality and balance.

8th House: death, sex, inheritances—all these apparently disparate things relate to Scorpio: transformation, profound feelings and control over the emotions and the values of others.

9th House: religion, higher education and long journeys—themes related to the expansiveness of Sagittarius.

10th House: career, achievements—if work in the sense of daily routine is related to the 6th house, its aspect of personal attainment is ruled by the 10th. People with a lot of Capricorn in their charts are considered to be ambitious.

11th House: friendships, interests—they express the eccentricities of Aquarius.

12th House: sacrifices interiority, enemies—expressing Pisces, this house always represents the submission of individuality; the expression of the hidden.

D: The Planets

Before continuing, I would like to return to Lévi-Strauss's theories to illustrate them one more time.

Choosing a non-intellectualist interpretation of totemic classifications, Lévi-Strauss continued according to the theory of Radcliffe-Brown, which postulates the existence of metaphorical relations between social units and the species they represent. However, although the exposition of Radcliffe-Brown's theory already indicated this, it did not warn of the danger of postulating simple, homologous, term-for-term relationships. His analysis of the symbolism of the falcon and the rook for the tribes of the Darling River in Australia shows us that these creatures are also represented as aspects of an opposition. The metaphor thus is not established between each group and each species, but between the relationships which organise the social and biological series. Lévi-Strauss relies, in his theories, on the structural character of symbolic thought to affirm that:

Contrary to what Radcliffe-Brown is still inclined to believe, it is this logic of oppositions and correlations, of exclusions and inclusions, of compatibilities and incompatibilities which explains the laws of association, and not the other way round (…).[79]

For a structuralist analysis, there is no unilateral correlation between the signified and its signifier, in other words, between the group represented and the species which classifies it. Trying to make more precise an excessively literal interpretation of the formulations of Saussure, Lévi-Strauss in earlier texts had already made clear that this relationship is not motivated *a priori* but is *a posteriori*.[80] This means that the relationship between the terms is neither as loose as Durkheim postulated, when he affirmed the purely emblematic character of the totemic animal,[81] nor as rigid as the Jungian theory of the archetypes (criticised at various points in his work, especially in *La Pensée Sauvage*).[82] Thus, of the two forms, the structural method privileges the relations at the expense of the terms or elements of a system; it is in the relations that it locates the universal element of the system and the production of the meaning of each element. Before passing on to planetary classifications, I would like to analyse the features already described in light of these conclusions.

The four elements, for example, are very often treated as 'universal archetypes' due to their central character in Western cosmology. Arroyo is at pains to show this, and in response to the presence of five elements in the Chinese classification system, he mentions Ether as the fifth element composing the Western system; this allows a transposition to be made between the two.[83] However, in Aristotelian physics, Ether is qualitatively different from the other elements, according to ancient and medieval cosmologies. Contrary to what happens with the five Chinese elements, Ether is situated on a different plane from the rest. Besides this, astrology selects only some of the possible meanings that could be attributed, in order to articulate them in a system which opposes its sensory qualities. The poetic evocations [evoked by these four], which Bachelard dedicated himself to collecting, transcend those which astrology attributed to them, given that the latter are motivated by the structure of the whole.

---

[79] Lévi-Strauss, *A Noção de Estrutura em Etnologia*, p. 166.

[80] Claude Lévi-Strauss, *Anthropologie Structurale*, (Paris: Plon, 1958) p. 105. [This is the original French publication of *Structural Anthropology*—Ed.]

[81] Lévi-Strauss, *A Noção de Estrutura em Etnologia*, p. 142.

[82] Lévi-Strauss, *La Pensée Sauvage*, p. 88.

[83] Arroyo, *Astrologia*, p. 102.

As far as the elements that are used in the classification of determined personality types, it is common to attribute human faculties to each one of them which, although present in every individual, attain greater or lesser development in each person. Thus fire is associated with the will, self-affirmation; air with intelligence, rational thinking; water with emotion; and earth with sensory perception, practical thinking and the bodily aspects of behaviour. This vague and general schema is widely disseminated. But in as far as certain astrologers try to define it more exactly, we can detect different formulations.

Those who follow a Jungian approach commonly associate the four elements with the four 'ectopsychic functions':[84]

Fire:	Intuition	Air:	Thinking
Water:	Feeling	Earth:	Sensation

We can understand this analogy if we take into account that Jung conceived the relationship between the functions in the form of a cruciform diagram in which each function is situated around the central Ego:

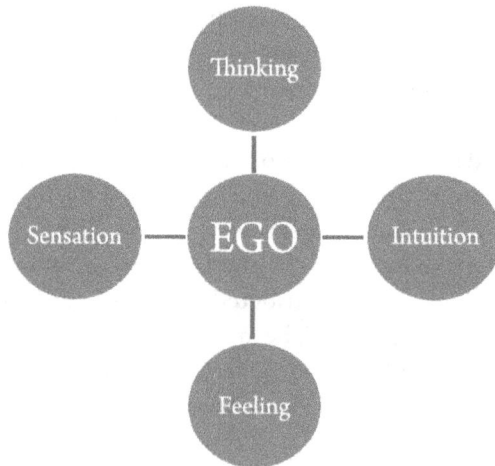

Fig. 4: (Adapted from original, after Jung[85])

---

[84] Ribeiro, *O Conhecimento da Astrologia*, p. 36.
[85] Carl Gustav Jung, *Fundamentos de Psicologia Analítica: As Conferências de Tavistock* (Petrópolis: Vozes, 1972), p. 31.

He explains this drawing, stating that, when conscious energy is concentrated in one of the functions, the opposite function is suppressed. It is thus the homology of the oppositional structure of these functions to that which is present in the astrological classification of the elements which allows this association. Thus:

Intuition : Sensation :: Fire : Earth
Thinking : Feeling :: Air : Water

The form by which Jung structures the oppositions is related to the way he defines intuition. It is 'the function by which one anticipates what is just around the corner, something which routinely is not possible'.[86] It is opposed, therefore, to sensation since it is able to 'sense' something that is not apparently accessible to the senses. This function is easily related, without much analysis, to the fire signs and attributes to them their concrete difficulties which stop them from exercising their expansive will. The analogy becomes more powerful when we take into account that Jung constructed a typology of these four functions, according to the greater or lesser development of each in the individual personality. In the whole of the Jungian functions, the structural factor of the classifications of the elements places their oppositions in the first rank. However, in a different example we can see how the hierarchical potential of the high/low opposition can be the privileged framework. Thus Oskar Adler suggested a classification of the 'natural kingdoms', linked to a second [classification] concerning the human faculties.[87]

(+ high)	Fire	–	Human kingdom	–	The moral I
	Air	–	Animal kingdom	–	Knowledge
	Water	–	Vegetable kingdom	–	Psychical
(- low)	Earth	–	Mineral kingdom	–	Bodily

In this picture, we can observe two traits of the thought of Adler's book published in the 1930s: the influence of evolutionist thinking (Darwin and Haeckel) and that of German critical philosophy (Kant and Schopenhauer). He made use of these sources to construct a hierarchical classification, given that the human kingdom is the only one that possesses all the other dimensions, subordinated to the exclusively human moral

---

[86] Jung, *Fundamentos de Psicologia Analítica*, p. 31.
[87] Oskar Adler, *La Astrología como Ciencia Oculta: el testamento de la astrología* (Buenos Aires: Kier, 1984), pp. 151–52.

dimension. Knowledge is simply related to elementary nervous activity, which distinguishes the animal kingdom from the vegetable, while the latter is separated from the mineral by the presence of water, which symbolises 'the kingdom of instincts and growth (…) which in the animal stage becomes the life of passions in impulsive seeking and instinctive flight (…) and which, in the human stage is converted into the total life of desire (…)'.[88]

The compartmentalisation of human faculties carried out in this more detailed form by Adler corresponds to those disseminated among the astrologers to whom he referred. Thus, following the high/low axis, water belongs to the inferior, being related to interiority. And some authors influenced by Jung, such as Arroyo, even associate intuition with the rule of emotions, classifying it as an attribute of people with water signs, not fire.[89]

Having reviewed some aspects of the previous descriptions in the light of the structural theory of the determination between signifier and signified in classificatory symbolism, I will now go on to describe the classification of the planets. With this in mind, it is interesting to reproduce the conclusions of Lévi-Strauss concerning a divinatory system elaborated by a tribe on the island of Borneo, consisting of seven birds:

---

[88] Adler, *La Astrología como Ciencia Oculta*, p. 69.

[89] As Vilhena notes, the relation between the traditional four Elements and Jung's four psychological functions is not straightforward. The correspondences previously given on pages 42–43 were proposed by astrologer Liz Greene, not by Jung, who commented that the Hippocratic four elements and their corresponding Galenic temperaments had a 'naivety which has long been apparent from the standpoint of psychological theory'. (C.G. Jung, H.G. Baynes and C.F. Baynes, *Contributions to Analytical Psychology* [London: Routledge and Kegan Paul, 1928], p. 295). Greene's set of correspondences is often taken as self-evident by astrologers, but it violates the structural integrity of the Elements; Fire (hot and dry) is the opposite of Water (cold and moist)—not Earth, whose qualities are cold and dry. A plausible solution (in my opinion) is to assign Fire to Thinking, understood as planning, analytical and goal-directed, while Air is related to Intuition, understood as a polysemic and imaginative function of the mind; Earth and Water can remain as they are in Greene's scheme. Since Jung also had an important third dimension contrasting Extraversion with Introversion, it would seem that a solid figure like the tetrahedron is more appropriate for trying to construct correspondences (Graham J. Douglas, *Physics, Astrology and Semiotics* [London: self-published, 1983]).—Trans.

The system chooses only a few distinctive traits, and attributes to them an arbitrary significance, limiting them to seven birds whose choice is surprising because of how unremarkable they are. But, although arbitrary at the level of terms, the system becomes coherent when we examine them as a whole (...). The terms never possess an intrinsic significance, their meaning is 'positional', a function of the cultural and historical context on the one hand, and on the other of the structure of the system in which they are called to take part.[90]

These words could be applied completely unchanged to ancient astrology, if we replace the word 'birds' with 'planets'. Evidently the choice of the latter was not arbitrary but was, for example, due to their association with the Greek pantheon of gods. Astrology also took advantage of certain sensible and astronomical characteristics of the planets in order to construct the system. My hypothesis is that the structure of the latter, if we consider only the seven traditional planets, is composed of successive oppositions on three different planes, from which we can extract the meaning that each of the terms acquires. The meanings attributed nowadays to the three planets which are invisible to the naked eye—Uranus, Neptune and Pluto—will be considered later.

On the first plane the two luminaries, Sun and Moon, can be opposed. Following Louis Dumont, I believe that we are looking at a hierarchical type of opposition which Dumont attempts to introduce into structural thinking alongside distinctive oppositions and complementarities.[91] The Sun possesses a pre-eminence not only in relation to the Moon but also to the rest of the planets, since it includes the first plane of oppositions which is hierarchically superior to the others. It is also the solar cycle which produces, according to the analogy we described, the meanings of the signs of the zodiac, thus determining all the rest of the planetary cycles. By occupying this structural position, it can be said to be linked to a symbolism of the *centre*. Hence, [this

---

[90] Lévi-Strauss, *La Pensée Sauvage*, p. 74.

[91] 'This hierarchical relation is generally between a whole (or a group) and one of its elements: the element forms part of the whole, and in this sense is consubstantial or identical, and at the same time distinguished from or opposed to it. This is what is meant by the term "inclusion of the contrary"'. (Louis Dumont, 'Vers une Théorie de la Hiérarchie', in Louis Dumont, *Homo Hierarchicus: Le Système des Castes et ses Implications* [Paris: Gallimard, 1979], p. 397); Louis Dumont, *Homo Hierarchicus: An Essay on the Caste System* (Chicago: University of Chicago Press, 1970), p. 401.

is] one of the reasons heliocentric cosmology did not represent such a violent blow to astrology.[92]

In the Ptolemaic system, the Sun occupies a central position among the planetary spheres, being the fourth in order. Such a position also marks its pre-eminence over the rest of the planets which, the ancients believed, were guided by it, 'the heart of the world' (*Cardia ton cosmon*).[93]

All the astrological manuals which I consulted, from the *Tetrabiblos* to contemporary examples, describe the properties of the planets according to the order of succession of the planetary spheres established by Ptolemy, with one exception: the description of the Sun is always given first place.[94] I am trying to show the relationship between the logical structural ordering of the planets in the astrological system and their positions in ancient astronomy. The latter do not appear as a simple linear progression, but attempt to translate the relationship to the rest of the planets, putting

---

[92] The astrologer Olavo de Carvalho exemplifies his symbolic methods of analysis through the Sun/Moon relationship (Carvalho, *Astros e Símbolos*, pp. 29–44). This analysis can be made on several planes, which succeed one another by their increasing order of inclusiveness. For him, above the rationalities of identity and difference, which statically oppose the two symbols, and that of causality and dialectic which opposes them dynamically, is situated the analogical method, according to which 'the Moon is not even opposed to the Sun, as in the reasoning based on static identity, nor as in dialectical reasoning, but rather subordinated to it'. (Carvalho, *Astros e Símbolos*, p. 36). To demonstrate this, Carvalho suggests a 'properly astronomical understanding' which teaches us that the Moon 'is even doubly subordinated, since it is the satellite of a satellite'. (Carvalho, *Astros e Símbolos*, p. 36).

[93] Cumont emphasises the important role which this star assumes in Roman astrology and astronomy which, as Ptolemy (for example) shows, were intimately linked during this period: 'The Sun is transformed into the conductor of cosmic harmony, the master of the four elements and the four seasons (…). Pliny already recognised it as the sovereign divinity which rules nature, *principale naturae regimen ac numer* (…). It will be seen by pagan theologians as the reason which controls the world, *mens mundi et temperatio*'. (Cumont, *Astrology and Religion*, pp. 72–73).

[94] Their succession was, according to Ptolemy, from the closest to the most distant from Earth: Moon, Mercury, Venus, Sun, Mars, Jupiter and Saturn. [Translator F.E. Robbins relates this information in his preface to Claudius Ptolemy, *Tetrabiblos*, Loeb Classical Library (Cambridge, MA: Harvard University Press, 1980), I.1, n.1—Ed.]

the Sun in a central position, an operation which post-Copernican astronomers have found to be unnecessary.[95]

The Sun's central symbolism is also revealed by the important role it plays in natal charts. In the psychological interpretation of a birth chart, the Sun sign is the fundamental datum in relation to which the other factors, which merely complement it and must be subordinated. Although the Ascendant may sometimes receive a similar emphasis, and its distinction from the Sun sign is not clear in the large number of manuals, generally the signs that are found in these two positions distinguish themselves through the opposition—if we continue with the same metaphor— between the centre and the periphery. This latter can be unfolded into a second contrast, which opposes appearance and essence. The Sun sign is the identity, the *self*.[96] Thus the Ascendant is generally associated with the way by which 'a person manifests himself, the personality or mask which they present'.[97] This identification with the external aspect of the individual, which Jung called the *persona*, is fortuitously linked to the fact that this is the sign which 'ascends' above the horizon, emerging from the darkness and 'appearing'. In the final analysis, the pre-eminence of the Sun in interpretation is explained by the character derived from the classification of the astrological houses in relation to the signs, which are defined by the solar cycle itself.

As I said earlier, the first plane holds a hierarchical pre-eminence with respect to the rest. Thus, on this level—and also in the other pole of the opposition which composes it, the Moon—it is still a question of attributes which I call central, individual, in contrast to the increasing exteriority represented by the symbolism of the other planets. The polarity positive/negative, masculine/feminine, which we already saw in the functioning of other sectors of the astrological system, organises equally all three planes of planetary classification. In the latter, its fullest expression is rightly found in the pair [of] Sun and Moon, whether from an abstract point of view, as we saw in the article commented on in note 92, or in the charts of individuals. Thus, Freeman avers that 'the Sun and Moon make up the basic integration of masculine and feminine in the

---

[95] Besides, it was not only for scientific reasons that the Sun obtained, in Copernican cosmology, the central place. He considered this place, 'following the Pythagorean tradition, and thus inverting completely the Aristotelian medieval scale (...), the best and the most important'. The Sun is due such privilege because of its 'supreme perfection and importance— the source of light and life'. (Koyré, *Do Mundo Fechado*, p. 38).

[96] 'Identity' is Freeman's definition in *How to Interpret a Birth Chart*, p. 20; 'self' is Hone's in *The Modern Textbook*, p. 251.

[97] Ribeiro, *O Conhecimento da Astrologia*, p. 191.

chart'.[98] In the symbology of Ptolemy, which is expressed in terms of temperature and humidity, these two planets embody this polarity paradigmatically, being defined respectively as hot and dry [Sun], and cold and moist [Moon].[99]

Although the symbolic properties of the Moon vary, they are always defined in relation to [those of] the Sun. Apart from their astronomical positions, other physical and visible traits of these planets are used as symbols of their opposition. The Sun is the source of light, radiation, while the Moon merely reflects solar luminosity. In comparison with the regular movement of the former, which determines the seasons, the second represents, in its sensible aspect, an instability represented by its various phases.

In a psychological interpretation of a natal chart the Sun represents the expansive aspects of the personality while the Moon is related to receptivity and passivity. The psychological approaches to astrology attribute to it the 'subconscious', the 'memory', the 'imagination', the 'instincts', the 'moods: in other words, the irrational or unconscious aspects of psychic functioning.[100] On the other hand, some followers of traditional astrology, among them Olavo de Carvalho, not only affirm that this system is a 'cosmological and not a psychological' science; they associate the Moon with the mind and reason, drawing support from Guénon himself.[101]

If we go to its source we will see that this second definition of lunar symbolism, linked to the brain, is opposed to the 'knowledge of the heart', represented by the Sun. If this statement is taken out of context, it can seem that the meaning of the opposition, such as was presented by astrologers of a psychological orientation, has been reversed. However this is not what we find if we analyse the fundamentals of the associations of Guénon. They start out from the Aristotelian and Thomist distinction between intellect and reason: intuitive knowledge of principles [on the one hand] and rational deduction of their implications [on the other].[102] In this way, the first is a source and the second a reflection; hence the first is solar and the second lunar.

Thus, I hope to have illustrated sufficiently how two astrological currents which possess seemingly irreconcilable presuppositions can, even through elaborating their

---

[98] Freeman, *How to Interpret a Birth Chart*, p. 21.

[99] Freeman, *How to Interpret a Birth Chart*, p. 19.

[100] Arroyo attributes the 'subconcious' to the Moon in *Astrologia*, p. 93; Hone attributes 'memory' and 'imagination' in *The Modern Textbook*, p. 26; Freeman attributes 'instincts' and 'moods' in *How to Interpret a Birth Chart*, p. 21.

[101] René Guénon, *Os Símbolos da Ciência Sagrada* (São Paulo: Pensamento, 1984), pp. 368–77.

[102] Guénon, *Os Símbolos da Ciência Sagrada*, pp. 374–75.

different definitions, remain loyal to the structure of the astrological system. I have tried, in this chapter, to define the constant character of the system, as Lévi-Strauss postulated for myths.[103] In this sense, I have been attempting to determine the underlying structure, of which all forms of astrology are variations. Contrary to what happens with the astrologer, who must take a position, it does not fall to the researcher to choose between these variants. Due to the modest pretensions and pilot nature of this study, its point of view of the whole (astrological) universe is considerably reduced; this could lead me to over- or under-estimate the capacity of the system to show transformations without altering the basic structures which define it. My conclusions have, therefore, a heuristic quality, and are not, in any way, represented as something definitive. They are based on the supposition that astrology must have a systematic character, since only this can explain the symbolism which it produces, and on the hope that its model can serve as a parameter for mapping the diverse specific manifestations of astrological practice, at the group or individual level, issuing from informants or theoretical currents and tendencies. For example, the hierarchical character of planetary classification is, on the one hand, emphasised by the religious approach of Guénon and his followers; [104] on the other, it tends to be minimised by psychological astrology which seeks to flatten the opposition contained in planetary symbolism, attributing it to different aspects of psychic functioning, without any one having pre-eminence.

Taking up the description of planetary symbolism, I will now consider Mercury. This planet is the mediator between the first plane (Sun/Moon) and the second (Venus/Mars). Its position in the Ptolemaic cosmology is curious. According to Willy Hartner, the criterion adopted by Ptolemy would have been the greater or lesser speed of orbital revolution of this planet.[105] However by being, in reality, situated between the Earth and the Sun, describing their true orbits around the latter, Venus and Mercury

---

[103] Lévi-Strauss, *Antropogia Estrutural* Vol. 1, ch. XI.

[104] 'Whatever the reason might be, the fact is that duality exists only from a relative and contingent point of view. If we take a different viewpoint, more profound and essential, in which we consider ourselves to be in the (divided) state that corresponds to it, then unity must be re-established. In this way, the relationship between the two elements, which appeared from the beginning as oppositional and later as complementary, becomes something else: a relationship of subordination'. (Guénon, *Os Símbolos da Ciência Sagrada*, p. 372).

[105] Willy Hartner, 'Medieval Views on Cosmic Dimensions and Ptolemy's "Kitab Al'Manshurat"', in *L'Aventure de l'Esprit: Mélanges Alexandre Koyré* (Paris: Hermann, 1964), I: p. 265.

have the same period of rotation around the Earth as that of the solar cycle. Projected onto the zodiac, they never move further from the Sun than 48° and 28° respectively. This latter figure could have led Ptolemy to locate the Venusian sphere further from the Sun than the Earth, since its motion is less determined by the Sun than that of Mercury. Today it is known that Mercury is further from the Earth than Venus; we may never know Ptolemy's reason for his choice. It is curious that they are very well adjusted to the structure of astrological classification.

The fact that Mercury never moves far from the Sun—which belongs, as we have seen, to the first plane—is used by Freeman to illustrate its 'meddling character'.[106] (He does not mention its similar astronomical properties to the motions of Venus.) Consistent with its structural position as a mediator, it is associated with 'communication in all its forms'. Other authors link it to thinking because of its associative and communicative abilities.[107] The mythological figure of Hermes/Mercury is also associated with this symbolism, in which he is pictured as the 'Messenger of the Gods' or, in other contexts, as a hermaphrodite. This last trait is linked to the thesis mentioned by several authors since Ptolemy: that it is a planet which is both masculine and feminine. As always happens in astrology, the characteristics of each symbol may have negative, [as well as positive] applications. Thus this planet is associated with duplicity, lying and theft.

If Mercury realises a mediation between the first and second planes, then the second plane similarly mediates between the first and the third planes which are contrasted on the axis of centre/periphery. If the Sun/Moon pair have as their theme the individuality or personality of the subject of a chart, the Jupiter/Saturn pair are concerned with all that surrounds the person, generally represented as external. Astrological manuals commonly associate the presence of Jupiter—the positive side of the opposition—with success, optimism, happiness and harmony, which are then manifested in the area of the chart which the planet occupies.[108] By contrast, Saturn will imply difficulties, restrictions and insecurity.[109] This opposition caused the ancient and medieval astrologers to define them respectively as the 'great benefic' and the 'great malefic'.

---

[106] Freeman, *How to Interpret a Birth Chart*, p. 22.
[107] Ribeiro, *O Conhecimento da Astrologia*, p. 122.
[108] Freeman, *How to Interpret a Birth Chart*, pp. 82–85.
[109] Freeman, *How to Interpret a Birth Chart*, pp. 85–89.

Venus and Mars correspond, in turn, to the lesser benefic and malefic. These two planets, occupying an intermediary plane, express the relationship of the individual with what surrounds them. The form of this interaction is also given to each of them according to their mythological symbolism: harmoniously in the case of the goddess of beauty [Venus], and aggressively in the case of the god of war [Mars]. In this opposition, we can witness the process of symbolic inversion which, according to Dumont, characterises the 'change of level'.[110] In the interior of the Kabylle House, as analysed by Bourdieu, the signs change places; on this plane the feminine pole has pre-eminence over the masculine.[111] On the third plane, with a further change of level, the original picture is re-established: Jupiter, the benefic, is almost always defined as the expansive principle; Saturn, the concentrator, represents a malign factor in the chart. Such inversions make sense given that, in contrast to the planes of the individual and their environment, where expansion and expression are valued, in relationships harmony is privileged as it allows these two poles to be in balance. Thus, although feminine, Venus possesses a hierarchical pre-eminence in that its specific plane (which is also expressed in the order of the planetary spheres) occupies the position before Mars.

The possibility that the planets may show malefic or benefic effects is basically linked to the peripheral pole of the opposition. Thus, as the use of the adjectives 'great' and 'lesser' implies, it [the opposition] is manifested more on the third than on the second plane. By contrast, the Moon, although of negative polarity and hierarchically dominated by the Sun, was never considered malefic.

The same opposition exists among the planetary aspects. The benefic aspects are those in which planets separated by certain angles are harmoniously related, while the opposite happens with malefic aspects. In the first group we find the Conjunction, in which both planets occupy the same sign, the Trine where they both occupy [signs of] the same element, and the Sextile where both have the same polarity of sign. In the Opposition they occupy opposite positions representing a negative tension. Similarly, the Square is labelled as the most malefic aspect as it puts in contact planets occupying signs of opposite polarity.

---

[110] Louis Dumont, *O Individualismo: uma perspectiva antropológica da ideologia moderna* (Rio de Janeiro: Rocco, 1985), p. 232.
[111] Pierre Bourdieu, *La Distinction: critique sociale du jugement* (Paris: Editions de Minuit, 1979).

INTERPRETATION

Before describing the topic specific to this section—the reading of a chart according to the astrological cosmology, interpreted on the basis of the symbolism of signs, houses and planets—I would like to take up the theoretical discussion again. Continuing, I will try to identify some principles on which this interpretative work rests.

I hope to have given some idea of how astrology shares some of the characteristics which define classification in the view of Lévi-Strauss: in other words, its internal consistency and its practically unlimited capacity for extension.[112] However, I believe that, with respect to the latter quality, although it does not surpass the extension of totemic systems (since nothing can exceed the limitless), it does represent a larger productivity. This dimension is shown in the features on which its divinatory and interpretative character rest: the secondary classifications.

We see that the relationship which establishes a homology between the different planes that make up a classificatory system is metaphorical in nature. Lévi-Strauss was exhaustively concerned with demonstrating this. The last chapter of *La Pensée Sauvage*, in which he distinguishes the logic of totemism from that of sacrifice, is metonymic in character; it is just the conclusion of a long argument with this goal in mind. He had previously examined the classic cases in anthropological literature on the question of totemism, showing that between the animal and social series linked by these societies there was a discontinuity, never a continuous relationship.[113]

But there is also another opposition implicitly superimposed. If we understand the reversible character of the totemic relationship, in contrast with the irreversibility of sacrifice, we will be able to understand the existence of a 'natural antipathy between history and classification systems'.[114] This is linked to the 'cold' character of totemic societies which, by taking the established divisions of nature as reference points for classification of their groups, subordinate transformations to structure. On the other hand, 'hot' societies, those which 'chose to explain themselves by means of their history', cannot be classified by finite groups. This would explain the problem of

---

[112] Lévi-Strauss, *La Pensée Sauvage*, p. 287.

[113] Lévi-Strauss, *A Noção de Estrutura em Etnologia*; for the Ojibwa, see p. 112; for the Tikopia, p. 116, and for the Maori, p. 119.

[114] Lévi-Strauss, *La Pensée Sauvage*, p. 307.

'totemic absence', in other words, Lévi-Strauss' claim that 'totemism seems to be remarkably absent from the areas of great civilisations in Europe and Asia'.[115]

I believe that the latter opposition must be interpreted more as the product of the deliberate choice of a contrastive perspective by Lévi-Strauss, and not the result of a simple binarism. In these observations he opposes the great historical civilisations to primitive societies, while all my effort in this chapter has been to bring their logical procedures closer together. This does not amount to a contradiction but is the result of a confrontation between two distinct perspectives; each, by themselves, does not exhaust the richness of reality. Up to this point I have been concerned with emphasising the similarities which exist between the totemic and astrological classifications; now I will begin to focus on their differences.

It is necessary to recognise that there are different ways of possessing a cyclic [view of] temporality.[116] In primitive societies temporality does not possess great depth, as can be verified by the example of the Nuer (quoted by Evans-Pritchard) for whom 'the tree on which humanity came into being was still standing, in the western Nuer region, a few years ago'.[117] This is linked, without doubt, as Goody and Watt observe, to the absence of writing.[118] But writing's introduction does not imply the end of any kind of cyclic [view of] temporality. Astrology is not alone as an example of this, as we are shown by the way in which its logic, without losing the pre-eminence of the metaphorical procedure, introduces metonymic elements into its temporal classification for the amplification of this depth [of temporality].

---

[115] Lévi-Strauss, *La Pensée Sauvage*, p. 308.

[116] The Greeks—who were responsible in great part for the modifications of Babylonian beliefs and for the origin of zodiacal astrology—also possessed a cyclic temporality, although with more depth than that of the Nuer. According to Paul Veyne, 'in this civilisation nothing was seen beyond a very recent temporal horizon: it was asked in the time of Epicurus if the world was one or two thousand years old, no more than this, or with Aristotle and Plato, if it was not eternal, but devastated by periodic catastrophes, after each one of which eveything began again as before, which led back to the way Epicurus thought'. (Paul Veyne, *Les Grecs, Ont-ils Crus à Leur Mythes?: essai sur l'imagination constituante* [Paris: Seuil, 1983], pp. 59–60).

[117] E.E. Evans-Pritchard, *Os Nuer: uma descrição do modo de subsistência e das instituções políticas de um povo nilota* (São Paulo: Perspectiva, 1978), p. 121.

[118] Jack Goody and Ian Watt, 'The Consequences of Literacy', in *Literacy in Traditional Societies*, ed. Jack Goody (Cambridge: Cambridge University Press, 1968), pp. 33–34.

Each map defines each instant as the intersection of different stages of various cycles.[119] The latter, therefore find themselves combined metonymically since their interrelation is made through the contiguity between planets and signs, cusps and signs, aspected planets, and other planets, etc. But in the last analysis, these relations only have meaning due to the metaphorical nature of the system as a whole, which starts from the presupposition that there exists an analogy between the planetary positions at that moment and the rest of the things that happen at the same time. Time is, in reality, the mediator of the metaphorical relations realised by the secondary classifications, since astrology establishes that each being is classified by the chart of the moment in which it arose. So as a chart is made for the birth of an individual, one can also be made for the birth of a country at the moment of its independence, or of a company at its founding, or for an astrology course, examining the planetary positions at the time of the first class. The astrological chart presumes, therefore, an analogy between a thing and the moment of its beginning.

These 'beginnings' can be multiplied; in mundane astrology, which analyses the history of collective events, the map of each date representing the start of an important phase for a given group or nation can be used in analysis.[120] They can also be placed in a metonymical relationship; in the method of synastry the charts of two people are compared and, through the aspects formed between the planets of each chart, an interpretation can be made about the relationship between the two people. The metonymical relationship can also exist between the natal chart and another given moment; using the technique of studying the 'planetary transits', the astrologer relates the position occupied by the planets in one given moment of time to those occupied in the birth chart. Their interrelationship can reveal the 'phases' through which the individual will pass.

---

[119] It is important to be clear that this procedure individualises each moment in an extreme way, amplifying the temporal profundity of the system, but it doesn't necessarily take them as individual and unrepeatable. The Stoics based their theory of eternal return on the idea that, one day, the stars will return to the places they occupied at the beginning of the world, which will provoke a repetition of everything that has occurred and will occur (Rodolfo Mondolfo, *O Pensamento Antigo II: desde Aristóteles até os neoplatônicos* [São Paulo: Mestre Jou, 1973], pp. 104–05).

[120] Astrologers rely on a similar principle to refute the criticisms that they should privilege the date of conception rather than that of birth. If the former could be obtained, it would be very important, but this does not diminish the value of the latter.

No interpretation technique is more used [in modern astrology] than the reading of the natal chart. As we saw the astrologer can, in this way, determine the personality of the subject of the chart through the positions of the Sun, Moon and Ascendant. Their way of relating to the world and the people around them, whether by affection or aggression, would depend on the places occupied by Venus and Mars, and so on. The presence of planets in the astrological houses and the signs in which their cusps fall would show the astrologer how and what each one of the areas of life they represent manifests. The symbolism of the planets and their positions combines according to the kinds of aspects they form. Finally, astrologers will have in front of them a multiplicity of 'units of interpretation', many of them mutually contradictory.[121] Although we can grade them into the primary and secondary they all are, in principle, considered significant. The talent of the astrologers manifests, therefore, in their capacity to select and synthesise, which permits them to transform the multiple combinations into a more or less coherent picture.

An old question is to identify the true nature of the relationship between the celestial and individual planes; in other words, how can the efficacy of astrology be explained? Some theories have tried to provide a scientific basis, attempting to show how the planetary positions cause gravitational or electromagnetic perturbations which create the effects detected in a chart. Arroyo, who seeks an 'energetic' language and cites an example of these schemas from T. Glynn, recognises that there is not 'at present any comprehensive and satisfactory theory to explain astrology in a causal framework'.[122]

If we continue following this hypothesis that I am maintaining, by which astrology possesses a logic which is homologous to those of magico-classificatory systems, we can agree with Arroyo and the other astrologers who don't believe in, or don't feel the necessity for, a causal connection between these two planes to explain its efficacy. As Evans-Pritchard demonstrated in an exemplary way when analysing Azande beliefs about witchcraft, magical thought neither postulates cause-and-effect relationships, nor ignores natural relationships; it simply tries to find an explanation for the particular

---

[121] 'Therefore, each unit of interpretation is simply a planetary energy expressing itself through a particular sign, focused in the particular house in which it is placed, and tied to the rest of the map by aspects'. (Freeman, *How to Interpret a Birth Chart*, p. 15).
[122] Arroyo, *Astrologia*, p. 53.

association of a number of causal chains that converge in one particular event.[123] There is in an astrological chart much more information than simply the personality and idiosyncrasies of an individual; information is also found there which depends on factors external to them, such as career, parents, etc. On the other hand, all the factors which compose the life of the individual are found *organised* in the chart, not shown merely as a chaotic accumulation of facts, but rather as a consistent whole visible through the configurations of the planets. This is not incompatible with the thinking of astrologers like Arroyo, who defends astrology by contrasting it with scientism and analytical positivism, which are, in his opinion:

> The extreme manifestations (...) of the scientific approach, which one can say is to seek the maximum abstraction and the minimum of meaning. And the human being needs meaning; and the understanding of the need which people have for meaning, is indispensable to any psychology of health and unity.[124]

This same opposition between the analytical determinism of science and the synthetic determinism of magic is formulated by Lévi-Strauss as follows:

> Between magic and science, the primary difference would be therefore, from this point of view, that one postulates a global determinism, while the other works by distinguishing levels among which only some allow forms of determinism, which are labelled as inapplicable at other levels.[125]

Behind the arguments of the astrologers cited in my bibliography and, as we shall see, of many of the interviewees, it is the belief in a unity and a coherence in the universe which explains the linkage between our life [on the one hand] and the planets [on the other] which are found so far away from us. Two terms used by modern astrologers themselves to express the relationship between these two planes are analogy and synchronicity.

When Lévi-Strauss tried to differentiate the metaphorical term-for-term relation between totemic species and social groups from the relation [that exists] between two systems in opposition, perhaps *analogy* wouold have been the best descriptive term. As

---

[123] E.E. Evans-Pritchard, *Bruxaria, Oráculos e Magia entre os Azande* (Rio de Janeiro: Jorge Zahar Editora, 1978), pp. 59–61.

[124] Arroyo, *Astrologia*, p. 33.

[125] Lévi-Strauss, *La Pensée Sauvage*, p. 19.

Michel Mirabail affirms 'analogy implies a similarity of relations, not the identity of the objects concerned'.[126] Hermetic philosophy elaborated a classical formulation to explain the efficacy of astrology, attributing it to the correspondence between the macrocosm and man defined as the microcosm.[127] According to Mirabail esoteric thought, for which analogy is 'the fundamental key of all investigation' is characterised by a constant search for an extension of this network of correspondences.[128]

Similarly, the term *synchronicity* was formulated by Jung to define the 'coincidence in time of two or more events, without causal relation, but with the same content of meaning'.[129] In doing so, he took precautions that do not appear to have merited much attention among his disciples. He expressly associated it to the affectivity of the subject who experienced it, or rather to *'the lowering of mental level'* which causes the emergence of instinctual and unconscious contents.[130] Thus if he made use of these qualifying concepts to explain certain 'coincidences' among the charts of couples he was studying, Jung believed that they were due to the expectation that he nurtured in relation to the possible results.[131]

Freeman, in making use of the Jungian concept [of synchronicity] to explain the efficacy of astrology, defines it as follows:

> Everything which happens at a defined moment receives the qualities of that moment. If we could understand the symbolic meaning of the form in which the sky is ordered at a given moment, then potentially we could understand the meaning of anything which happened at that moment.[132]

Really, these two notions [analogy and synchronicity] apply the global correspondence between planes, which classificatory logic tries to establish in its constant search to contain reality, to spatial and temporal domains. The revealed tendency of magical thought to exclude [the operation of] chance, making it always reducible to the

---

[126] Michel Mirabail, *Dictionnaire de L'ésotérisme* (Paris: Marabout, 1981).

[127] Cf. Festugière, *La Révélation.*

[128] Mirabail, *Dictionnaire de L'ésotérisme* , p. 13.

[129] C. G. Jung, *Sincronicidade, Obras Completas* Vol. 8/3. Trans. by Padre Dom Mateus Ramalho Rocha, OSB. (Petrópolis: Vozes, 1984), p. 19.

[130] Jung, *Sincronicidade*, pp. 24, 28.

[131] Jung, *Sincronicidade*, p. 51.

[132] Freeman, *How to Interpret a Birth Chart*, p. 8.

premises of the system, corresponds to the type of operations that it carries out, in terms of their exhaustiveness and all-inclusiveness:

> For a [system of] thought founded in the dichotomous opposition, the principle of all-or-nothing does not just express a heuristic value, it expresses a property of being: everything offers a meaning: otherwise nothing has a meaning.[133]

We can see here one more example of how astrology at the same time approaches and moves away from the magical systems found in primitive societies. Comparing the thinking of African societies, which he describes as traditional, Robin Horton employed the terminology of the philosopher Karl Popper to classify those societies as 'closed cultures'.[134] It is known that, for Popper, science is an undertaking which is never finished and whose formulations must always be falsifiable, being able to be refuted by experimental data. According to Horton, in African societies there would be 'a lack of understanding of alternatives' in relation to traditional ideas. This would lead them to remain closed to such ideas, since outside of them there would only be chaos.[135] Thus the hyper-determinism which characterises traditional thought represents a constant attempt to re-affirm its premises, which can never be falsified.

This contrast between the two forms of knowledge, open and closed, was examined earlier, especially when I compared the concept and the sign as they were defined by Lévi-Strauss. He argued that magical thought 'elaborates structures to organise events', while science 'produces, in the form of events, its means and its results, thanks to the structures it is constantly building which are its hypotheses and theories'.[136] The problem with the connections made by Horton is in the risk that his ideas contain a residue of evolutionism; it appears that he believes that traditional thought would lose its reason for existence if alternative systems arose. In addition to the anthropological literature on contact between cultures—which shows that sometimes the alternatives end up reinforcing the tradition—the study of astrology could help to contextualise these hypotheses.

In this sense we see that, on the one hand, the valuing of tradition was emphasised by astrologers of different theoretical orientations; on the other, their legitimacy was

---

[133] Lévi-Strauss, *La Pensée Sauvage*, p. 228.

[134] Robin Horton, 'African Traditional Thought and Western Science', in *Witchcraft and Sorcery*, ed. Max Marwick (Harmondsworth: Penguin, 1970).

[135] Horton, 'African Traditional Thought', p. 352.

[136] Lévi-Strauss, *La Pensée Sauvage*, pp. 32–33.

based, in the end, more on their ability to manipulate the system than on a traditional authority. What is becoming understood in the development of the present work is that astrological practice almost always seeks this authority. But this attempt is ambiguous because its goal is always a tradition which does not belong to [contemporary] society, and whose origin appears lost in time. The need of the astrologers to refer themselves to this source derives precisely from the nature of their procedures. It is the only form through which the user of a closed system of knowledge—who is not seeking to create new structures, but to capture events in his established symbolic net—can legitimate himself in a pluralistic society. This unfolding will be illustrated in later chapters with empirical examples; at the moment I am concerned with commenting on this particular *modus operandi*. It can be clearly understood in the way astrology reacted to the discovery of the new trans-Saturnian planets. We saw [above] how the seven visible planets made up a closed structure which is connected with the classification of signs through the allocation of a ruling planet for each zodiacal sign. In this form astrology tries to construct an analogy between these two distinct classificatory planes. Ptolemy attributed to the signs of summer, which represent the longest days of the year, the rulerships of the Sun and the Moon, respectively Leo and Cancer: a masculine sign to the former and a feminine to the latter. Of the remaining ten signs which succeed those ruled by the luminaries, [the two adjacent signs] were associated with Mercury which was made the solar ruler of Virgo and the lunar ruler of Gemini. And the connections continued so that as the times of year covered by the signs get colder they are ruled by planets which are further from the earth, according to the Ptolemaic system (see fig. 5).

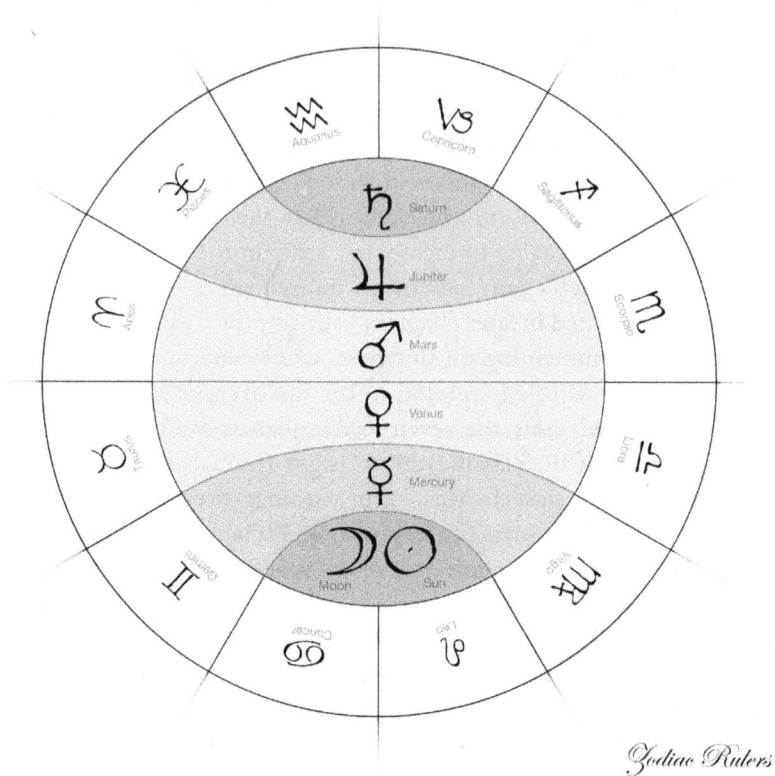

Fig. 5: The relation between the signs and planets in ancient astrology[137]

Settling the meaning of the trans-Saturnian planets was carried out within the existing structure, extending the continuum of centre/periphery and allowing them, naturally, [to govern] the furthest extreme [of that periphery]. This position is also related to the extreme slowness of their movements, which cause them to remain in one sign for several years. It is therefore said that these planets indicate generational traits or global events while they occupy a particular sign. An example of the latter is the association of AIDS with the entrance of Pluto into Scorpio, both associated with the symbolism of

---

[137] [This illustration is from 'Vic DiCara's Astrology', http://vicdicara.wordpress.com/2010/06/04/the-ancient-myth-behind-the-zodiac/ —Ed.]; for a discussion, see Claudius Ptolemy, 'Of the Houses of the Several Planets' in *Tetrabiblos*, 1:17, pp. 79–83.

transformation: in other words, sex and death. Another example of the consequences of the structural position of these planets can be found in a book by Arroyo in which he connects them with karmic features of the chart, those which come from past lives.[138] In the only book I consulted written before the discovery of Pluto, there is an evident tendency to reproduce the dual relationships which governed the original system in the characterisation of the new planets. For Alan Leo, the two planets [Uranus and Neptune] would be the 'higher octaves of Jupiter and Saturn'.[139] If we were to consult Freeman's manual, which I used as a basis for the characterisation of the planets, we would see that Uranus and Neptune can be viewed as the constitutive opposition on a fourth plane: the presence of the first is associated, almost always, with the possibility of sudden transformations, emerging from creativity and originality; the latter expresses an idealisation of the world which would make the individual, in the areas related to this planet, little able to manage practical affairs. Both represent a break with the daily practical reality which surrounds the individual: in the case of Uranus through its capacity to transcend it and, with Neptune, through difficulty in understanding it. It is symptomatic that the last two signs come to be ruled by them, exactly those which are least individualised. The positive sign, Aquarius, is associated with Uranus and the negative sign, Pisces, with Neptune.

In 1930 however, Pluto was discovered. After a while it must have seemed natural to astrologers to associate the planet named after the god who ruled hell with the sign of Scorpio. However, could we not ask what motives led astronomers, possibly ignorant of astrological symbolism, to baptise these planets with (names of) certain characters of the Greek pantheon? Freeman does not appear perturbed by this. He tells us that the astronomer Percival Lowell did not baptise the planet thinking of mythology, but actually accepted the suggestion of an eleven-year old girl who liked the dog of the same name, Mickey's companion in the cartoons of Walt Disney. At the end of this surprising account, Freeman comments: 'Strange are the ways of synchronicity'.[140]

I believe this is a striking example of the effort of astrology to expel chance and contingency, consistent with its magico-classificatory logic. Thus, the actual historical moments of discovery of each of the new planets receive symbolic interpretations; the original Uranus emerged during an era of revolutions; the confused Neptune had its

---

[138] Stephen Arroyo, *Astrologia, Karma e Transformação* (Nem Martins: Europa-America, 1979).
[139] Alan Leo, *Astrología Para Todos* (Barcelona: Teorema, 1980), p. 429.
[140] Freeman, *How to Interpret a Birth Chart*, p. 30.

discovery marked by mistakes and misunderstandings; the transforming and at times deadly Pluto is linked to the discovery of psychoanalysis and atomic energy.[141]

On the other hand, it must be agreed that this effort may result in the loss of some of the consistency with which astrology claims to support itself. The relationships between the ruling planets and their signs, for example, were fairly symmetrical in Ptolemy: the two luminaries were related to one sign each, while the other signs possessed two rulers, one lunar and one solar. The adaptations added after the discovery of the new planets disorganised this symmetry. Only Mercury and Venus remain uniquely associated with two signs. A number of solutions have been proposed for this. Some astrologers attribute Virgo and Libra to the rulership of two asteroids situated between Mars and Jupiter: Ceres and Pallas. Others are awaiting the discovery of two new planets: Vulcan, which was added by some astronomers to explain perturbations in the orbit of Mercury, and a second which would explain those of Pluto, sometimes called Planet X. Despite its greater productivity, astrology still shows, like other classificatory systems, a more rarefied structuring in its extremities as a consequence of diachrony.[142]

This type of determinism has, however, another inverse side. In order to play the classificatory role that the logic of astrology demands, its signs (in Lévi-Strauss's sense of the word), have to be extremely inclusive losing, in the process, exactness and determination, qualities in which the concept [as distinct from the sign or referent] is outstanding. A similar 'unity of interpretation' can be interpreted in different ways, and even the most cookbook-style manuals try to make this clear to the reader. I tried to communicate this when I sought to show that the criteria and qualities that each sign expresses can manifest both as benefits and defects.

Although in my description of planetary classification I was more preoccupied to point out the hierarchy which exists within it, these same comments also apply there. In this sense, several astrologers have tried to relativise the opposition of planets and benefic/malefic aspects. This warning to avoid formulaic and dichotomous classifications very often comes from astrologers of the psychological movement, who draw attention to the fact that it is precisely the difficult and complicated traits in a chart, which permit growth and self-development. On the other hand, the convenience in taking advantage of what, according to the chart, comes easily could degenerate into vices.

---

[141] Freeman, *How to Interpret a Birth Chart*, pp. 27–30.
[142] Lévi-Strauss, *La Pensée Sauvage*, pp. 210–11.

In spite of this, I would like to invoke an example of this question from the past, from Renaissance astrologer Marcilio Ficino. On one hand, in his book *Libri di Vita*, he opposes to malefic Saturn 'the luckiest, happiest most life-giving planets, of which the principals are the Sun, Venus and Jupiter'. At the same time, he links the intellectual life to the former, since 'contemplation and profound and abstract study belong to Saturn, which is also the planet of the melancholic temperament, and the star which is antagonistic to the vital forces of life and youth'.[143] This picture by Ficino can also be found in the portrait of Albrecht Dürer entitled *Melancholia*. The taciturn image which these sages have of themselves does not necessarily imply any pessimism. The concentrating character of Saturn is what permits them to extract rigorous wisdom in their thinking, as a slogan which was very common at the time had it: 'wisdom will overcome the stars'.[144]

The criticism of a Manichaean treatment of the planets is linked to an emphasis on a certain freedom of choice, which permits individuals to 'work' with their chart. This does not mean that the chart ceases to have any influence; the patterns that are represented can simply be expressed in a more conscious and mature way. Neither do I want to lose the hierarchical character of the oppositions which, as we saw, constitute the structure of planetary classification. At certain times this is emphasised through an apparent inversion: astrologers can praise Mars and Saturn and the square aspects for the challenges they represent through which the individual can develop.

I have tried in this chapter, to give the reader a general idea of the complexity of astrology and the multiple possibilities it offers. Rather than an exhaustive description, my objective was to provide some basic information about the common beliefs of my informants, and to show how they can be defined as forming a system, with a specific structure and logic. With the exception of some brief suggestions in the article by Steve Kemper on astrology in Ceylon (1980), and in the work assembled by Morin, I have not found any attempt to analyse the system of astrology in itself, considering each of its principal elements in detail.[145] I have made a first attempt in this direction seeking, in the last analysis, a characterisation of astrology which is sufficiently flexible to give an account of its many applications, but also to take seriously the belief that its users

---

[143] Frances A. Yates, *Giordano Bruno and the Hermetic Tradition* (London: Routledge and Kegan Paul; Chicago: The University of Chicago Press, 1964), p. 63.

[144] Jean Delumeau, *La Civilisation de la Renaissance* (Paris: Fayard, 1967), p. 399.

[145] Kemper, 'Singhalese Astrology'; Edgar Morin, Philippe Defrance, Claude Fischler, and Lena Petrossian, *O Retorno dos Astrólogos: Diagnóstico Sociológico* (Lisbon: Moraes, 1972), Ch. IX.

nourish about its continuity. This latter is not just related to the logic of the system itself, as it can have practical consequences which reinforce it; it leads many astrologers to study ancient astrological literature (for example, Carla (one of my informants) read Ptolemy).

Modern anthropology, since its first criticisms of [explanations of cultural phenomena based on] diffusionism, has been more and more concerned with not isolating the traits of a culture from their context. My hypotheses do not deny these concerns, since they do not take astrology to be immutable and trans-historical, but rather a system made up of a structure of oppositions which can be filled with different contents, as long as the structure is preserved. In principle, I have simply tried to compare interpretations from the different theoretical currents in the intellectual field of modern astrology, and draw out examples of the different moments of its historical trajectory. In addition, we will see how these variants are not merely due to different visions of the world held by its users. The latter may be aware of astrology in different degrees, from only being able to make more 'superficial' interpretations or to explore the poly-semy of its symbols more profoundly. For didactic reasons, I have based almost all my characterisations of the planets on the book by Freeman which, despite the prestige of its author (ex-president of the Faculty of Astrological Studies in England), is more summarised and deliberately more stereotypical.[146]

---

[146] Freeman, *How to Interpret a Birth Chart*.

CHAPTER 2:
ASTROLOGY AND MODERNITY

Modernity is a theme which periodically assumes an important position in intellectual debates. Although this debate is once again in vogue today, it should not be forgotten that many of its roots are found in the beginnings of social theory. In fact, a good number of the pioneers of social theory dedicated themselves, at different times and with different perspectives, to attempts to define the traits which distinguished the radical novelty of industrialised European society (in which they lived) from the other forms which history and ethnography have recorded. Far from being recent, the question of modernity is as old as the social sciences.

Due to its complexity and long history, this question cannot easily be described in a brief summary without losing several of its important features. However, it is possible to say that one of the theoreticians of this crisis, Daniel Bell, identified a central point in mentioning the debate on 'whether modern society is characterised by a growing depersonalisation or by a growing freedom'.[1] According to Bell this affects not only sociology, but the intellectual world as a whole. For him, the root of this debate would be [found], respectively, in the works of Max Weber and Emile Durkheim. While Weber associated modernisation with a growing process of bureaucratisation and rationalisation of daily life, Durkheim, by means of his concept of organic solidarity, identified it with a diversification of roles in industrial society, giving the individual a range of free choice previously unknown in history.

Bell's claim is that authors who unilaterally privilege the thesis of one of these inclinations formulate [only] a partial picture of modernity, given that both tendencies are present within it. Thus, we can easily state that political as much as scientific revolutions were equally important for the affirmation of modern ideology, in which the valuing of the individual and rationality were established. Although this claim is not entirely new, two authors are notable for an attempt to integrate these two aspects: Louis Dumont and Georg Simmel. Both have served as basic theoretical sources for the anthropological literature on the Brazilian middle classes, and I will comment on them later.

---

[1] Daniel Bell, *The Cultural Contradictions of Capitalism* (New York: Basic Books, 1976), p. 92.

Besides its purely theoretical aspect, the question of modernity offers a specific value to the study of astrology. Like all concepts useful to the social sciences, it is not used exclusively in academic debate. Thus, in the same way in which interpretations linked to concepts of race, class struggle, culture, etc., are acted on in social life—independently of the scientific use they may have, without even necessarily using the word *modern*—the individuals who make up a contemporary society develop theories to explain and describe the particular historical conditions in which they live.

This problem is especially acute among my informants, precisely due to the fact that they know they are utilising a system whose legitimacy is contested by scientific knowledge, which is taken as the principal criterion of truth in their society. In contrast to what took place in the Middle Ages, astrology is no longer a part of regular teaching curricula. Those who are interested in it are obliged to study by themselves, having very often had to overcome prejudices about it. Identifying the opposition between modern and traditional societies with that between West and East, Ruth (one informant) describes how she tried to develop her initial curiosity for astrology:

> (...) I found that the information which people had about oriental culture, which didn't include astrology, caused them to disbelieve a lot. And it was exactly this which attracted me; I thought I needed to find out about other teachings (...). I was always very studious (...), wanting to know about everything, but it never gave me real satisfaction. I thought that there were other things besides what colleges and universities normally teach.

Describing English history, Keith Thomas showed how, from the eighteenth century onwards, astrology would experience a complete ostracism which would be repeated in other modern Western societies. In recent decades however, interest in the subject has been growing, which has led many theorists to associate this resurgence with the crisis of modernity. My informants also came to similar conclusions:

> I interpret the return of astrology in the same way as many people, as a change of the Era, as a change of the social system (...) of values. In these times of crisis, something from the past and alternative proposals always emerge, not necessarily from the past, but a lot from the past, and from other cultures, as a possible reference point (Haroldo).

In this chapter, initially using anthropological literature produced in Brazil on the urban middle classes as a means of exploring certain aspects of modernity, I will try to characterise the entry of astrology into this historical period by, in the next chapter, providing a succinct characterisation of what I will call 'the world of astrology in Rio de Janeiro', where my informants can be contextualised sociologically.

THE STUDY OF THE URBAN MIDDLE CLASSES IN BRAZIL

To achieve a critical balance on current debates about modernity and the crisis happening to it, Sérgio Paulo Rouanet defines it as the 'autonomisation of the axiological spheres (...) until then incorporated into religion: science, morals and art'.[2] The mention of these three spheres evidently evokes the work of Immanuel Kant and his three Critiques. At the same time Rouanet's use of the term autonomisation echoes the hypotheses of Weber, according to which the ascetic rationalisation represented historically by Calvinism would dissolve the 'acute and permanent state of tension about the world and its orders' in which were found the great 'prophetic and redemptive religions'.[3] In the writings of Louis Dumont, the study of the importance of this process of autonomisation for the constitution of modern society and its ideology will be added to the analyses of the French School of Sociology (of which Dumont is a professed descendant) about the development of the modern conception of the individual.

The novelty introduced by Dumont in relation to the themes of Weber is due to the fact that his reflections about modern society were born from the study of another culture whose values, as he was able to claim, are distanced from those which sustain us. So he situates the logic which would define the Indian caste system in the principle of hierarchy in which *'the elements of all are ordered in relation to a whole'*.[4] The difficulty experienced by the first researchers in understanding this society would reside in the fact that modern ideology is based on the valuing of the individual: in other words, of the element at the expense of the totality which it composes.

In relation to the traditional approaches to that system, the innovation of Dumont's analysis represents more than a simple use of a native value. He recognises in the idea of hierarchy the real correlate of valuation: 'to adopt a value is to introduce a hierarchy'.[5] Contrary to what happened with earlier investigators, the caste system is

---

[2] Sérgio Paulo Rouanet, 'A Verdade e a Ilusão do Pós-Moderno', in Sérgio Paulo Rouanet, *As Razões do Iluminismo* (São Paulo: Companhia das Letras, 1987), p. 231.

[3] Max Weber, *Ensaios de Sociologia*, p. 376.

[4] Dumont, *Homo Hierarchicus*, p. 66.

[5] Dumont, *Homo Hierarchicus*, p. 20.

not seen as an anomaly nor as the product of the ignorance of certain concepts which had been recognised in the West since the Enlightenment. In Dumont's work Indian society is the product of an extremely sophisticated elaboration of a universal principle.

Another of the errors pointed out by Dumont in his predecessors' work was a confusion of the hierarchy of castes with political power. For him the autonomisation of the political sphere is not universal; in a holistic society, it finds itself subordinated to religion. Thus, the distribution of power is not made according to a battle of conflicting political forces but as a reflection of a cosmic order, taken to be universal. If temporal power is found in the hands of the king, then that is due to the 'religious nature of his function', since 'religion is the form which universal truth assumes in these societies'.[6]

Besides carrying out a comparison between distant societies, Dumont concerns himself also with the historiography of the genesis of individual value and of modern ideology which he studied from the basis of medieval cosmology, closer (to Western culture) than Indian holism. Following Weber, he finds in Calvinism one of the culminating points of this process, with the movement from the idea of 'the individual out-of-the-world', exemplified by Christian monasticism, to the 'individual-in-the-world'.[7]

My intention in briefly describing Dumont's theories was to complete the direction of the previous segment and to illustrate the interest that his work offers to Brazilian anthropology: constructing a definition of modernity in terms of 'a comparative anthropology' at the level of cultures and 'civilisations'.[8] However, the mechanical use of his opposition between holism and individualism can make it difficult, not only to understand a 'specific historical conjuncture' as Gilberto Velho warns, but also to understand the contradictory and ambiguous aspects which constitute modernity. In relation to the first question, the example provided by Dumont's analysis of Indian unbelievers shows us that there are possibilities of individualisation 'even in the most "totalised cultures"'.[9]

---

[6] Dumont, *Homo Hierarchicus*, p. 252.

[7] Dumont, *O Individualismo*, pp. 62–71.

[8] Gilberto Velho, *Individualismo e Cultura: notas para uma antropologia da sociedade contemporânea* , 2nd ed. (Rio de Janeiro: Jorge Zahar Editora, 1987), p. 23.

[9] For Dumont's analysis, see *Homo Hierarchicus*, pp. 184–92; For Velho's, see *Individualismo e Cultura*, p. 24.

In his analysis of the position of the individual in modernity, Dumont recognises the difference between his abstract definition—concerned with establishing a global opposition (of individualism) in relation to holism—and the specific forms which it assumes in each society. The comparisons that he points out between the individualisms in the French and German national 'subcultures' are understood in this sense.[10]

On the other hand, Dumont's own theory gives us grounds for hypothesising that the emergence of valuation of the individual is no longer seen in terms of a renunciation of the world, but as the basis for the ideology which structures society [and] contributes to an extreme fragmentation of this society. The autonomisation of the axiological spheres of science, morality and art, to which I referred earlier, have their most complete formulation in the philosophy of Kant, who dedicated his three critiques to each one of these spheres. It is curious that Kant concluded his *Critique of Practical Reason* defending the necessity that two things be distinguished, which for him 'fill the soul with the spirit of admiration and veneration (...): the starry sky above me and the moral law within me'.[11] In his commentaries, he refers to an earlier epoch, where reason still has not taken account of the 'sublimity of the object', confusing its specificity and resulting in astrology. To avoid such errors, concludes Kant, it is necessary to be inspired by chemistry and realise the '*separation* of the empirical and the rational', abandoning the hopes of 'imaginary treasures' offered by 'adepts of the philosophical stone'.[12] We see, therefore, that in the idea of separation between the worlds of knowledge and action defended by Kant occult sciences are explicitly rejected, with their representation of nature governed by criteria of perfection, value and harmony. For Dumont, this is one of the first versions of the typically modern distinction between fact and value:

> The dimension of value, which until then projected spontaneously into the world, was restricted to what is, for us, its only true dominion, in other words, the spirit, feeling and will of man.[13]

---

[10] Louis Dumont, 'Religion, Politics and Society in the Individualistic Universe', *Proceedings of the Royal Anthropological Institute of Great Britain and Ireland*, no. 1970 (1970): pp. 33–35.

[11] Immanuel Kant, *Crítica da Razão Prática* (Lisbon: Edições 70, 1984), p. 183.

[12] Kant, *Crítica da Razão Prática*, p. 184.

[13] Dumont, *O Individualismo*, p. 240.

There is no doubt that the study of Kantian philosophy provides us with important assistance for the analysis of the consequences of the emergence of valuation of the individual as a constituent of modern ideology. It holds a strategic historical value since it was an attempt to supply a foundation, not only to the democratic ideals which culminated in the French Revolution but also to the Newtonian system, whose genesis signified the decline of astrology.

However, above and beyond this abstract investigation of individualist ideology, it is necessary to recall, as Velho reminds us, that 'there is no single individualism'.[14] In the study of Brazilian society, this contextualisation becomes especially acute if we take into account that the process of modernisation that is occurring there has a limited extent, not having reached all its [societal] sectors, as well as being able to display particular characteristics due to its delayed manifestation in relation to European societies. Finally, it should be emphasised that there is the possibility of encountering in some sectors of modern society a holistic vision of the world, as is the case among the working classes, according to Luiz Fernando Duarte.[15]

In Simmel's version of the historical emergence of individualism, Kantian philosophy emerges as 'the highest intellectual sublimation' of the eighteenth century's conception of individuality.[16] Stimulated by the discovery of natural laws, there arose at this time the idea of the 'natural man' as a general concept, in which idiosyncratic differences are left aside. The struggle for political freedom sought the flowering of the root common to all men. Thus, the ideals of freedom and equality were not in contradiction. In the same way (in Kant), if the 'I' is a source of moral law, it is a question of the transcendental 'I', 'not the accidental, psychological, individual "I"' but expressing itself in the formula of the 'categorical imperative'.[17] In the nineteenth century however, the unity between the two ideals is broken. Modern individualism ceases to be characterised as two types: the quantitative—on which is based the idea of economic free competition emphasising equality between men—and the qualitative— the basis of the division of labour—which values the original and irreplaceable character of each individual personality.[18] Simmel is not thinking in terms of two static

---

[14] Velho, *Individualismo e Cultura*, p. 50.

[15] Luiz Fernando Dias Duarte, *Da Vida Nervosa nas Classes Trabalhadoras Urbanas* (Rio de Janeiro: Jorge Zahar Editora; Brasilia: CNPq, 1986).

[16] Georg Simmel, *The Sociology of Georg Simmel* (New York: The Free Press, 1950), p. 69.

[17] Kant, *Crítica da Razão Prática*, pp. 69, 72.

[18] Kant, *Crítica da Razão Prática*, pp. 83.

types; for him they express a tension between two modern tendencies that are combined in different ways:

> Probably no particular man is guided exclusively by either one of these two tendencies, liberty and equality. Perhaps also, the exclusive realisation of one of them alone would be completely impossible. Even so, this does not prevent them from manifesting themselves socially as fundamental types of character difference.[19]

Simmel argues that this tension has its privileged *locus* in the [world's] great urban centres.[20] There, the two types which Bell would identify in the sociological literature are manifested. On the one hand, the monetary economy homogenises, converting everything into values, while the measurement of time, mathematised by clocks, loses its relation to the rhythms of nature. Metropolitan life becomes highly intellectualised, dominated by 'punctuality, calculability and exactness'.[21] This process possesses a correspondence in the reserved attitude assumed by individuals faced with the multiple impressions and fragmented experiences to which they are exposed. The *blasé* attitude (characteristic, according to Simmel) of the inhabitant of large cities reflects a preoccupation with preserving the *self* in the face of the 'threatening currents and inconsistencies of their external environment'.[22] In this way qualitative individualism emerges as an attempt, through an emphasis on originality and the particular, to exaggerate the 'personal element' rejected by the modern world and preserve the identity of the subject.[23]

This fragmentation and individualisation of modern life can reach extreme levels. In one of his last texts, where Simmel took as his theme what he called 'conflict in modern culture', he tried to show the symptoms of this process in the society of his time. Using a philosophical language, he defined the history of culture as a product of a contradiction between the vital creative impulse and the autonomisation of the forms by which it is expressed. Cultural change would be caused by the exhaustion of the formal aspects of one historical moment, forcing the expression of life to adopt new forms in which to make itself concrete. In this context, culture assumes a larger

---

[19] Simmel, *The Sociology*, p. 74.
[20] Simmel, *The Sociology*, p. 423.
[21] Bell, *The Cultural Contradictions of Capitalism*, p. 413.
[22] Simmel, *The Sociology*, p. 410.
[23] Simmel, *The Sociology*, p. 422.

meaning, quite close to that which was being developed by anthropology at the time, covering diverse areas from economy to art.[24]

For Simmel, modern culture presents a particularity in relation to this dynamic; in it, this conflict deepens to a point at which disagreement no longer targets a traditional form in order to benefit another which is emerging, but challenges 'forms *as such*': the principle of form itself.[25] He situates the basic impulse for this conception in what he calls 'philosophy of life' within which, through texts like this one, Simmel's work itself is included. He also analyses the art of his time as dominated by the idea of the vanguard, according to which the artist must always be seeking new languages of expression, trying to avoid being taken over by any formal convention. In one way, his thesis is no different from a generalisation of the Weberian hypothesis about the modern economy, which is described as an unceasing overtaking of traditionalism, constantly revolutionising its means of production and expanding itself. At one point in his article, Simmel seems to anticipate the theorists of the crisis of modernity, showing that conflict and contradiction are constitutive of modern life itself, not necessarily implying its end:

> (…) the basic impulse underlying contemporary culture is negative, and it is for this reason that, differently from men in all previous epochs, we have lived without any common ideal, even without any ideal at all.[26]

Several of the works which make up the literature on the middle classes have focused on the phenomena related to the rapid pace of modernisation which accelerated in Brazilian society from 1950, at the peak of the developmentalist movement of the 'Brazilian miracle', etc.[27] Tania Salem constructed a description of part of this tradition based on her studies of families, in which she frequently examined their tendency

---

[24] 'We are speaking about culture wherever life produces certain forms in which it expresses and realises itself: works of art, religions, sciences, technologies, laws and innumerable others'. (Georg Simmel, *On Individuality and Social Forms* [Chicago: University of Chicago Press, 1971], p. 375).

[25] Simmel, *On Individuality and Social Forms*, p. 377.

[26] Simmel, *On Individuality and Social Forms*, p. 380.

[27] Velho, *Individualismo e Cultura*, p. 70; Sérvulo A. Figueira, 'Introdução: Psicologismo, Psicanálise e Ciências Sociais na "Cultura Psicanalítica"; Modernização, Família e Desorientação: Uma das Raízes do Psicologismo no Brasil', in *A Cultura da Psicanálise* (São Paulo: Brasiliense, 1985), p. 144.

toward nuclearisation. This would represent one more manifestation of fragmentation and individualisation (although referred to as a 'collective individual'), which typifies modernity.[28] But such investigations do not reveal a linear and determined evolution from the traditional family model to the nuclear. The modern pole and the traditional (the latter more hierarchical than the former) coexist in many situations composing, in the last analysis, a social fragmentation of the larger society.[29]

Attempting to identify the social causes of the emergence of psychoanalysis, Sérvulo Figueira classified it as a response provoked by the 'disorientation' of individuals under the influence of these two family models: represented in his book based on Foucault's model, which opposes the mechanisms of alliance to those of sexuality.[30] The analytical experience could offer subjects a new 'map' which would allow them to tolerate this 'paradoxical and tense coexistence'. For Figueira (following Simmel) the process takes place through one of 'individuation', in which a 're-creation by individuals of that which society has stopped providing for them, takes place'.[31]

In this way, although they represent those sectors which simultaneously channel and are also most exposed to the ideology of this modernisation, the middle classes deal ambiguously with this cohabitation which places them 'dramatically (in) the dilemma of to move or to stay'.[32] These two alternatives are generally expressed through moving [either] away from or closer to their families of origin and the values associated with them. Since this positioning can happen on different levels, there is always a considerable 'field of possibilities' open to these subjects, to combine the alternatives in different proportions.

This explains the methodological approach assumed in these studies: an attempt to recognise the great heterogeneity which is in evidence in these classes, and to criticise any attempt to tie these variations to purely socio-economic criteria.[33] It is in this context that a concern with identifying symbolic boundaries is placed (to which I referred in the introduction). The present work has also proposed—as will be discussed at greater length in the next chapter—a familiarity with and practice of astrology as a useful criterion in creating such boundaries. These boundaries must not

---

[28] Salem, 'Família', p. 11.
[29] Salem, 'Família', p. 14.
[30] Sérvulo A. Figueira, O Contexto Social da Psicanálise (Rio de Janeiro: Francisco Alves, 1981), p. 35.
[31] Figueira, O Contexto Social da Psicanálise, p. 271.
[32] Velho, Individualismo e Cultura, p. 108.
[33] Salem, 'Família', pp. 3–4.

however be reified, but understood as 'an identity in situation or relation with other social identities', being capable of frequent re-negotiation or re-elaboration.[34]

To exemplify these mechanisms, I would like to cite some of the groups studied in this literature whose *ethos* and lifestyles are closest to [those in] the present study, although they repeat standards present in other groups [which are] faced with the traditional/modern polarity. Thus, one of the sectors studied by Gilberto Velho in *Nobles and Angels* is described as made up of young people who frequent a sandwich bar in the South Zone [of Rio]; their characteristics, apart from the use of drugs (the central topic of the study), are the desacralisation of sex, hedonism and a playful spirit which challenges the morality of productivity, something which very often brings them into conflict with their families of origin.[35] This could easily lead us to identify them as belonging to a 'counterculture', due to their rejection of 'day-to-day behaviour', defining a 'conflictual theme' in relation to the 'evolving culture', in agreement with the concepts of J. Milton Yinger.[36] Besides theoretically contextualising the term 'counterculture' itself, Velho describes how its members operate mechanisms of exclusion to mark their boundaries from other countercultural groups coming from more modest social classes: 'the museum hippies'.[37] Despite everything, they value the sophisticated standards of consumption which feed their hedonism, relying on the social and economic position conferred on them by their families of origin, which in other contexts are despised.

Salem warns that the 'crisis of the expectant couple' doesn't solely reside in purely practical difficulties; in other words, it doesn't represent a simple abandonment of modern ideals in favour of the convenience of family support. The latter is put into action in the form of a threat exercised by the family as an inclusive unity of its elements, 'resisting the individualisation of its component members'.[38] In the tension between the 'collective individual' and the 'individualised subject', features of the 'hierarchical' pole are presented as compromise solutions to the dilemma of modernity itself.

---

[34] Salem, 'Família', p. 5.
[35] Gilberto Velho, *Nobres e Anjos: Um estudo de tóxicos e hierarchia* (São Paulo: USP. Tese de Doutorado, 1975), pp. 122–23, 138, 150.
[36] Velho, *Nobres e Anjos*, p. 141.
[37] Velho, *Nobres e Anjos*, pp. 4–5, 143–48.
[38] Salem, 'Família', p. 54.

My objective here was to show how questions raised by the literature on the urban middle classes and the theories that inspired them are capable of amplifying the relativising influence of anthropology which, in its early days, was focused on primitive societies, emphasising their specificity in relation to modern society. At a later time, this allowed it to nuance certain schemas which can emerge from such a contrastive classification. The study of the family, a traditional topic of ethnology whose importance has been minimised in modernity, reveals itself as a powerful instrument for understanding modernity's featured ambiguities and contrasts. It is not by chance, the axis along which Salem laid out the details of this literature.

In relation to these studies, astrology presents us with some unique features. In the first place, boundaries between the modern and the traditional become more tenuous because when they attack 'traditional knowledge' the informants refer themselves to science as it is defined by modernity. That can cause its 'avant-gardism' to assume, as was the case with the expectant couple, a rather archaic tone. At other times, tradition and religion will be re-valued, but always from the 'occult' point of view or that of its 'esoteric' sectors. Thus the secret and initiatory character is highlighted which astrology, along with other occult systems, has assumed during its history.

These observations do not get in the way of the fact that *the networks* which are formed around these practices are constructed on the basis of 'personal choice and preference', as is typical of the modern pole of the middle classes.[39] This is in addition to the fact that astrology is nowadays part of the means of mass communication, also making the 'avant-gardism' of its practice problematic.

The description of the complex game by which these symbolic boundaries are constructed, making astrology a system which takes part in the fragmentation of modernity—even while being opposed to some of its aspects—can be more fully appreciated in the two final chapters. The statements of the informants show that, behind their common belief in astrology, there exist specific forms by which they dedicate themselves to their 'personal lived experience of heterogeneity', so common in the middle classes.[40] Before this, however, I would like to discuss the pertinence of this belief being chosen as a significant criterion in the construction of these boundaries.

---

[39] Salem, 'Família', p. 16.
[40] Velho, *Subjetividade e Sociedade*, p. 93.

BELIEF IN MODERNITY: THE CASE OF ASTROLOGY

In the study of astrology, it is natural that the first types of symbolic frontiers evoked to identify its apprentices would be beliefs in its validity and/or efficacy. However in describing 'the modern belief in astrology' (in a book edited by Morin) Lena Petrossian tries to establish 'a scale of belief, which runs from faith in astrology to an anti-astrological position, passing through attitudes of scepticism and indifference'.[41] In the middle of this scale we find '"intermittent belief", semi-playful belief, undecided, truncated belief, ambivalent but believing'.[42] The 'semi-believer' hesitates between the impulses of their 'rational-critical mind' and their unconscious (without the author defining these terms precisely), changing their opinions of astrology at different times.[43]

Although I am not convinced of the suitability of Petrossian's concepts, the impression that her observations provoke in anyone who maintains some contact with astrology is that she is talking about a phenomenon with which she is familiar. It is true that I worked basically with individuals who are found at the extreme positive end of the scale; the majority were fully convinced of the efficacy of astrology. However, either through the accounts of informants about their contact with people less involved with astrology, or through the comments of people I knew, [I discovered that] there is undeniably a nebulous area where curiosity, mistrust and ambiguity about astrology are mixed together.

The difficulties in understanding this situation can be attributed to some particular features of the anthropological tradition; according to Rodney Needham, 'belief' has become a 'standard descriptive term'.[44] Being accustomed to studying simple societies where cultural heterogeneity is considerably reduced, and in part being the inheritor of Durkheim's concepts of representation and collective awareness, which possess a strong substancialising content; his tradition rarely problematised the uncritical use of the term. However several authors, not exclusively linked to anthropology, have recently attempted to contextualise this term.

This has been done in two complementary ways. The first attempts to recognise the cultural relativity of the notion of belief, such as it is described in our own culture. Thus

---

[41] Morin et al., *O Retorno dos Astrólogos*, p. 152.
[42] Morin et al., *O Retorno dos Astrólogos*, p. 153.
[43] Morin et al., *O Retorno dos Astrólogos*, p. 155.
[44] Rodney Needham, *Belief, Language and Experience* (Oxford: Basil Blackwell, 1972), p. 4.

the statement that the natives of this or that society believe in this or that has quite convenient descriptive power for the ethnographer. But if it is not accompanied by supplementary explanations—which specify exactly (for example) the meanings of the native word which is translated by the verb *to believe*—this can be a source of serious errors. Based on the reflections of Evans-Pritchard, Needham carried out an extensive investigation of the term, approaching it not only from the point of view of comparative ethnology, but also from that of philosophy and etymology. His conclusion was that belief does not correspond either to a particular experience to which can be attributed a trans-cultural existence, nor to a homogeneous notion within our own culture.

The second line of debate tries to expand the question raised by Needham from a philosophical point of view, examining the coexistence of apparently contradictory beliefs in particular societies. For example, the historian Paul Veyne described a number of different ways by which the Greeks viewed myths.[45] To the plurality of worldviews which made up the world of classical and Hellenistic Greece, and the specialisation of knowledge which was sketched out in this period, there correspond criticisms of the ingenuous literal belief in myths which, however, do not entirely disqualify them. Thus the rise of historiography caused Veyne to dissolve the heterogeneity between the mythical and contemporary worlds, stripping myths of their fantastic aspects, but not their reality.[46] On the other hand, philosophers such as Plato took these stories as allegories whose essence is covered with exaggerations explicable in terms of their hierarchical cosmology:

(...) in Plato philosophical allegory is half-truth, corresponding at the same time to the participation of the sensory in the reality of ideas, and no less to the impossibility of a rigorous science of the sensible world.[47]

Even if, as Veyne appears to show, the coexistence of contradictory beliefs were universal, it is undeniable that the development of social heterogeneity makes it more visible. Related to this, for example, is the theory of Simmel, that through the *blasé* attitude typical of those who live in the metropolis, modern individuals avoid a total involvement with the phenomena that surround them, not allowing any particular experience to absorb them totally. In this way, describing the coexistence of rationalist

---

[45] Veyne, *Les Grecs.*
[46] Veyne, *Les Grecs,* p. 45.
[47] Veyne, *Les Grecs,* p. 75.

and 'irrationalist' worldviews in a middle class group discussing the idea of passion, Gilberto Velho refers to:

> ...the complex nature of the social construction of reality in contemporary society. There is no (...), linear consistency between codes and values. It is good to remember that, in other contexts, some of those who have been studied, rationalists and materialists etc., had recourse to astrology, Tarot and other esoteric and/or occult activities. Although this group may be rare, there are one or two people who have turned to spiritualist centres.[48]

Without doubt Needham's work can be considered the most complete on the subject, [both] for its exhaustiveness and concern to be comparative. After approaching it from the most varied angles, his conclusions are not very optimistic for the possibility of a general theory on the subject. He recognises its complexity from the beginning, admitting that it had been 'the most difficult thing' he had so far undertaken.[49] Thus, contrary to the earlier segment included in this chapter, it is not a matter of summarising some more-or-less established traditions. Here I will be obliged to venture into a question which is less resolved and studied in the bibliography of the social sciences, and in which there are few certainties. I believe it is possible to describe some aspects of modern astrology related to the question of belief, starting from an article by Jean Pouillon on this concept, which proposes to take up Needham's terms again, while employing them differently.[50]

Like Needham, Pouillon begins his investigation through the analysis of language, but specifically the meanings of the French verb *croire*. We can identify three meanings for it:

> *croire a..., to affirm the existence of*
> *croire en..., to have confidence in*
> *croire que..., to represent something in a certain way.*[51]

---

[48] Velho, *Subjetividade e Sociedade*, p. 94.
[49] Needham, *Belief, Language and Experience*, p. 11.
[50] Jean Pouillon, 'Remarques sur le Verbe "Croire"', in *La Fonction Symbolique: essais d'Anthropologie*, eds. Michel Izard and Pierre Smith (Paris: Gallimard, 1979), p. 46.
[51] Pouillon, 'Remarques sur le Verbe "Croire"', p. 43.

Without being able to so easily distinguish them, by the type of transitivity or by different prepositions in the rulership of the verb, the three meanings exist in the (Portuguese) verb *crer*, or its more colloquial synonym *acreditar*. They can equally express existence, confidence or opinion.[52]

The condensation of these three meanings into a single word is not accidental, as we shall see further on. However this must not lead us to confuse them. Each of the three implies different degrees of certainty. Someone who has confidence in something has no doubt of its existence: 'this is not believed but perceived'; hence, according to Pouillon, 'to enunciate existence is to open the possibility of doubt'.[53] In its turn, 'to believe that something will happen' means precisely not being sure of its occurrence. In this way, from the second to the first meaning and from there to the third, there are decreasing degrees of certainty.

Analysing the indications of Benveniste on the origin of the word (also commented on by Needham),[54] Pouillon locates its original meaning in the chapter on 'economic obligations', related to the idea of credit and, therefore, to the second of the three meanings. Again, the analysis of the vocabulary of the Dangaleat, a primitive society of Central Africa, shows us that only this meaning is used on the religious plane; in modern culture, on the contrary, it is this plane which 'permits the unification of the three constructions of the verb', without exhausting them. Thus, *àbidè* means 'to fulfil the rites faithfully', designating the act of serving God, in the biblical sense. The other verb used in a religious sense is *àmniyè*, which implies the idea of confidence. Again, the concept of existence, either as certain or doubtful, is expressed by other verbs which are not used in a religious sense (*ibinè, pakkine*).

Pouillon concludes that it is possible to translate the three meanings of the verb *croire* into Dangleat 'with the exception of the verb itself'.[55] The non-existence of this

---

[52] In the Aurelio dictionary, the first possibility corresponds to meaning (1) ('to take as correct, or true'), which is transitive direct; the second to meanings 2 and 5 ('to have confidence'), respectively transitive direct and indirect; and the third to numbers 3 and 4 ('to judge, to suppose'), direct and transobjective (Aurélio Buarque de Holanda Ferreira, *Novo Dicionário da Língua Portuguesa* [Rio de Janeiro: Nova Fronteira, 1986], p. 497). Colloquially, however, it is common to use the first as transitive indirect. Thus if a Christian affirms that he believes in the Devil, he cannot be accused of satanism, because he is just affriming the existence of this Being, even if he only has confidence in God.

[53] Pouillon, 'Remarques sur le Verbe "Croire"', p. 44.

[54] Needham, *Belief, Language and Experience*, pp. 107–08.

[55] Pouillon, 'Remarques sur le Verbe "Croire"', p. 48.

synthetic word, also present in other Western languages such as English, is verified by several missionaries, such as Eugene A. Nida, who took on the prickly task of translating the Bible into tribal languages. Nida recounts that, in Anauak, the words *yiey* and *ngadho* are not adequate for expressing *belief* or *faith*, because the first 'implies only an intellectual agreement', while the other 'is closer to *hope* or *trust* than to *faith*'.[56] In a manual for translators of St Mark's Gospel, written in conjunction with Robert Bratcher, Nida states that finding equivalents for the word *belief* is very difficult 'because expressions such as *believe a report*, *believe a person*, and *believe in a person* are frequently treated in other languages as different types of expressions'.[57]

The reasons which Pouillon identifies for this phenomenon go in the same direction as the initial thoughts on the question of belief formulated by Evans-Pritchard in *Nuer Religion*. He says that it does not make any sense for a Nuer to say that God exists, 'because the existence of God is taken as a given for the whole world'.[58] The equivalent expression, *kwoth a thin*, means 'God is present'; it reminds the Nuer of this truth at difficult times. For primitive societies God and the spirits are not simply believed in, their presence is experienced. Similarly, as Needham has exhaustively shown, supported by Wittgenstein, a *belief* is not an experience. The fact that people in turn convert to Christianity or Islam, abandoning their traditional worship of the *margoi* (spirits), does not perturb a Dangaleat: if he experiences these spirits, 'this experience is in principle, local; such spirits are not necessarily present everywhere'.[59] They do not belong, then, to a supernatural domain given that this society, like the Azande in relation to witchcraft, does not make a distinction between this domain and the natural.[60] So through not knowing transcendence this religion, contrary to Christian and Islamic monotheism, does not possess evangelism. This characteristic is symptomatically exclusive to the religions in which belief implicitly contains doubt.

For Robert Bellah, the notion of disbelief arose historically with Plato, when it became the reason for severe punishments in *The Laws*. It was the product of the

---

[56] Cited in Needham, *Belief, Language and Experience*, p. 32.

[57] Robert G. Bratcher and Eugene A. Nida, *A Handbook on the Gospel of Mark*, (United Bible Societies, 1961), p. 83. The English expressions compared by Bratcher, which are analogous to those evoked by Pouillon, can be roughly translated by 'to believe a story', 'to believe (have confidence) in a person', and 'to believe in (the existence of) a person'.

[58] E.E. Evans-Pritchard, *Nuer Religion* (Oxford: Clarendon Press, 1956), p. 25.

[59] Pouillon, 'Remarques sur le Verbe "Croire"', p. 50.

[60] Pouillon, 'Remarques sur le Verbe "Croire"', pp. 49–50; Evans-Pritchard, *Bruxaria*, pp. 69–71.

intellectual revolution of the Sophists and Socrates: in other words, of the emergence of the 'first stratum of free intellectuals (…) in human history'. Such a concept was entirely foreign to the Bible given that Bellah states, corroborating the hypotheses of Pouillon, that:

> Where the word 'belief' is used to translate the Hebraic or Greek bibles, it does not mean the 'belief that' of Plato, but 'belief in', a question not of cognitive agreement but of faith, confidence and obedience.[61]

For Bellah, Plato's concern, that would later become that of Christian and Islamic theologians, is due less to the fear that the masses possess a tendency to devalue religion—given that they were less characterised by 'disbelief'—than of their 'excess of belief'.[62] Thus the preoccupations of the religious elites were focused on assuring fidelity to the dogmas and the orthodoxy, expressed in the religions most influenced by Greek thought, which Bellah labels as the 'objectivist fallacy, in other words, a confusion of *belief* and religion' (using this first concept in the sense of knowledge).[63] We have, therefore, one more example which can be added to those offered by Veyne, of how the growth of social heterogeneity implies the multiplication of forms of belief and the development of the critical tradition.

Another author who considered this question was Alfred Schütz whose theoretical instruments, according to Velho, 'are focusing definite types of human experience which, if not exclusive, are characteristic enough of modern complex society'.[64] In his well-known theory of 'multiple realities', Schütz argues that beyond 'the daily world of work', there exist various 'finite provinces of meaning', such as the worlds of religion, art, science, dreams, etc., each of which is ruled by its own logic.[65] In this sense an individual could, on different occasions, move from one to another of these other realities, acquiring contradictory beliefs.

Although Schütz treats this question from an abstract and philosophical point of view, there is no doubt that this phenomenon becomes more evident in the

---

[61] Robert Bellah, 'The Historical Background of Unbelief', in *The Culture of Unbelief*, ed. Rocco Caporale (Berkeley: University of California Press, 1971), p. 39.

[62] Bellah, 'The Historical Background of Unbelief', p. 40.

[63] Bellah, 'The Historical Background of Unbelief', p. 43.

[64] Velho, *Individualismo e Cultura*, p. 81.

[65] Alfred Schütz, *Collected Papers I: The Problem of Social Reality* (The Hague: Martinus Nijhoff, 1971), pp. 207–59.

fragmentation of modern life. So the specificity of 'the world of art' becomes much clearer when it becomes autonomous, ceasing to be a vehicle for necessarily religious, mythical or cosmological values, etc. His own definition of the specificity of the scientific sphere refers to modern ideology when he claims that it furnishes the idea that theory 'does not serve any practical purpose', and that its only objective is 'to observe and possibly to understand'.[66]

Although I will look more deeply into this topic in Chapter 4, in general terms the belief in astrology—insofar as it is represented by the informants—possesses a number of these traits. The interest in the study of nature, awoken in the twelfth century by scholastic philosophy, expounds more forcefully the contradictions of the 'objectivist fallacy' to which Bellah refers, which was defended through its attempts to reconcile faith and reason. In the midst of the multiple tensions of this period in which astrology took part, Calvinism articulated, as Weber shows us, a new accommodation in which the knowledge of nature became autonomous from religion, abandoning considerations of value and opening the way for the advent of modern science. The development of the modern science, even in Catholic countries, generally tended to devalue magical systems such as astrology.

Faced with the plurality of values which are established in modern society, the value of science in part, remains, given that it limits itself to the domain of facts while, as Bellah emphasises, the power of religious authority to impose its dogmas has weakened.[67] So as not to be contradictory in relation to science, I tried to show in Chapter 1 [that] it possesses its own logic; astrology is incorporated into the domain of the supernatural and magic, from which it had tried to escape in the medieval epoch by means of the idea of 'natural magic'.[68] In this way, it is allocated to another 'finite province of meaning' distinct from the scientific: that of mysterious phenomena, the inexplicable, sometimes called (as Velho does) the sphere of the irrational. The informants' first interest in astrology is always explained by them as due to the fascination exercised by this domain, defined according to various categories:

I was always attracted by these things (…), attraction for mystical things, for the occult side (Sônia).

---

[66] Schütz, *Collected Papers I*, p. 245.
[67] Bellah, 'The Historical Background of Unbelief', p. 44.
[68] Yates, *Giordano Bruno*, p. 80.

I always had, then, an interest for the mystical side of things in general, not only for astrology; for the concepts behind things (…). I was interested in UFOs (…); always the idea of when the world is going to end; of the mother-ship, these really fantastic ideas, I was always super-interested (Jaime).

I am of Irish descent (…) and the Irish are very superstitious, very interested in the beyond, they believe in gnomes and dwarves, those things (…). Besides this I had my grandmother who read the cards. From there I came to encounter the side of astrology to do with seeing the future (Helen).

(…) I always had a tendency to believe in those things I didn't know how to explain. But in my group of friends, people always said I was a Macumbista (Bárbara). [Someone who takes part in Macumba—Trans.]

We can see how the informants define this common sphere in different ways, whether through the 'modern' references of Jaime or the 'traditional' of Helen. But such curiosity does not indicate an unequivocal attachment to astrology. With the exception of Bárbara, all others quoted above described an initial interest that only later would become consolidated.

The predictive aspect of astrology did not constitute for Helen, 'the true reason for astrology', but 'the icing on the cake, the thing that attracts and makes it sweet'. As I stated in the introduction and will make clearer in the following chapters, their position as 'students of astrology' gave the majority of my informants this particular view of its system.

A basic component of this view is the idea that it is a knowledge which is acquired slowly, through the study of the techniques and symbolic classifications which comprise it. Having acquired some competence, they are able to draw charts for friends who have the same curiosity as they did when they started. As Carla said, 'no one believes, but everyone asks for their chart; there's no point in that'.

Other informants said they didn't pass through this stage as they were 'sceptics' initially. Because of this, their approach to astrology was a long journey in which belief was the product of slow study. The category of 'sceptic' is sometimes used as an accusation against those who would have an intolerant attitude towards astrology. On the other hand, as Teresa comments, demonstrating a strong critical spirit when speaking about astrologers she knew, this scepticism produces the best astrologers because it leads them to deepen their study.

We see then that the association of belief with knowledge is strongly present in the groups studied, due in part to what I have called the rational authority of astrology.

Given the attraction which modernity has for this association, it creates a curious convergence between astrology and modern values. In this sense, despite the fascination she felt for divination, Helen stated that she would not go to a *jogo de buzios*, because she felt afraid of the mysterious character of the proceedings of the *pai-de-santo*.[69] Even Bárbara, the only person interviewed who showed no interest in knowing the techniques of astrology, established a hierarchy in which 'I thought astrology was the least threatening of all these half-strange explanatory systems'. So, with its exact astronomical positions and its mathematical calculations, astrological divination offers itself to the eyes of its clients as a compromise solution between the 'magical' and the 'scientific'.

The close linkage of knowledge and belief among my informants can be better illustrated by describing an episode during the interview with Helen and Ruth, in which Vánia and Alice took part. Questioned about the relationship of astrology to reincarnation, they became very hesitant to take a position on the subject. They seemed to have a tendency not to believe in the theory of *karma*, but well-known astrologers supported the idea and they opined that 'the people who have books on this are those who have a basis to speak about it'. Helen, in the course of these doubts, concluded:

> I don't believe because I'm a Libra, you understand? If I believe in justice, how is it that I did something in a past life and now I'm going to pay for it?

This is just one example of something which happened in almost all the interviews: informants generally justified their attitudes in relation to aspects of astrology or the system as a whole on the basis of traits in their natal charts. In this way they succeeded in keeping the arbitrary character of belief at a distance, determining and explaining it by rational arguments based on the determinism of astrology itself.

Going back to the 'scales of belief' cited by Petrossian, on one side of what he termed the 'no man's land' of semi-belief, which mixes curiosity and scepticism, there is the position of my informants and, on the other side, that which he called anti-astrologism. This concept would define the militant position of writers and institutions—such as the Rationalist Society —which vehemently criticised the spread

---

[69] The *jogo de buzios* is a divination technique of throwing cowrie shells, and the *Pai-de-santo* is the priest who officiates in Candomblé, and similar religions with strong West African roots brought to Brazil during the time of the slave trade—Trans.

of astrology in modern society.[70] Among these writers, Paul Courdec, chief astronomer of the Paris Observatory, asks:

> In the name of this aberrant liberalism (…) must we, how can we, give the verdict in favour of the enemies of reason, to the doctrinaires of unproven statements, to the proselytisers of the most antique superstitions?[71]

As far as I can see, attacks on astrology today in Brazil are far less violent than those recounted by Petrossian referring to France at the beginning of the 1970s. I don't know of any organised campaign against the diffusion of astrology, even though it continues to advance in our country. It is true however that, by the nature of my investigation itself, I did not come into much contact with those in this area. Ronaldo Rogério de Freitas Mourão, one of the Brazilian astronomers who is most employed by the media, recently wrote a rather moderate article. He tried 'to show how important a knowledge of astrology is for the general culture, since it has been involved in the actual development of the most diverse sciences and even in the history of peoples'. He ends by acknowledging that it is 'more of a problem for sociologists and psychologists than for astronomers', although personally he considers it 'an irrational escape route' adopted by modern man, 'insecure about the future of humanity'.[72]

More vehement are the opinions of D. Marcos Barbosa, a Benedictine monk and occasional contributor to the *Jornal do Brasil*. He condemns astrology, quoting St Augustine's defence of free choice, while conveniently omitting the opinions of St Thomas Aquinas and St Alberto Magno which were favourable to aspects of astrology.[73] Apart from this, readers of this newpaper occasionally write letters of protest from time to time against the great spread of astrology allowed by the media. One of the letters of protest suggested to this newspaper (19/12/1987), states that 'they interview astronomers, priests and pastors on the subject' to demonstrate how it is 'inconceivable that today in the "century of science"', people still believe in astrology.[74]

---

[70] Morin et al., *O Retorno dos Astrólogos*, pp. 163–65.

[71] Courdec, *L'Astrologie*, p. 127.

[72] Ronaldo R. de F. Mourão, 'Importância Histórica da Astrología', *Jornal do Brasil*, (31 Dec., 1986): 2, Caderno B.

[73] Dom Marcos Barbosa, 'Astrologia', *Jornal do Brasil*, (29 Dec., 1987): 2, Caderno B.

[74] Dom Marcos Barbosa, 'Astrologia'.

The place of this system in modern society, which goes against some of the most basic values by which it is defined, will be described in the next chapter. However, we can already contextualise this opposition to some extent since we have seen that, even among those who adhere most strongly to astrology, it is possible to find statements according to which this belief would have been born from 'study' and 'knowledge'; this demonstrates a convergence [of viewpoint] in its students with one of the traits of modernity defined by Jean Pouillon, as I have tried to show.

CHAPTER 3:
THE WORLD OF ASTROLOGY

A paradox from the previous chapter faces any attempt to study modern astrology: how to reconcile the incompatibility of modern values with astrology, which manifests itself as much on the theoretical plane as in the discourse of users, with its presence in contemporary society? Much of the answer is already to be found in the statement that modernity cannot be defined statically; contradiction is one of the mechanisms which defines its logic. Nevertheless, these problems return when we try to bring our analysis down from the theoretical plane in attempting to describe the presence of astrological practices in modern society, specifically that of Rio de Janeiro. I will make a description of the 'astrological world of Rio de Janeiro' and try to apply to it some hypotheses which allow us to better understand the practices and the discourse of the informants. But first I will briefly sketch the questions which run through the literature of the social sciences on this subject. Although limited and of recent origin, it will reveal a degree of consistency, which probably reflects its attempt to resolve the paradox mentioned above.

This literature very often associates the study of the insertion of astrology into modern society with two questions: one, the 'means of mass communication' and the other the noted 'crisis of modernity'. Both have been explored from the most diverse perspectives, generating a number of important debates. Astrology is included in each of them and plays an important strategic role in the work compiled by Edgar Morin, which is probably the most complete so far on modern astrology, articulating these two questions.[1]

There were more than a few occasions in which this articulation was made. As Umberto Eco illustrates, for a long time the debates around the so-called 'industrial culture' remained, in general, a confrontation between the antagonistic positions of the 'apocalypticists' and the 'fundamentalists'.[2] While the latter were more concerned with producing a proper 'mass culture', it basically fell to the first to construct various theories about it. And these, as the adjective with which Eco names them already indicates, often consisted of catastrophic diagnoses which identified a sign of terrible

---

[1] Morin et al., *O Retorno dos Astrólogos*.
[2] Umberto Eco, *Apocalípticos e Integrados* (São Paulo: Perspectiva, 1970).

decadence that would assault our culture through the spreading of means of mass communication. This opposition already appears in the divergent articles of the organisers of one of the first collections on the subject, published in the USA [for the first time] in 1956. Thus, while for Bernard Rosenberg 'mass culture threatens not only to cretinize our taste, but to brutalize our feelings, and at the same time open the way to totalitarianism', David M. White showed the possibilities offered by modern media for the diffusion of primary works of art and culture from the past.[3]

In spite of the good sense that many found beneath White's words, this didn't stop the arguments of the apocalypticists from having a great impact. It is among these that we find the first mentions of a concept which is very fashionable today for defining the crisis and the possible overthrow of modern values:

> Rather than being able to transcend himself man is being dehumanised. Rather than being able to raise his mind, it is being blunted. (…) The mass is growing; we are more like each other than ever; and the sensation of having fallen into a trap and being alone is stronger. (…) In sum, the post-modern world offers the world all or nothing.[4]

In a tone of desperation, post-modernity is defined as a betrayal of the promises of early modernism. The possibility of the participation of the masses in the consumption of cultural products would end with the banalisation of the latter and not with the democratisation of access to them. The consumer of media, anaesthetised by a bombardment of alternatives of variable aesthetic value, will also become unable to appreciate the great works of Western culture that modern means of communication finally offered to the larger public, as the 'fundamentalists' hoped. Squeezed between commercial jingles and popular music conceived for easy consumption, listening to Beethoven's Fifth Symphony would lose all its interest; the principal theme of its first movement would become just a tune to be whistled, without the listener being motivated to experience the structural complexity of the work.[5]

In attempting to make a brief summary of this debate, it is possible to say that the noted mass culture exercises—in the view of its critics—a damaging influence on the

---

[3] Bernard Rosenberg, 'A Cultura de Massa nos Estados Unidos', in *Cultura de Massa: as artes populares nos Estados Unidos* , eds. Bernard Rosenberg and David M. White (São Paulo: Cultrix, 1973 [1956]), p. 22.

[4] Rosenberg, 'A Cultura de Massa', p. 17.

[5] The example of Beethoven's Fifth Symphony is that of Theodor Adorno, cited by Eco in *Apocalipticos e Integrados*, p. 41.

three levels into which modern cultural production is divided. We see how the fruition of 'high culture' is damaged by its levelling with other forms. On the other hand, although they rarely show any appreciation for the tastes of the masses, the critics lament that they have lost the spontaneity of the noted 'popular culture'. This occurs [they say] through transformation into a powerful consumer market which would allow the formation of a cultural industry which begins to feed them with standardised works of easy consumption: controlled from above. But what appears to be most threatening for these authors is the development of an intermediate level of cultural production, which finally makes impossible the separation between the erudite and the popular which was prevalent before cultural massification. It was what Dwight MacDonald would call *midcult*, the sector in which the subjects of erudite culture are 'domesticated', becoming suitable for consumption by [those of] middle taste who are incapable of understanding them, but avid for the [cultural] legitimation that they offer them. As we saw in the previous chapter, modern art is characterised by the search for new languages, through which it seeks constant innovations which make understanding it increasingly difficult for the general public. MacDonald thus interprets the last phase of the artistic avant-garde as a reaction to mass culture.[6] However, it doesn't manage to avoid its themes being re-appropriated and banalised by this culture at a later stage, losing their creative vigour.

> The modernism of Bauhaus ended, spreading naturally in a degraded form, through our furniture, cafeterias, cinemas, electric toasters, pharmacies and railway trains. Psycho-analysis is explained easily and superficially in popular magazines, and the psychoanalyst replaces the eccentric millionaire as a *deus ex machina* in innumerable cinema films.[7]

We can see that among the more perceptive critics of mass culture, the phenomenon of massification can be seen broadly as something which does not restrict the artistic domain including, for example, the composition of what Sérvulo Figueira will call the 'culture of psychoanalysis'.[8] Although astrology, in the way it is usually defined, cannot necessarily be seen as belonging to erudite culture, it develops among its sectors relations which reproduce this tension existing on the larger cultural plane. On the one

---

[6] Dwight MacDonald, 'Uma Teoria da Cultura de Massa', in *Cultura de Massa: as artes populares no Estados Unidos*, eds. Bernard Rosenberg and David M. White (Sao Paulo: Cultrix, 1973), pp. 81–82.

[7] MacDonald, 'Uma Teoria da Cultura de Massa', p. 82.

[8] Figueira, 'Introdução'.

hand it is incorporated into the media; on the other some students have come to reject this astrological vulgarisation. Among them are included several of my informants.

INTERPRETATIONS OF MODERN ASTROLOGY AND 'ESOTERIC CULTURE'

The book coordinated by Edgar Morin condenses the conclusions of an investigation undertaken by the *Diagnostic Sociology Group*, linked to the *École Pratique des Hautes Études*.[9] As the name of the group suggests, its purpose was to 'diagnose' the *Return of the Astrologers* to which its title refers. Thus the analysis of the history and structure of the [astrological] system receive less space (two of the nine chapters) in comparison to [the study of] its various appropriations in modern French society. The choice of object is explained through the definition of the objectives of the group, presented at the beginning of the book: it is dedicated 'to the study of unexpected events and new phenomena'.[10] The declared interest in 'diagnosing' such phenomena carries a biologistic bias, present in the whole work, which can easily be demonstrated in this extract, written by Lena Petrossian:

> The problem of the diffusion of astrology in modern society is, in a certain sense, similar to the propagation of an infectious germ: will it depend on the virulence of the germ or the weakness of the organism which is attacked? (...) the force of propagation of astrology is linked to the intensity of the need provoked by the development of individualism, and also to the weakness of its [society's] defences.[11]

The analysis of the rise of astrology in French society occupies a place in Morin's work as one more example of the complex interrelation which he identifies between the expansion of 'the culture of the masses' and the 'crisis of modernity'. This is shown by the conclusions of the research in the second of the two volumes of the collection dedicated specifically to this interrelation.[12] In the first of these, Morin attributes to the media a double effect: they integrate the individual into bourgeois society, offering them imaginary consolations for their bureaucratised routine which otherwise would

---

[9] Morin et al., *O Retorno dos Astrologos*.

[10] Morin et al., *O Retorno dos Astrologos*, p. 9.

[11] Morin et al., *O Retorno dos Astrologos*, p. 161.

[12] Edgar Morin, *Cultura de Massas no Século XX: o espírito do tempo I, nevrose* (Rio de Janeiro: Forense Universitária, 1977); Edgar Morin, *Cultura de Massas no Século XX: o espírito do tempo II: necrose* (Rio de Janeiro: Forense Universitária, 1986).

lead them to apathy and conformism.[13] It is in exploring the first effect that Claude Fischler, the contributor to the book who deals with the presence of French astrology in the media, presents his conclusions.[14] In his view, the horoscopes published by the press try to accommodate 'the world to the destiny of the individual, expelling unhappiness'.[15] There is however another sector of astrology, characterised by Morin as 'erudite'; this would reach a more restricted audience. In this would be reflected aspects of the crisis of modern society which began to take up more and more space in mass culture from the second half of the 1960s [onward].[16] In this way, 'erudite astrology's' theorists, in developing the suppositions of the astrological system, were able to formulate an 'anthropo-cosmology' which would attempt to unite the subject— [who has become] atomised by modernity, to the cosmos.[17]

In referring to this aspect of modern astrology, Morin included it in a much larger movement, which he calls 'New Gnosis'. Under this heading he tries to include a cultural movement which not only marks the resurgence of interest in the systems and philosophies of which ancient occult thought was composed, but which incorporates new elements. Defrance places it on the periphery of erudite astrology, attributing its central theme to the 'examination of all the questions left unanswered by science'.[18] Having as the principle vehicle for its ideas the journal *Planète*, this movement popularises the ideas of erudite astrology which seek to re-instate the unity of man [and] cosmos by means of fantastic hypotheses about lost civilisations, extra-terrestrial beings, and 'unexplained' phenomena. In so doing it is rejected as much by the astrological as by the scientific *intelligentsia*.[19]

The tendency of astrology to integrate into itself collections of beliefs and systems grouped together syncretically was already noted in my introduction and can be confirmed in several of its historical periods. This feature is also present in modern astrology and can easily be found in the interviews [with my informants]; however, its assimilation by the mass media, and consequently a great popularisation of its ideas, confers on it—in modern society—an incomparable richness and fragmentation. It

---

[13] Morin, *Cultura de Massas I*, pp. 169–70.
[14] Claude Fischler, 'A Astrologia da Massa', in *O Retorno dos Astrologos* , eds. Morin et al. (Lisbon: Moraes, 1972), pp. 29–66.
[15] Fischler, 'Astrologia da Massa', p. 50.
[16] Morin, *Cultura de Massas I*, p. 9.
[17] Morin, et al., *O Retorno dos Astrologos*, pp. 120–22.
[18] Morin, et al., *O Retorno dos Astrologos*, p. 101.
[19] Morin, et al., *O Retorno dos Astrologos*, p. 103.

thus becomes a challenge for any researcher of its various manifestations to try to cover the larger context which seems to surround the object [of their study].

Recently, several social scientists have sought a definition which includes all of this heterogeneous collection of beliefs and practices. In general terms, it attempts to pick out a linked set of principles which constitute a vision of the world common to all of them. Before describing and analysing the subject of his dissertation, 'the World of UFOlogy' in Brasilia, José Fonseca Ferreira Neto, for example, states that this world would be part of the 'alternative culture', which he defines as 'a lifestyle outside of "the system" or of consumer society'.[20] Ferreira Neto enumerates four characteristics which distinguish it: its 'ecological awareness' expressed in the idea of the 'natural';[21] its 'orientalism'; its religiosity which gives preference to mystical, oriental, and esoteric forms in contrast to the great religions of the West; and finally 'its eschatogical or millenarian perspective'.[22] Another distinguishing trait of the alternative culture (as he defines it) is its pluralism; not only does it offer a great diversity of doctrines and systems, but also 'for the same person' they are 'not mutually exclusive; in other words, there is not much radicalism involved in choosing any one of them'.[23]

As far as I know, the work of Ferreira Neto constitutes the apparently unique attempt of this kind in Brazil; in the USA, from the 1970s onward, a significant bibliography on this subject was being produced, whose debates are summarised by the sociologist Danny Jorgensen.[24] Although it is not appropriate here to make a detailed analysis of all the literature on what Jorgensen prefers to call 'the esoteric community', one recurring feature which jumps off the page for any reader can be noted. This is the difficulty of clearly locating the exact boundaries of this vision of the world in the terms which Ferreira Neto ventures to use. All these authors agree that the systems included by this 'culture' define themselves as 'deviant' in relation to what would be the 'dominant' values of the surrounding society: hence, epithets such as 'alternative', 'occult', 'esoteric', etc. Such deviance is highly valued by its members even though they may suffer discrimination as a result. However, besides the contents of

---

[20] Jose Fonseca Ferreira Neto, 'A Ciência dos Mitos e o Mito da Ciência'. (Master's Dissertation, Brasília: UnB, 1984), p. 18.

[21] This idea can also be found in the representations of 'expectant couples' studied by Tania Salem, which were commented on in the previous chapter (Salem, 'Trajetória', p. 40).

[22] Ferreira Neto, 'A Ciencia dos Mitos', pp. 18–25.

[23] Ferreira Neto, 'A Ciencia dos Mitos', p. 22.

[24] Danny L. Jorgensen, 'The Esoteric Community: an ethnographic investigation of the Cultic milieu', *Urban Life*, Vol. 10, No. 4 (Jan., 1982): pp. 383–84.

these beliefs, such a description only defines their relation to the values labelled as dominant, which are also rarely defined clearly. In Ferreira Neto's definition, for example, this recurrent trait underlies the first and third characteristics which he proposes. [Counting the first as a lifestyle outside the system and the third as a rejection of western religion—Trans.] Beyond this vague attitude, there don't appear to be any other traits consensually recognised by the different researchers in esoteric culture, who seek to define it in terms of a common vision of the world. We have already seen how such a common vision cannot be postulated in astrology.

It might still be premature to try to resolve this debate; even so one common tendency can already be found in the majority of the debate's participants: several describe the substantive features of the esoteric world in terms of the inclinations of the particular segment which they studied. The choice of terms itself reflects this. Ferreira [Neto] defines the 'alternative culture' chiefly as a lifestyle to the extent that the Project he studied implies the formation of communities outside the main centres, where the standards of sociability, work, consumption, etc., are altered. This kind of radical choice is much rarer among the students of astrology that I met. Hence, Morin and his team occupy themselves with a system of ideas that attempts to answer the impasses of science, which is a question that Morin proposes to deal with in other contexts.[25]

Another example is cited by Jorgensen:[26] the debate between Marcello Truzzi and Edward Tiryakian, which appears more clearly in the collection edited by the latter.[27] Tiryakian proposes the development of a 'sociology of esoteric culture'—the title of one of his articles—defining it by its secret, initiatory, magical, deviant, etc.,

---

[25] Antoine Faivre, a student of esotericism whose ideas I will discuss in Chapter 4, identifies a 'neo-Gnostic' current, defining it in a slightly different way from Morin. He describes, instead of the mass culture phenomenon, the 'erudite' side of this tendency which would manifest itself through contemporary scientists and epistemologists who, seeking to determine the theoretical consequences of the new scientific paradigms which have abandoned Newtonian cosmology, move back towards esoteric thought. Although he acknowledges that Morin may not accept the epithet, Faivre included him in this movement stating that, in *La Methode*, he didn't avoid making use of hermetic symbolism (Antoine Faivre, *Accès de l'ésotérisme Occidental* [Paris: Gallimard, 1986], p. 331).

[26] Jorgensen, 'The Esoteric Community', p. 384.

[27] Edward Tiryakian, 'Preliminary Consideration: toward the sociology of esoteric culture', in *On the Margins of the Visible: sociology, the esoteric and the occult*, ed. Edward Tiryakian (New York: Willes, 1974).

characteristics.[28] Although he believes that the 'occult *revival*' holds modern values in check, he views the phenomenon optimistically; he believes that esoteric culture and the groups it represents 'are the main sources of cultural and social innovations'.[29] On the other hand, Truzzi—also with generalising intentions in his analysis of 'occultism'—prefers not to emphasise its secret character, but 'its mysterious element, while commonly being very open and public'.[30]

Although the proposals of each one offer an undeniable utility to the student of the subject, being worthy of several commentaries, I would like to refer only to the areas of relevance in each of them. Tiryakian, in the collection he edited on the theme, reveals a notable curiosity for the study of witchcraft (which takes up one of the three parts into which the book is divided) and for the emergence of satanic sects in the 1960s; similarly, Truzzi is the author of an article on 'the revitalization of occultism as a popular culture'.[31] His particular interests in 'occultism' separate the two themes through which the social sciences normally focussed on it (the crisis [of modernity] and the mass media), making occultism's true nature even more mysterious.

That the only point of agreement in the definitions of this sector is on their 'alternative' and 'marginal' character is not at all surprising. As we can easily check, it is a definition claimed by the members themselves. But it is important to note that this is not a distinctive trait of a view of the world, but of the relationship which members of groups of the 'esoteric culture' establish with other groups. We must dissolve these notions in the same way that anthropology tried to do with the category of deviance.[32] We are faced here with a self-attributed deviance, positively valued and, in principle, not stigmatising. As also happened with other types of deviance, social scientists

---

[28] Tiryakian, 'Preliminary Consideration', pp. 1, 4, 6, 10–12, 263–75.

[29] Tiryakian, 'Preliminary Consideration', p. 273.

[30] Marcelo Truzzi, 'Definition and dimensions of the Occult: towards a sociological perspective', in *On the Margins of the Visible*, ed. Tiryakian, p. 224 [*sic*]. [The listed page number may be a typo, as it does not fall within the page range of Truzzi's chapter in Tiryakian's book, which is listed as pp. 243–55.—Ed.]

[31] [Marcello Truzzi, 'The Occult Revival as Popular Culture: Some Random Observations on the Old and Nouveau Witch', in *On the Margins of the Visible* , ed. Tiryakian. This article is not in the bibliography but is mentioned here as a possible source for the quote, both because Vilhena appears to refer to a different article and because the first part of its title duplicates the words of the quotation.—Ed.]

[32] Gilberto Velho, *Desvio e Divergência: uma crítica da patologia social*, 5th Ed. (Rio de Janeiro: Jorge Zahar Editora, 1985).

tended to reify it, classifying it very often as a social pathology, as was noted in the biologism of Morin and his team. The fact that certain sociologists have pointed out the positive characteristics of 'esoteric culture'—as Tiryakian does, in praising its innovative qualities—does not free us from these criticisms. In the article cited, Velho shows clearly how a view of social pathology produced by functionalism was also sympathetic to the idea that 'the deviant of today can be the civilising hero of tomorrow'.[33]

Noting the impasses present in the literature on 'esoteric culture', Jorgensen tries in a recent article to move the focus away from the search for abstract definitions of the supposed common view of the world, and towards a description of the social networks made up of its members. Although he does not abandon the attempt to indicate some concrete contents of their doctrines, the main interest of his approach is in showing how this culture develops complex relationships with the outside world. An example of this is events such as *psychic fairs* where their products are sold and their ideas propagated, thus making contact with the environment outside the community. Besides generating income, they

> serve as places to make new friends, exchange ideas and skills, strengthen existing relationships, develop business, present a positive public image, and as a means of making converts and recruiting new members.[34]

Despite using the term 'esoteric community' to describe it, his view of these groups is not closed, recognising that the esoteric community must be treated as a continuum. He also employs the categories of 'the curious' and 'clients', which might also be taken as examples of an intermediate position between the 'community' and the surrounding society.

This approach constitutes a real alternative to biologistic views, such as those found in North American social sciences, which explain adherence to theories they define as 'non-scientific' by means of a supposed 'deprivation' of its members.[35] Such approaches pass over the political aspects inherent in the question of deviance; as Velho reminds us, 'the deviant (...) is an individual who is not so much outside his culture but rather "reads it" differently'.[36]

---

[33] Velho, *Desvio e Divirgencia*, p. 15.
[34] Jorgensen, 'The Esoteric Community', p. 391.
[35] Jorgensen, 'The Esoteric Community', p. 403.
[36] Velho, *Desvio e Divirgencia*, p. 27.

I have not made such a wide-ranging ethnographic survey as Jorgensen of the 'social network' which makes up the world of astrology; the descriptions and commentaries that I will make refer mainly to the sectors of society frequented by my informants. However I will attempt to use and expand the theoretical indications of Jorgensen in the treatment of this *network*, because I believe that they allow us to escape from various theoretical dilemmas which I have noted. Although characterised by the presence of 'marginal beliefs', Jorgensen believes that the esoteric community has means of interacting with the surrounding society. These [means] are basically made up of events such as congresses, fairs, and workshops where the community makes contact with individuals who do not necessarily share their beliefs.[37] We will find in these situations, negotiations, and conflicts the different definitions of reality which the rest of society puts up against the esoteric and alternative culture. We can thus relativise the notion of deviance [through] understanding, along with the interactionists, that it is constructed by social agents through conflicts and accusations instead of existing as a property of the groups involved.[38] The attribute of deviance therefore can be negotiated or manipulated to mark out and reconstruct frontiers between the groups.

Modern esoteric culture is constituted as a privileged case in which such mechanisms remain clear, since the attribute of deviance is claimed by the group itself; it builds its identity from a rejection of the values of 'the system' or of 'Western culture'. Through these concepts, the members define their opposition to the larger society in simple categories; sociologists who characterise them only by their deviance are uncritically reproducing this reification, [which is] practically efficient but analytically impoverished. As Velho points out, the deviant is not so in all areas of behaviour; several members of the alternative world are forced to make compromise solutions with the outside world in a process of mediation, either in their ideology, as in the use of scientific-sounding language to which I referred earlier, or in practical terms, as in the sale of their products. This process of negotiation has repercussions in the form of creating boundaries inside the group itself, where 'purist' elements can accuse others of having been 'co-opted' or 'sold themselves out', etc.

---

[37] Jorgensen, 'The Esoteric Community', p. 401.
[38] Velho, *Subjetividade e Sociedade*, pp. 23–26.

THE WORLD OF ASTROLOGY IN RIO DE JANEIRO

In this section I will use the concept of 'social world' in the precise sense that Howard S. Becker attributes to it in the study of 'artistic worlds': to define the social organisation of astrology in Rio de Janeiro in the way suggested by Jorgensen as 'complex networks of friendship, business and communication'.[39] The expression *world of astrology* could be framed merely as an inclusive label in which the word *world*, as used in expressions like *world of art* or *world of sports*, has the function of embracing a poorly defined totality, in the same way as we use words like *universe* or *domain*. As far as art is concerned, Becker suggests going beyond this usage in a 'loose metaphorical way' to give the concept a more technical sociological meaning.[40] For him, the 'world of art' (for example) constitutes the network that enters into cooperation through the making of the artworks which characterise it. Traditionally the creation of the latter was always seen simply as a product of the creative power of the artist. Becker, following the line of investigation which he developed, intends to show that art can also be studied as a product of 'collective action'.[41] Becker includes material and institutional resources in this network; in other words, products of collective action that are not exclusively connected with the work of the artist—such as the production of paper or the existence of means of printed communication—and similarly the beliefs and values which transcend them, such as the tradition shared by the creator(s) and their public. So it can be said that Becker provides us with two possible definitions of the artistic world: one more extensive and the other limited. In the first case it would include not just the personnel involved in the creation of works of art, but also those who provide the conditions for these activities, then those who provide them for the second group, and so on, successively, in an infinite progression.[42]

In this case Becker's model can be represented as a succession of concentric circles whose central sector is composed of those who are engaged in their work with the deliberate intention of producing the work which defines the world of art. This sector has the greatest probability of developing a constant and regular cooperation. At other

---

[39] Jorgensen, 'The Esoteric Community', p. 402.

[40] Howard S. Becker, preface to *Art Worlds* (Berkeley: University of California Press, 1982), p. x.

[41] Cf. Howard S. Becker, 'Arte como Açâo Coletiva', in *Uma Teoria da Açâo Coletiva*, ed. Howard S. Becker et al. (Rio de Janeiro: Jorge Zahar Editora, 1977).

[42] Cf. Becker, 'Arte como Açâo Coletiva', p. 35.

points Becker declares that this routinisation produces the 'standards of collective action which we can call [typical of] the world of art'.[43] It is this more restricted definition that I will attempt to use to discuss the world of astrology, which will only include those networks based on the deliberate intention of producing interpretations and astrological works. However autodidactic individuals might be, they relate to this world by means of the books and magazines produced by it.

Even in the central circle conceived by Becker there is a segmentation, whose limiting criteria may also be subject to variations. Distinguishing themselves from their support staff and from the public, artists would define themselves through their ability to carry out the 'central activity' which characterises that world.[44] Although this activity tends to be seen as essential inside the network, its importance and its place [in society] varies greatly, both historically and culturally.

So, as modern society possesses—borrowing an expression from Pierre Bourdieu—a 'market of symbolic goods' with a relative autonomy which allows it to function according to its own logic, the world of astrology—to the extent that it is developed in our society—begins to constitute an 'intellectual field', with creators, a public and its own resources.[45] Astrologers—more than in the artistic world in general, perhaps because they receive less social recognition from the larger society—meet frequently at events such as congresses and meetings, attempting to spread knowledge of astrology. In Rio there exists an association which tries to gather them together, the SARJ (*Sociedade de Astrologia do Rio de Janeiro*), founded on 18 September 1980.

We can find in this world the same three characters who make up the central circle of the world of arts: the support staff, the public, and the one responsible for the 'central activity', the astrologer. My interviews did not include any representative of Becker's first group and only four astrologers. Among the consumers, I also privileged a specific sector: the 'students of astrology'. These choices do not simply depend on the circumstances of the research, but also on the kind of astrology that I took as my subject, [practised in] urban middle class sectors with intellectual and psychological interests, as will become clearer further on. My description of the extent of the astrological social network will also privilege the environments most often frequented

---

[43] Becker, *Art Worlds*, p. 1.

[44] Becker, *Art Worlds*, p. 18.

[45] Pierre Bourdieu, 'O mercado do bens simbólicos', in Pierre Bourdieu, *A Economia das Trocas Simbólicas* (Sao Paulo: Perspectiva, 1982), pp. 99–181.

by this type of consumer. It was in this context that I myself was involved during my fieldwork.

According to Morin and his team's investigation of the world of French astrology, the distribution of the consumption of its products varied basically according to social class. For Claude Fischler, although astrology might be 'trans-class'—or rather, it manages to reach all classes—it 'changes its tone from one class to another'.[46] In this sense, the astrology produced by each class varies in content in a way parallel to cultural consumption as a whole. There will be in some way an adjustment between the astrological discourse and the social class it touches.

In the same way that studies of cultural consumption work with large dichotomous categories which can be unfolded into smaller units in a specific analysis—such as 'high culture' and 'popular culture' [Gans's terms], or 'refined taste' and 'raw taste'[47]—the work coordinated by Morin operates with a general distinction between 'astrology of the masses' and 'erudite astrology'. Philippe Defrance locates them as two extreme polarities:

> Between the daily newspaper horoscope and the esoteric and para-scientific speculations of erudite astrology, all grades are possible.[48]

Following these principles the authors distinguish several modes of astrology anchored to firm socio-economic reference points. The erudite pole is described as an 'astrology of the rich', since 'the favoured classes, protected against material difficulties, are those most naturally disposed towards a speculative astrology'.[49] Still within these classes, but having more immediate pragmatic interests, we will find the consumption of astrology 'by the upper classes of the bourgeoisie, by technical and managerial directors and by the liberal professions'.[50] Consistent with the needs dictated by their social position it would serve, on the one hand, 'as an aid in decision-making; on the other (…) as a tool of psychological inquiry allowing, "the establishment of a human relation"'.[51] We would have two distinct forms of 'bourgeois astrology': 'praxo-astrology' and 'psycho-

---

[46] Morin et al., *O Retorno dos Astrologos*, pp. 111–12.

[47] Herbert Gans, *Popular Culture and High Culture: an analysis and evaluation of taste* (New York: Basic Books, 1974); Bourdieu, *La Distinction*, pp. 31–33.

[48] Morin et al., *O Retorno dos Astrologos*, p. 95.

[49] Morin et al., *O Retorno dos Astrologos*, p. 113.

[50] Morin et al., *O Retorno dos Astrologos*, p. 67.

[51] Morin et al., *O Retorno dos Astrologos*, p. 71.

astrology', respectively, 'indicating the exact moment to act and clarifying [relationships] with partners', by means of which 'astrology improves the fortunes of the unfortunate'.[52]

The analysis of mass astrology that these authors carried out was strongly influenced by a phenomenon of the French mass media at the time: the programme of Madame Soleil, an astrologer who gave consultations over the radio replying to listeners' letters and became a national figure through her success.[53] She also became a symbol of the characteristics attributed by Morin to mass culture; with advice which was at the same time consoling and encouraging, she 'joined and re-joined together ceaselessly'. They supposed that in the 'lower classes' there would be a demand for an astrology which supplied direct and immediate answers to practical problems. It is the kingdom of 'emergency rescue astrology'.[54]

These analyses seem to leave aside some of the characteristics of mass culture pointed out earlier by Morin himself. In his first work on this culture, he acknowledged that the differentiation existing in the consumer public 'is not exactly the same as the social classes'.[55] Umberto Eco also affirms that the three levels by which consumer culture is stratified 'do not correspond to those of social classes'.[56]

As far as astrological consumption is concerned, where considerations completely extrinsic to mere cultural competence play a part—such as the disposition to believe in the [astrological] system itself—such a correlation, locked onto social stratification, becomes less plausible. In contrast to this hypothesis, I will try to show how Becker describes, by means of the concept of 'convention', the internal principle through which not only consumption, but the positions [of the players] in the artistic world as a whole are structured, and thus to demonstrate its utility in the analysis of the social organisation of astrology.

Howard S. Becker used the term 'convention' to define the knowledge of particular rules and values which facilitate communal cooperation, based partially on consensus, within an artistic world. In practice, knowledge of these rules defines the participation of each individual in a sector of the artistic world. Becker's analytical schema allows us to conceive of differential behaviours in artistic consumption according to its own

---

[52] Morin et al., *O Retorno dos Astrologos*, p. 74.
[53] Morin et al., *O Retorno dos Astrologos*, p. 35.
[54] Morin et al., *O Retorno dos Astrologos*, p. 116.
[55] Morin, *Cultura de Massas I*, p. 40.
[56] Eco, *Apocalipticos e Integrados*, p. 54.

logic, which is not automatically subordinated to social stratification; for him, it is the conventions which define the existence and organisation of the world of art:

> To speak of the organisation of the world of art—its division into different kinds of publics, and producers and support staff of various kinds—is another way of talking about who knows what and uses their knowledge in order to act collectively.[57]

Such principles, which organise cooperation among members of the artistic world, and which allow their public to understand the works that they produce, can equally be either intrinsic or extrinsic to this [artistic] world. The latter belong to the cultural contexts in which these works are produced; such is the case, for example, in the distinction between masculine and feminine rôles constructed in ballet. However there are other conventions which 'arise inside the world itself, and are only known to those who work with them in some form'.[58] In the case of the world of astrology these conventions refer to a greater or lesser mastery of the techniques and classifications described in Chapter 1. Theoretically, the other types participate as much as those in the production of the symbolic goods offered by this world. However, they are not only exclusive to the astrological network, conferring its identity [upon it], but are also the most relevant for defining the specific social sectors to which my informants belong.

For Becker, the intrinsic conventions would have two functions in the world of art. In the role of a specific language for each kind of art, they permit bases for cooperation in creative work and communication with the public to be established; in the form of aesthetic judgements which create hierarchies among works of art and their styles, they justify the demands of their creators 'for the resources and benefits commonly available to people who produce this kind of art'.[59]

The worlds of astrology are distinguished from those of art in relation to both these functions. In the latter case, it is important to note that astrology does not seek explicitly to satisfy a purely aesthetic pleasure. It defines itself as a form of knowledge with claims to a degree of practical efficacy. Because of this, its attempts to achieve some legitimacy are based much more on epistemological than on aesthetic criteria; and however much these two criteria might be related, this is a crucial difference. In theoretical terms, a work of art does not aspire to have a truth value; however, it is necessary to remember that certain people may go to an astrologer simply for

---

[57] Becker, *Art Worlds*, p. 67.
[58] Becker, *Art Worlds*, p. 47.
[59] Becker, *Art Worlds*, p. 132.

amusement [and], that many people also condemn romantic fiction or films because they believe them to be vehicles for certain ideas. Therefore, in practice, this distinction may lose its sharpness.

However, the analysis of the operation of the first type of convention makes the specific features of astrology much clearer. The language of astrology articulates a conjunction of techniques and classifications whose structure, as I tried to show in the first chapter, reveals a degree of stability. But on the contrary, each form of artistic expression manifests in terms of its own language proper to its cultural and historical context. It may be possible to find common traits among different musical languages, although our tonal and harmonic system includes conventions not shared by those born into other musical traditions.[60] Besides this, one of the most widely known values in modern art is the search for new languages and forms of expression, which forms part of the idea of the artistic avant-garde. So there exists, although based on different principles, a competition for legitimacy in the two types of 'worlds': while in that of astrology it is uncommon for autonomous subgroups typical of the art world to arise and come to exclusively dominate a particular language of the avant-garde, in the way that Becker describes.[61]

On the other hand, by its necessarily epistemological character, the internal debates of astrology can create these types of subgroups. The various currents which comprise it [the world of astrology] each try to offer better explanations for the efficacy of the techniques and classifications that they share. Each [current] can add to the latter [shared techniques and classifications] a technical vocabulary from one or more authors, such as Jung or Guénon, which claims the ability to define the true nature of astrology. The themes put forward by these doctrines will be described in the next chapter. It is important to keep in mind that, in spite of their differences, they remain as common references as long as they continue to use the language of astrology.

In his definition of what he calls 'cultures of taste', Herbert Gans is interested in describing them as *partial* cultures'.[62] Except for the professional creators involved in cultural production, who would occupy the inner core of the world of art, these cultures do not involve the whole life of an individual. For him, 'they have to do with those values over which individuals have some choice'.[63] So it relates to those aspects of

---

[60] Cf. Becker, *Art Worlds*, pp. 40–42.
[61] Becker, *Art Worlds*, pp. 61–67.
[62] Gans, *Popular Culture*, p. 13.
[63] Gans, *Popular Culture*, p. 12.

modern life which are understood as free, related to the domain of leisure. Although sometimes Gans can be observed to have some difficulty in contextualising these values, it cannot be denied that they form part of the constructions on which contemporary cultural consumption is based.

These features permit us to understand how 'taste cultures' are not necessarily tied to social stratification. The most important way by which the latter influences cultural consumption is, as Gans emphasises, through education: in other words, through their relationship with the formation of 'symbolic codes' and of the acquisition of distinct grades of 'cultural capital'.[64] Beyond this Gans also recognises the importance of variables such as age and ethnic origin.[65] The first factor draws its influence from the fact that youth in Western society constitute 'an idle class, at least if they are affluent'.[66]

Free time alters the balance between 'taste cultures' precisely to the extent that it facilitates the specialisation necessary for participation in high cultures. The more one ascends in this hierarchy, the more the autonomisation of cultural consumption is emphasised. In this way, a distinctive feature of the segment of each art belonging to *high culture* is to become, in the expression of Gans, *creator-oriented*: in other words, to begin to judge the works in terms of the needs of the creator and not the consumers.[67] Closer to the inner core of this artistic world, this *taste-public* begins to take on the point of view of those responsible for the core activity, defending the freedom of creation and the creator. We would have here also a great similarity between the conventions of the artist and those of the public.

The similarities noted above between Gans and Becker were acknowledged by the latter, as is shown by his complimentary references to his colleague.[68] He also points out that their differences flow from the fact that, in contrast to the former, he is not interested in constructing a social theory from the aesthetic point of view, seeking to value the conventions in themselves, focusing, instead, on 'questions of social organisation'. My work, on the other hand, is halfway along the road; in being concerned to describe this organisation, I approached astrology as a whole principally in terms of its beliefs. For Becker, the conventions can just as easily be values and

---

[64] For Gans' views on how education inflruces cultural consumption, see *Popular Culture*, p. 70; for Velho's views on symbolic codes, see *Individualismo e Cultura*, pp. 19–23; for cultural capital, see Pierre Bourdieu, *Le Sens Pratique* (Paris: Editions de Minuit, 1980), pp. 191–207.

[65] Gans, *Popular Culture*, pp. 70, 100–02.

[66] Gans, *Popular Culture*, p. 70.

[67] Gans, *Popular Culture*, p. 62.

[68] Becker, *Art Worlds*, p. 144.

symbolic systems as simple schemes for coordinating collective actions. However I am interested in them primarily in the first sense.

Being a classificatory structure which can be combined with different values, the zodiacal system and the language associated with it organises the world of astrology. It is by the differential distribution of this language that I hope to explain the relations between the astrology of the masses and the erudite variety, without mechanically linking them to the structure of the surrounding society.

My interviewees, especially those described as 'students', often referred to astrology as 'a language'. Through the evocative power that they possess, astrological symbols such as signs and planets have an ability to express multiple realities, forming a vocabulary applicable even to contexts not specifically related to the practice of this divinatory technique. This will be explored more systematically in the next chapter, but it can be confidently stated that it supplies terms applicable not only to the personalities of individuals, but also to situations, relationships, etc. In the words of one informant:

> To the extent that you absorb this symbolism to a certain level of understanding (…) it starts to become part of your life, it will lead you to use it for whatever you want (…); so I am beginning to relate these symbols to real life, my own and those of people that I see. For example, watching a child (…), you see the kind of relationship they have with the world; the old person is different. There you can compare the moon with Saturn (Claudio).

On the subject of the influence of this phenomenon in the interactions between individuals, I witnessed a curious event during my socialising with the informants with whom I shared a friendship. A group of people with very different levels of interest in astrology were together when Beatriz arrived, talking about a film she had recently seen and which, although it had not been on posters for long, had already provoked a lot of interest within this circle. It was *The Purple Rose of Cairo* by Woody Allen. Praising several features of the film and revealing her difficulty in defining its qualities, she commented that the film was, in her opinion, 'Pisces with Cancer'. In fact, she had wanted to refer (as she was able to say later) to the discussion that the film encompassed about 'illusion' and 'imagination', characteristics of these two signs. She found out straight away however, that her commentary provoked complaints from the uninitiated who accused her of a certain pedantry.

The use of the expression 'to become literate' to define the process of apprenticeship in astrology and of its vocabulary was made by three informants (Alice, Beatriz and Helen); in so doing, [they] converged with one of the members of Morin's team, Philippe Defrance. He defined 'astrological literacy' as the absorption of the themes of erudite astrology into more external contexts, forming the 'astrological culture'.[69] This hypothesis allows us to distance ourselves from an approach in which the world of astrology would be organised exclusively by external criteria, which the work coordinated by Morin sometimes appears to suggest. We can say that this culture, insofar as it is infused by erudite astrology, is a condensation of the conventions which characterise and distinguish the world of astrology and determines, through its distribution, the structure of astrological consumption.

The main characters of this network, the astrologers, seem to be more at ease in an environment of *creator-oriented* consumption. The four interviews I arranged with them did not allow me to establish a complete picture of the attitudes they held. But Rosa, a member of SARJ, described in her interview some aspects of the tense relations that can arise between astrologers and the media:

> At the moment there is a fight going on, if you can call it a fight, between astrologers and the press: people only give interviews now if what we say is what they print. (…). For example, a short time ago we (the astrologers of SARJ) had a discussion and we decided that we would not give interviews about stories in the news (…), intending to show that astrology has much more to say for itself than 'you will die of this, you won't die of that', 'who will win, who won't win the election'. This kind of use of astrology doesn't interest me (…), it ends up as a business so superficial, so misrepresenting, that it demoralises you even more.

Rosa is concerned that the simplifications of astrology in the media might lead to the loss of the prestige it gained in the last five or six years, 'when a competition began (…) a sophistication' of the system, as it began to interest 'intellectuals, thinkers, people of a good level, intellectual level'. This pragmatic, popular astrology is reflected in the kinds of clients she receives. She accepts that the majority of people who call her come with very concrete questions, wanting exact answers such as 'will I or won't I sell the business?', 'is it good to buy the house or not?' Others 'have a lover and a husband and want to know if they should stay with the lover or the husband'. In the same way as Rosa, José also admits to feeling dissatisfied with these cases:

> Recently I made a chart for a young woman. Her main question was whether she was going to get married. I mean the biggest, the only question was if she was going to get

---

[69] Morin et al., *O Retorno dos Astrologos*, p. 95.

married, have money, a simple answer is very difficult to give. And this is one thing that as well as irritating me a lot, bores and frustrates me.

Both of them, despite the difficulties, make efforts to lead their more pragmatic clients towards ideas of self-development, features of the sector of astrology which I have privileged and will more fully explain in the next chapter. Rosa said that, contrary to other astrologers, her approach, in working with such a client, is 'to speak a bit with them, familiarising them a little with astrological language'. José, for his part, talks about making 'an approach like this, for people to know themselves better, for people to become more aware of themselves'.

Regina, an astrologer with more prestige, and belonging to the group of four for longer, stated that, four years from now, she will only have three clients a week and

> People that someone recommends, that are working a lot with their interior life, who are already searching within, and have an intellectual level like, a bit better (…); any human being can come here, from a domestic worker to impresarios and bankers. But I'm not interested in working purely superficially with anyone: 'you are going to get a better job', 'you will win the election' (…)

When the astrologer does not reveal a tendency to select their clients they are very often concerned to see a few clients a day for the longest possible time. Rosa affirmed that, although she knew professionals who see eight clients a day, which she considered 'an exhaustion', she limits herself to two a day, trying to get them to come back a month later after listening several times to the tape recorded during the first session. In one conversation Roberto revealed his admiration for an astrologer who, according to what he told me, spent a whole year analysing one chart. He compared him to a colleague from Sao Paulo who, although having a pioneering role in developing the system in Brazil, was always cited as a representative of the commercialisation of astrology. Roberto told me that he spends thirty minutes with a client, counted on the clock, limiting himself to interpreting those parts of the chart which the client requests.

As we can see, the astrologers I interviewed represent a very specific sector within the astrological world in Rio de Janeiro. Given that my entry into this world happened basically through contact with astrological students and from attending courses and congresses, it is natural that most of my informants should be closer to [the pole of] erudite astrology. If, as I try to show in the last chapter, their discourse can be understood through the use they make of the category *symbolism*, this means that they are, to a large extent, interested in examining the structure and techniques of the astrological system itself. We shall then see that this privilege conceded to the symbolic logic underneath astrology takes them away from the merely pragmatic applications of its divinatory capacity.

However not all astrologers share this creator-oriented vision; the commentaries reproduced above show that. Given that the majority of my interviewees complained that many of their clients were not interested in astrology as an instrument of personal transformation, it is to be expected that there would be professionals more allied to a deterministic relationship between the individual and the planets. They reduced the psychologisation of astrology to the *public relation* to which Fischler referred, and in the opinion of many informants would not understand the poly-semy of its symbolism; this would be due to them occupying a more peripheral position in the diffusion of astrological culture. We will see, in the account of the interviews in the next chapter, how this distinction which Morin drew between *praxo*-astrology and *erudite* astrology is recognised by all the informants, even when they prefer the first.

Although it is always possible to point to the limitations that each context imposes on the content that it transmits, these two types of astrology must not be too tightly associated respectively with the media versus private consultations. For several years the Rio newspaper *O Globo* has been publishing the chart of the week every Friday. It supplies the planetary positions for that week, trying to help the reader with a reasonable level of astrological knowledge but who doesn't possess an ephemeris. On the other hand *O Jorno do Brasil* (1 December 1987) published a report mentioning astrologers [who] specialised in the provision of predictions for financial investments, marriages, etc. The professionals I interviewed, as we saw, rejected this type of practice.

Besides individual consultations—their main source of income—they [astrologers I interviewed] all gave weekly courses, with the exception of Roberto, who only organised study groups. The latter, after the interview, collaborated for a while with a non-specialist monthly magazine. Aside from him, only Rosa said she wrote regularly for the mass media. From the conversations which we had at this time her intentions seem to have been to exercise the same educational influence, which she describes as follows:

> We try to use the media to say 'look, this isn't good, astrology is different from what it appears; it's no use to keep on talking only about the sun sign, that the sign is only one part'.

The three main types of products offered by astrologers determine the three types of consumer. The biggest group, who only read the astrology of the mass media, were not included in my interviews. The second group would be the clients who, more or less often, consult astrologers, acquiring in the process a better knowledge of their own charts and of the language of astrology. But what distinguishes them is a lack of interest, due to some combination of lack of time and curiosity, in becoming able to work with the astrological system themselves. To differing degrees, they remain interested in the 'oracular' aspect of astrology, in its ability to give definite answers to specific practical questions.

The third group consists of those who study astrology; they make up the largest proportion of my informants being, therefore, the principal transmission vehicle of the values described in the next chapter. Their place in the world of astrology is defined by the fact that, besides sometimes going for astrological consultations, they attend courses and study groups coordinated by astrologers. They are therefore more allied with the values of the latter, who are obviously ex-students as well. I try to show, however, that this professionalisation exhibits some variations.

To a large extent, they [third group] are the product of the *boom* that astrology experienced in Rio de Janeiro in this decade, mentioned earlier by Rosa and characterised by a proliferation of courses and consultations. A number of astrological study centres arose, with lecture halls in which the courses were delivered. The majority of interviewees had only been interested in astrology for a few years. The great exception, Gloria, although she can be called a student, appeared not to share, as we will see, the views of the majority of my informants on symbolism.[70] The values that she articulates therefore seem to be largely associated with this *boom*.

The signs of this expansion can be observed in the reports which newspapers in Rio periodically devoted to it. The *Jornal do Brasil* of 5 November 1987 asked: 'In 1970 did anyone know any astrologer except Omar Cardoso and Zora Yonara?', referring to two figures associated with the mass media who, at that time, wrote columns in magazines and presented radio programmes. Today private consultations would be the norm, with about a hundred professionals in Rio de Janeiro who charge between 1000Cz$ and 3000Cz$ for a ninety-minute consultation.[71] Among these [astrologers], according to another report, about thirty belong to the SARJ which has, according to its president, six hundred members.

Besides the routine activities of the world of astrology through which it offers these three 'products', there are also 'events' which have grown greatly in popularity during

---

[70] This interviewee is absent from the list of interviewees in Appendix 1—Trans.

[71] The name of the Brazilian currency at this time, a period when hyper-inflation required frequent revaluations—Trans.

this recent period. It is in the congresses, meetings and debating circles that astrologers meet, who otherwise belong to separate sectors of the world of astrology, where they try to create a panorama of the theoretical production of astrology. They also set themselves up in some of the privileged areas [of Rio], in which students can be found.

The biggest of these events was certainly the Second International Congress of Astrology, which took place on 5, 6, and 7 November 1987 in the meeting rooms of the Hotel Copacabana Palace. Drawing astrologers to their workshops from all over Brazil, Europe and the USA, it had an attendance of six hundred people, according to information obtained from the organisers; this included the speakers, journalists and the audience, who paid six OTNs to attend.[72]

As we shall see, the conversation of these informants is marked by a great intellectual curiosity which is rarely limited to astrology, leading them to attend courses and ask for readings on different topics. We can link Gans's observations on the 'leisure classes', in the formation of *taste cultures*, with the fact that my study's three groups were made up mainly of students and housewives. Vánia, talking about her initial interest in astrology is explicit on this point:

(...) I began to go to classes out of curiosity (...). Since I had nothing to do, letting myself learn something interesting, enriched me a little, to leave the children behind a little. That's how it was for me.

In the case of the young people, this 'enriching knowledge' also came about by studies in the areas of the human sciences provided, for example, by teachers in the basic level of the universities—where very often they did not complete the courses.[73] In the specific case of this group music also played an important role, given that several of them sang in a choir. This activity offered a dilettante contact with the world of music which, for some offered the possibility of a future profession or of cultivating their creator-oriented view of this art.[74] However, the chief areas of interest for these

---

[72] The OTN (Obrigaçao do Tesouro Naçional) was a certificate of public debt used as payment during the period of economic crisis at the end of the military dictatorship between 1986–1989, and was calculated as equivalent to 106.40 Cruzados.

[73] They could potentially form part of the professional 'taste-culture', which, according to Gans develops around the erudite production of human sciences like sociology (Gans, *Popular Culture*, pp. 73–74).

[74] Becker draws attention to the importance of art students in the worlds of art, as a strategic audience for knowing different conventions. He notes also that in the USA, the number of art

astrology students are the systems and beliefs associated with the 'esoteric world' or 'alternative culture', whose networks interlink with those of astrology. As we see, they belong to various taste-cultures where they can exercise their 'freedom' and 'curiosity'.

There are many types of contacts between the world of astrology and the world of the alternative, which was made clear in my interviews. In the first place, clients and students rarely refrain from using other divinatory techniques (tarot, numerology, etc.) or 'alternative therapies' (homeopathy, acupuncture, etc.). Some of the professionals in these [other] areas are often invited to take part in events such as congresses. Rosa, revealing what appears to be a common practice among other astrologers, has a list of these therapists to whom she sends clients if a chart reading reveals some serious problems which require a specialist's approach.

There also exist points in common which link the different alternative networks. This is the case, for example, in specialised bookshops where literature referring to various aspects of this culture can be found, including a large stock of imported material. In the model of psychic fairs described by Jorgensen,[75] the Esoteric Fair has taken place already several times in Rio de Janeiro; the second produced a profit of about three million Cruzados during its eleven days (*Jornal do Brasil*, 5 November 1987). During this fair the visitor could, after paying 170 Cz$ entrance fee, go around the stalls where astrological consultations and shell divinations were on offer (both costing 600 Cz$) or Tarot (1200 Cz$), in addition to books, publications, food, and clothes linked to the 'alternative lifestyle' described by Ferreira.[76]

The astrological study centres are usually founded by very successful astrologers, [either] alone or with associates; they take over some rooms in a commercial building and offer a programme of intensive courses and workshops. These latter are rarely limited to astrology, but may include other systems or approach more philosophical themes: attempting to include and define an 'anthropo-cosmology', to use Morin's expression, of esotericism. In these places, as in the bookshops referred to above, specialised periodicals of the alternative world with a limited circulation are for sale which, being more orthodox in their defence of alternative lifestyles and views of the

---

courses is much greater than the demand for professionals (*Art Worlds*, pp. 52–54). Are we not, once more, faced with a logic particular to the market in symbolic goods, motivated by choice and by the 'wish to enrich oneself', about which our informant spoke?

[75] Jorgensen, 'The Esoteric Community', pp. 390–91.
[76] Ferreira Neto, 'A Ciencia dos Mitos', pp. 18–33.

world, seek to distinguish themselves from those which reach a larger public, avoiding being included in mass culture.

The consumer of mass astrology appears in the conversations of my informants, as we shall see later, as the *Other* in contrast to whom they construct their identities. Although it may be in these places that 'astrological literacy' begins, an individual's contact with the erudite culture of this world means an immediate rejection of their initial views of the astrological system. Because of this I don't want to draw a precise picture of this consumer, in order to avoid falling into stereotypical definitions which would certainly be shown to be false. It is also in this sector that another character in the world of astrology that I have left aside gains importance: the member of the support staff. In the erudite sector, profoundly creator-oriented as it is and where the language of astrology shows few variations, the ideal is that these personnel facilitate the activity of the astrologer without interference. The latter gains more importance in the area not covered in the present work, in the figure of the editor or director of the mass media.

EXPERIENCES AND TRAJECTORIES

As I stated in the introduction, Chapter 4 will be dedicated to the description of my interviews, using as a guideline the notion of symbolism through which, for the interviewees, astrology is explained and justified. Before this it was necessary not only to describe the astrological system, but also to examine the place of astrology in modern society, showing the variety of ways in which it is used. Without this analysis—which is completed in this section—being exhaustive, it still serves to allow the reader to contextualise the informants and their views. I will conclude the description of the world of astrology with an overall look at the group interviewed, showing how its members take part in this world so that, knowing the ways in which each one experiences astrology, we can better understand the similarities and differences between them.

With the aim of understanding how each of them came to be included in the study and what rôle each played in its development, I will present a report of my fieldwork. The latter moved away from classical parameters established by anthropological tradition as I tried to find my own solutions to certain problems that afflict researchers in the urban environment. It does not share the homogeneity and reduced scale very often attributed to primitive societies: the privileged object in which the tradition [of anthropology] was developed. Although I have tried to show that, in the last analysis, astrological students are part of a vast network, the latter is not just extensive, but is also very heterogeneous; it presents different kinds and degrees of belonging. Even among students of astrology—those who do not practice it professionally and who have the biggest involvement in this system—it only makes up one part of their daily concerns, immersed as they are in professional and family relationships where astrology is not always present.

As I recounted earlier, I frequented two study groups who met once a week. The first, Group **c**, was composed of Alice, Vánia, Ruth, Helen and Theresa; it was run by a quite well-known astrologer, A.[77] The group met in the house of Alice who was Vánia's mother-in-law, and had already been running for two years. The participants already had enough mastery of the astrological system to analyse, under the guidance of **A**, charts of clients which he provided for teaching purposes or of the family and friends of participants, nearly always with the aim of helping them with problems they were experiencing. The meetings lasted two hours and, after the coordinator had left, some of the members stayed on to chat. I usually took advantage of this period to conduct my interviews and take part in discussions.

I stopped attending these meetings at the beginning of October 1986, after attending them from the middle of the previous July. A short time later the meetings stopped because **A** found himself too busy, preparing the work he was due to present at the First International Congress of Astrology, which took place 22 to 24 November at the Hotel Gloria in Rio de Janeiro. This being the last group of studies that he coordinated, he decided to bring it to an end, not only because he was becoming more and more busy with consultations and courses, but also because—as he said in the last meetings I attended—they had already 'learned everything', and were limited to exercising their knowledge.

I was able to meet Alice and her group thanks to Beatriz, her niece and my friend. It was through her, and another person I knew who was taking astrology courses, that I made my first contacts with this system. Both of them enthusiastically recommended

---

[77] Following the customary practice in urban anthropology of keeping the people studied incognito, the astrologers only appear with their real names in this book as public personages: in other words, when they write books or articles or deliver conferences. Those I interviewed, like the rest of my informants, have been given fictitious names. However a number of them figure in the statements of the informants and, in order to illustrate the common connections within the astrological network, without muliplying the number of names, I will just use initials to identify them. As one more means of ensuring their anonymity they will all be treated as masculine (the gender which, in the Portuguese language is employed to refer to both sexes jointly), although some are men and some are women.

Arroyo's book and gave me information about two weekly introductory courses that I attended in these three months, run by astrologers B and C.[78] Some weeks later, at the invitation of A, I began to take part in his weekly course. Unlike the other two, he was not concerned only with astrology, narrating several Greek myths and interpreting them with the use of Neo-Platonic theories as well as those of René Guénon. He also cited well-known researchers of myths such as James Frazer. We had begun to arrange an interview but since, at the time, I was not still interviewing astrologers it didn't take place; afterwards I lost contact with him. Nevertheless, from the few conversations we had it was possible to know that in general terms his view of astrology was strongly influenced by Guénon and his disciples.

Beatriz, with her sister and Luísa, formed Group **b** of students, led by Roberto, Alice's son and a professional astrologer, meeting weekly in Alice's house (Alice was not able to attend). However, Alice was able to take part in a group which met at night, which I have called Group **a**, led by the same astrologer and composed of several of my acquaintances, among them Cláudio, Jaime and Marcos. To get to know some members of these groups outside of astrology I was able, to some extent, to share their movements after the dissolution of this group at the beginning of the following year, precipitated by Roberto's trip to Europe. Although several members already had a fairly advanced knowledge of the astrological system—knowing how to erect a [birth] chart and make a preliminary analysis—the group discussed its basic principles in each meeting, analysing each sign, its symbolism, and meaning.

During this period, which preceded the editing of my first work on astrology, I interviewed the first nine informants listed in Appendix 1. Among them only one person who did not belong to any of the three groups is included: Sônia, who I met in the course run by C, where she was learning the fundamentals of astrology on the recommendation of an astrologer who had read her chart. However, due to the line followed in that course, her view of astrology was as much permeated by the symbolist approach as was that of two other informants, who had absorbed influences both from traditional astrology and the Humanistic trend of Arroyo.

From the beginning of my investigation, also influenced by my first readings, I was always concerned to identify the different appropriations made of astrology. Without having fully developed hypotheses on this, I already understood the relativity of the information I obtained from my interviewees. I understood that, aside from the theoretical and philosophical disagreements in the world of astrology, the interviews

---

[78] Arroyo, *Astrologia*.

showed a perspective strongly marked by the fact that the groups investigated and described in the previous chapter were composed of students. Thus, in the initial study to which I referred I tried to analyse those characteristics and only held an interview with Roberto—with whom I had discussed astrology a great deal since I began to attend the study group—after writing this analysis. The interview with Roberto took place on the evening before the First International Congress of Astrology, I was able to meet several members of group **c** again and see Sônia, who I knew had progressed in her studies.

From the first interviews, three themes emerged clearly. The most intriguing was that of esotericism, once I had settled [on] the definition of the object I had chosen to study. The syncretism in which astrology is immersed made me ask to what extent esotericism constitutes a system of beliefs sufficiently important for the classification of that group. Practically all of its members admitted to feeling at least an interest in other divinatory and therapeutic systems generally associated with the esoteric or alternative world. Generally the informants recognised all of them as valid routes to self-knowledge and the choice of astrology sometimes seemed quite casual. In the field of religions, there was also a great deal of tolerance, and the idea of a convergence among almost all of their manifestations.

For an anthropologist trained to concern himself with 'differences', this pluralism seemed extremely enigmatic. Obviously there were mechanisms of exclusion which were evident from the beginning, and about which I will speak later. But what I am trying to describe now is the emphasis on tolerance which (not by chance) several social scientists interested in studying the esoteric world have noted. That is perhaps the most complex of the topics I encountered in the interviews, besides being the least studied. I will treat it only as it concerned the group studied, maintaining a degree of caution against general theorising. This is motivated precisely because, contrary to the way it is often presented, the esoteric world is extremely heterogeneous.

From the beginning of my interviews, attempts to describe the nature of astrology frequently compared it to religion on the one hand and to psychoanalysis on the other. Likewise the purpose of the [astrological] system was unanimously linked to self-knowledge which would also be, as mentioned above, a function of the other esoteric systems. For the informants, more than being a means of obtaining predictions of the future or becoming successful, astrology represented a powerful tool with which they could come to know their weaknesses and potentials through a process of self-development. From the beginning this obviously suggested a closeness between psychology and this system, something which had already been suggested to me from reading Arroyo's psychological approach.

But astrology, as described by the informants, presents unique features compared to psychoanalysis and psychotherapies: it is, in the words of Beatriz, 'a sacred science'. Although the astrological system is not necessarily linked to any stated religious principle, several informants related its efficacy to the existence of a 'cosmic harmony', expressed sometimes by the redefinition of the Jungian concept of synchronicity. While (according to the group) the search for self-knowledge in psychoanalysis does not take spiritual or cosmic factors into account, astrology—on the contrary—would tend to view man as belonging to a totality which encloses him, permitting this self-development to move in the direction of a greater harmony with the universe which surrounds him.

That does not imply, on the part of the interviewees, a total adherence to religion. If that representation of a totality which astrology may possess is associated by some of them with God, it does not imply the acceptance of a specific religious creed or their regular participation in services. It is true that their positions on religion were much more varied than those on psychoanalysis. But the informants' attitudes towards the totality which astrology allowed them to glimpse was almost always much more a question of intellectual reflection than devotion or faith. It did not lead them to the performance of any kind of ritual, nor adherence to groups related to any of the common religions.

With the exception of Vánia, Sônia and Jaime—of Jewish origin, who according to them had not received any religious education—the members of the first group interviewed had received a Catholic education and had chiefly studied in Catholic colleges. The younger the informants, the more they seemed to have moved away from the religion they had been taught, although they admitted having experienced, until adolescence, a great influence from this education. Thus only Helen and Alice declared themselves to be Catholics. But even in their interviews, the differences between astrology and 'religion' as defined by the informants were also evident. So already in the first interview, Alice stated that the condemnation of astrology made by the Pope some months before the interview did not make her feel a 'sinner'; in her judgement there was no incompatibility between her faith and astrology, the study of which had just strengthened her belief in a 'superior force'; this affirmation, as I said, was quite common in the interviews.

However, while talking about the compatibility between her religion and astrology, she made one observation: 'but the dogmas for me are dogmas, I don't question them'. She moved on to recount the arguments she had had with her professor of religion at a course in library management which he gave in a Catholic university. That professor,

[who] apparently identified with a more liberal strain of Catholicism, relativised the doctrine of Immaculate Conception, which led her to protest:

> Imagine if I wanted to question the virginity of Mary in a class! So, I am like that: (…) for me dogmas are dogmas full stop. Mary is a virgin (…) her son was born from the Holy Spirit; for me he was born and that's it; I don't want to question it. I just believe in that, I'm not going to question it.

This was in conflict with the attitude she presented to me on astrology, and which I would see repeated in all the interviews, so much so that I took it almost as a standard of the 'students'. According to this no astrological knowledge is excused from debate and each person continues their studies according to their own personal preferences for the kind of astrology they choose. Seeing this, I tried to examine this contrast in detail and in this way Alice confirmed what I suspected:

> In astrology for me, there is no dogma at all, everything can be questioned. Everything is a subject for you to discuss, study and reach a conclusion, even if that disagrees with your teacher.

The dogmatic feature attributed by the informants to religion, in contrast to astrology, was more marked in other interviews, sometimes acquiring a pejorative connotation for the former. It can be said that the way the astrological system is open to appropriation will always be pointed out, determining not only its qualities but also sometimes its defects. On that first occasion, Cláudio was the informant who had a more religious approach to astrology, criticising some members of the group for having a 'consumer relationship' with the system, only wanting to get practically useful information (something which would probably be denied by them). However, even while claiming to be seeking in astrology 'a transcendence', he accepted that astrology 'is a personal choice not a commitment', as happens in a religion.

After these first interviews astrology appeared, to me, to occupy an intermediate position between the two poles of psychoanalysis and religion, attempting to reconcile the individual and the sacred. This was suggested to me by the informants themselves, and illustrated, in exemplary fashion, in the fifth interview, in which Helen and Ruth took part together. On asking each of them for their personal definitions of astrology, I could see that the differences between them could be described in terms of the position they attributed to the system on the continuum between the two poles, bringing it closer to one or the other. So, while Helen talked from the beginning about the Catholic and superstitious character of the Irish culture she came from, Ruth disagreed and stated that she did not try to associate astrology with religion. She then compared it to self-analysis, allowing the individual 'to know him- or herself better (...), understand others' and 'get on better with others'.

However, although the definitions of astrology show variations, the criterion that maintains its uniqueness is the self-description of the 'students' to which I have been referring. In the same example, Helen acknowledged that all religions have 'their imposed norms, while in astrology there is freedom'. On the other hand, Ruth affirmed that the benefit of self-analysis in comparison to psychoanalysis resides in the fact that the latter has a dangerous tendency to foster a dependency of the client on the analyst, something entirely incompatible with the subject's *ethos* of independence present among the astrology students I interviewed.

In the following year a series of personal problems prevented me from continuing my research at the same [level of] intensity as I had previously been working. Thus, only in the second half of the year was I able to take it up again. In the following year I took part in only one more astrology course whose material I had already mastered. My main interest was not just the opportunity for observation but to get closer to the astrologer who delivered it, who had an important position in the world of astrology in Rio de Janeiro. After some months I was obliged to abandon it. My failure was not due to the unwillingness of the astrologer, but to his extremely busy timetable. Thus, direct contact with the most prestigious representatives of the astrological *boom* in Rio became difficult due to their success which, in itself, would have made these interviews interesting. For the [astrologers], who normally had a full diary for the following four months, time was literally money.

In the end I succeeded in interviewing three more astrologers besides Roberto. Two of them, José and Rosa, had been practising for a short time and, although reasonably successful, were not part of the group of 'stars' of the world of astrology. The first declared himself to have a more psychological view of astrology, while the second admitted that he was beginning to wake up to the limitations of that approach, feeling a strong attraction for the idea of traditional astrology, without knowing at that time how he was going to incorporate it into his professional practice. Regina, the most successful astrologer I interviewed, a pioneer in Brazil, linked herself more explicitly to Jungian psychology without being so taken by writers in the humanistic movement. The ease of interviewing her was perhaps due to the fact that she accorded herself the luxury of giving consultations only twice a week. As the reader can understand, despite the differences, similar issues arose as in the first interviews. This was true also of the difficulties I have already described, given that the first astrologer I sought out, whose success led him to be preferred by politicians and businessmen, maybe had a more

utilitarian and pragmatic view of astrology—which Morin called 'praxo-astrology'—
than Regina who condemned such a view.

My goal in the second phase of the research was—while at the same time
deepening my bibliographical investigations and attending new astrological events at
which I almost always re-encountered my informants—to extend the view of astrology
I had obtained in the first interviews. However this widening was limited and did not
include a proliferation of interviews which, although it might have given a more
inclusive portrait of the growth of astrology in Rio, would have gone beyond my
objectives, which were always to carry out a case study. If my privileged case was that of
students of astrology, I tried not only to interview other students with different
contacts in the astrological network, but also the astrologers mentioned and some
clients, in order to evaluate the extent of the specificity I attributed to the former [the
astrologers]. I will take an opportunity to comment on each case, which will discuss the
variations between informants and the way they do or don't connect themselves to the
rôle that each plays in the astrological network.

Three clients were interviewed. Bárbara had already been to three astrologers,
whom I will designate as D, E and F. Although I had contacted her for personal reasons
which had nothing to do with the first informants, the professionals that she
frequented were known to them. The majority of the members of Group c also went to
classes with D, and after some years of attendance began to study with F. After
finishing the course at which I met her, Sônia went [on] to study with E. By Bárbara's
own definition it can be said, roughly speaking, that the first [D] is more pragmatic
while the latter [E and F] are more psychologically oriented. The other informants
generally agreed with that description of D, which didn't stop some of them, like Alice,
from enjoying his classes; according to her, being a Taurean astrologer and hence 'very
objective', he provided her with a more concrete vision of astrology, being able to
compensate for the abstract view of A, the group coordinator. So we see that the
pluralism which makes up the *ethos* of 'the students' allows the acceptance of views of
astrology from which they themselves have moved away.

Both Bárbara and Renato, the other client I interviewed, were intrigued by 'magical'
matters, although they distinguished astrology from these others, considering it more
'scientific'. Francisco, a friend of Renato, could also be described as just a client, even
though he had a more psychological view of astrology. This was due to his profession
of psychoanalyst. He revealed that he used it sometimes with reference to his clients
and their signs in his analytic practice, but he didn't use it systematically as he had not
completely mastered the subject. He had visited six different astrologers, among them

C, the only astrologer consulted by Renato in Brazil, since he had lived abroad for a long time.

Carla and Haroldo can be called students of astrology and their interviews share several common features with those of the first phase, except for a few peculiarities. The first, from the beginning, insisted on his association with humanistic astrology, while the second was mostly interested in astrology's curative possibilities, since he was a homeopathic doctor. These two issues can be related if we recall that Arroyo himself, besides his Jungian influence, reveals in his books a great concern for the so-called 'holistic' theories; these take man as a whole in which the psychic aspect is integrated with the various physical ones, and cannot be approached in isolation; these theories frequently use the language of 'energy' which we saw Arroyo employ in Chapter 1.[79] Despite its specificity homeopathy can, especially in its purist variety, be included in this wider category. The convergence [of views] between these two clients is particularly explained by the fact that at the time of the interview, both were taking part in a homeopathic study group, and I had been introduced to them by a third member of this group.

Earlier, I interviewed two students who presented some interesting peculiarities within the group that I studied. In the interview with Eliana I was very surprised by how different she was from the rest of the group, which gave me a better idea of the limits of my earlier conclusions. She did not interpret astrology in the explicitly symbolic way my other informants described. Thus, during the analysis of this interpretation she will be invoked as a counter-example. I believe that her attitude was due in part to her having begun to study astrology in 1972, and hence before the *boom* of which I believe the majority of my informants are typical. Besides this she admitted to being, as far as astrology was concerned, 'completely disconnected from Brazil', not frequenting the world of astrology in Rio and having learned the system independently by reading foreign authors. Characteristically, the only astrologers that she said she knew were D and G, the latter classed by Teresa as very deterministic.

Another special case was Laura. She spoke of the same attraction for magic as Bárbara and Renato, even of having already consulted clairvoyants. She then ended up consulting G and D, beginning to visit the latter once a year. She stated that she felt 'fascinated by the divinatory character' that astrology offered her in these consultations, and described D as 'a person of accomplishment'. However, shocked by an interpretation which she judged exaggerated, of a conjunction of Lillith and Pluto

---

[79] Arroyo, *Astrologia*, pp. 197–204.

that would take place one year, and encouraged by a conversation with an astrologer friend, she decided to study the system. After a certain time, she was able to construct and analyse her own chart and its transits although, according to her, she had typically done it [herself] by private study. The odd thing is that, even feeling the same lack of interest shown by Eliana in attending courses, congresses or astrology groups, Laura showed in her interview the same symbolic vision as the other informants.

This difference [between these two and the other informants] can be explained by several factors which were not purely dependent on the particular place that each of them held in the astrological network. Obviously being self-taught did not mean a lack of contacts with this network. The publications they read belonged to it; speaking of its flexible view of determinism in astrology, Laura used such expressions as 'that is there, in all the books'. Beyond this, the intervention of the third astrologer with whom she had contact, from frequenting the same ones that Eliana knew, appears to have been decisive. Although not cited in any interviews, he had published articles explicitly speaking about the symbolic character of astrology.

However, this example (along with others I could cite) shows us aspects of social life which appear especially often in the study of the middle classes. Being the product of a market of symbolic goods built on the basis of criteria described by the agents themselves as 'choices' and 'affinities', the astrological network is a significant example of what is, in the words of Salem, 'the typical form in which sociability is organised in urban areas, or at least among these classes'.[80] On the plane of its consumption of symbolic goods, it can be viewed as one more example of 'media culture'—if we accept the considered conclusions of MacDonald—with its syncretism, bringing together, in different proportions in each case, [both] erudition and vulgarisation. Using the terminology of Morin, the informants are situated between the *intelligentsia* and the 'New Gnosis'.

Therefore, the actions of individuals cannot be reduced to sociological causes; the particular social organisation itself which each group takes on presupposes the existence of a 'field of possibilities', such as was defined by Gilberto Velho: balancing itself between valuing both subjectivity and the specificity of the 'possibility of communication' of their individualising projects.[81] There are idiosyncratic aspects of the paths followed by these two informants, not just in what concerned them at the time and possibilities offered to each of them, but the very specific details which

---

[80] Salem, 'Família', p. 7.
[81] Velho, *Individualismo e Cultura*, pp. 27–28.

distinguish them. For example, Laura decided to study astrology as a result of a prediction which impressed her because she didn't agree with it, leading her to question and relativise astrological determinism. Eliana began to be interested by the system after having had a consultation with G, in which she correctly identified several details of her past, leaving her, as she herself said 'with eyes this big!'. Thus for her, astrology 'is a science', being characterised by its extreme precision.

I could add more examples that would help us understand the motives of the 'preferences' and 'choices' of each informant. Still referring to these two informants, more commentaries will be made in the following chapter. What is important to make clear at the moment is that, although I will later present an *ethos* which I judge to be characteristic of the astrology students I interviewed, attributing certain qualities to other characters in the field of astrology, this *ethos* is traversed by various tensions, expressed in the particular paths taken by each informant. So, like the projects to which Velho refers, these pathways seek 'to give meaning or coherence to a fragmenting experience'.[82] As Velho said elsewhere,[83] I could concentrate here on the life story of each of the informants; since this was not the initial intention of my research, my interviews did not have the intensity or duration for that. By the end of my study I managed to interview three friends—Marcos, Luísa and Paulo—the first two belonging respectively to groups **a** and **b**, all ex-students of astrology at the time of their interviews who, together with Roberto, developed an interesting pathway; following their experiences with astrology, they moved closer to other systems such as homeopathy and religious orthodoxy. So if their study and contact with astrology constituted a synthesising experience, creating an identity to some degree among the members of the esoteric network, permitting the 'possibility of communication' based on a common language, this experience can have different meanings within the field of possibilities of each individual. So in the next chapter, I will attempt to discuss the beliefs and opinions of the informants: not as a closed system, but as a combination of tensions which, expressing themselves in the particular trajectories of each informant, allow us to understand 'the individual lived experience in all its detail'.[84]

---

[82] Velho, *Desvio e Divirgencia*, p. 31.
[83] Velho, *Subjetividade e Sociedade*, pp. 58–74.
[84] Velho, *Subjetividade e Sociedade*, p. 53.

CHAPTER 4:
ASTROLOGY AND SYMBOLISM

Since Chapter 1 an opposition between two distinct lines of reasoning has arisen under different guises, one attributed sometimes to modernity and scientific thinking, the other to astrology and systems related to it. Although very often constructed using different theoretical guidelines, this distinction was formulated by a number of the authors I have cited; for example Lévi-Strauss distinguished domesticated from wild thought, and Robin Horton elaborated the concepts of open and closed systems. Dan Sperber summarised this opposition, often used in cognitive psychology and anthropology, designating the two poles as rational thought and symbolic thought.[1]

In one way or another several of these authors identify the first pole of these oppositions more markedly with modern society, while the other has been rejected or repressed by it. That does not prevent them from refining this association, admitting the existence of symbolic thought in certain sectors of modern society.

Such a distinction in general terms can also be found in common belief which relegates not just astrology, but divinatory and esoteric systems in general, to the domain of the occult or irrational. This classification is re-appropriated by the adepts of these systems, in the course of a critique of modern society and its forms of knowledge, attributing a degree of favourability to the alternative and esoteric character of the former.

The category 'symbolism' takes on a strategic role in the discourse of the users of astrology with whom I had contact, contributing to its self-definition. Right from the first interviews, the symbolic character of astrology appeared as one of the great attractions mentioned by the informants that explained their interest in this system. So in this chapter I attempt to describe the main themes of these interviews, keeping closely, as a guideline, to the form in which 'symbolism' appeared in them. This concept, on the one hand, serves the informants as a reference point for the construction of their own values, as well as those they attribute to astrology in general; in contrast, 'modern ideology' would be viewed as a rejection of the symbolic dimension of reality. And, moreover, within the field of astrology the user groups that I identified as members of its erudite branch, [when] following the theorists on whom

---

[1] Dan Sperber, *Le Symbolisme en Général*, (Paris: Hermann, 1974), p. 19.

they rely, contrasted themselves to mass or commercialised astrology by their greater fidelity to this same dimension.

However, I will show in this chapter how this use of the concept permits not just the construction of boundaries between the world of astrology and the surrounding society, but also allows us to see some [of the] ways in which this separation is compensated. As Dan Sperber tries to show, the notion of symbol 'is a secondary cultural development of the universal phenomenon of symbolism'.[2] This notion, although present in a secondary manner in Western society—in which astrology is generally seen as marginal—is not present in all cultures. It 'is not universal but cultural, present or absent, different from culture to culture or even within the same given culture'.[3]

In the book I am quoting Sperber attempts to criticise the idea, intrinsically associated with the idea of the symbol, that it would have signification as its distinctive feature: in other words, the ability to transmit an unequivocal meaning which can then be deciphered. To demonstrate this thesis, Sperber develops his argument on two levels. On the first he tries to show how, in certain societies such as the Dorzé, this notion [of symbol] does not exist. In this culture 'What does this mean?' (in the native language 'awa yusi?') can only be asked 'about a word, a phrase, a text or a behaviour which can be directly paraphrased such as a nod of the head'.[4] In other societies such as the Ndembu studied by Victor Turner, the notion of symbol is defined differently, leading Sperber to propose the same kind of critical analysis for this concept as that developed by Needham for belief (which was summarised earlier).[5]

On the second level Sperber discusses theoretically the arbitrary character of what he calls the semiological illusion: the idea, defended by semiology and by psychoanalysis, according to which symbolism constitutes itself in the form of messages which can be interpreted unambiguously. Such theories are mistaken by attributing to symbols, in the last analysis, arbitrary forms and meanings in the face of the multiplicity of possible manifestations of symbolism and its polysemy. Structuralism would represent the culmination of this tradition but at the same time, for Sperber, would mark its end. He disagrees in this sense, with the semiological interpretation which Lévi-Strauss puts forward of his own work; for example,

---

[2] Sperber, *Le Symbolisme en Général*, [no page number given.—Ed.]
[3] Sperber, *Le Symbolisme en Général*, p. 61.
[4] Sperber, *Le Symbolisme en Général*, p. 95.
[5] Sperber, *Le Symbolisme en Général*, p. 61.

according to the latter, myths do not contain messages, but are in reality cognitive mechanisms. So the methods which each culture possesses for the 'interpretation' of symbols constitute one more element of its symbolism, which must be included in a global analysis of the latter, contributing to its construction. In this way the semiological illusion

> Is not just a theoretical datum limited to a university audience. It frequently constitutes a cultural phenomenon, a conscious theory which the natives—Westerners or the Ndembu for example—possess of their own symbolism. This indigenous theory reacts back on the symbolic practice itself. It defines symbols to be certain manipulable elements. It leads to the exegetic unfolding of symbolism. It privileges certain forms of symbolic configurations.[6]

Astrology, although with different emphases in different contexts, always presupposes the idea of the symbol having implicit forms of exegesis in its symbolism. The planets and their positions are organised into a system which allows their interpretation from a divinatory point of view. However, as several astrologers recognise, such an exegesis is never unequivocal. The only thing that remains consistent in the system is its structure, since its ultimate signification is the subject of debates which vary between the different cultural contexts in which it is used. At the same time, in the conscious elaboration of its symbolism astrology finds common ground with modern ideologies, which also carry out this type of elaboration as, for example, aesthetics or psychoanalysis.[7]

However concise I try to be, it would be doubtless impossible to try to summarise the trajectory of Western semiology, as much as to describe its various 'theories of the symbol'. This latter expression is the translation of the original French title of a book by Tzvetan Todorov which distinguishes various particular traditions in Antiquity, which find, in his understanding, a synthesis in the works of St Augustine.[8] To this extent, the latter would represent the 'birth of Western semiology', the title of his first

---

[6] Sperber, *Le Symbolisme en Général*, p. 60.

[7] For a summary of the aesthetic theories of Romanticism, which are characterised precisely by their concept of the symbol, see Tzvetan Todorov, *Théories du symbole* (Paris: Éditions du Seuil, 1977), pp. 179–259 . On the theories of symbolism in Freud, see Todorov, *Théories du Symbole*, pp. 285–321 and Sperber, *Le Symbolisme en Général*, pp. 46–58.

[8] Todorov, *Théories du Symbole*.

chapter. One of these traditions, designated as 'hermeneutic', could be directly related to ancient astrology. It would be abundant and multiform, since

> The recognition itself of its object appears to have been acquired from the end of Antiquity, taking place only in the form of an opposition between two regimes of language, direct and indirect, clear and obscure, logos and mythos, and in consequence two modes of reception: comprehension for one, interpretation for the other.[9]

As we see, since Antiquity the need was already established that certain [textual] contents should not be given a literal interpretation in the way that happens in day-to-day communication; in this way they gain the character of symbolic qualities. For the latter, certain exegetic procedures are established which, in summary, divide them into two series 'well separated one from the other' according to Todorov: the commentary of texts, principally Homer and the Bible, and divination, in the most varied forms in which it was known in Antiquity.

Regrettably, Todorov's text gives us few details about this rich tradition [of textual analysis]. But I believe that, developing the observation made earlier, some hypotheses can be put forward about its flowering in the 'peak of antiquity', exactly the period of the introduction of oriental cultures into the Roman world, of religious syncretism, and the arrival of Christianity. Without doubt, the practice of divination often included a conscious elaboration of its symbolic content, since it represents the interpretation of particular signs, requiring from its exegete certain particular characteristics; as I have been suggesting, these can be in idealised terms, either of a traditional, charismatic, or rational nature. The oracle of Delphi, for example, represents a case which combines the first two of these features, since the priests interpreted the confused discourse of a sybilla in trance.[10] According to Heraclitus, this oracle 'doesn't say anything and doesn't hide anything, but it signifies'.[11] But the principal reflections on this subject belong to a later period: that of the authors cited by Todorov such as Plutarch, from where this fragment of pre-Socratic philosophy was taken. That period is characterised by two features which reach their peak in modernity: social fragmentation and the cohabitation of distinct cultural traditions. The book by Veyne is no more than a

---

[9] Todorov, *Théories du Symbole*, p. 28.

[10] Cf. Contenau, 1951, p. 139 [*sic*]. [This is the only information given for this reference. It is probable that the author is Georges Contenau since he is mentioned in the Conclusion. Which of Contenau's writings is being cited is unknown.—Ed.]

[11] Cited in Todorov, *Théories du Symbole*, p. 28.

description of all the strategies of interpretation of the Greek myths, developed by philosophers and historians as a reflection of the different 'programmes de verité' used by these intellectuals in relation to the masses, who took them literally.[12]

The exegesis of sacred texts would reach its peak with the Augustinian system, which was to be for several centuries the basis of Western Christianity. Christianity was born in the midst of a proliferation of oriental mysticisms and neo-Platonism, absorbing influences from both. For example, the date chosen for the birth of Christ corresponds to pagan festivals of the winter solstice, represented as the rebirth of the Sun; similarly, a number of pagan festivals were associated with Christian saints and incorporated into the Catholic calendar.[13] At the same time, the need arose for the rising religion to come to terms with the precepts of the Jewish tradition from which it was descended. For these reasons, the hypotheses of the neo-Platonic Jew, Philo of Alexandria, were important; he proposed an allegorical interpretation of the scriptures, which facilitated his attempt to assimilate the Hebraic tradition with Greek philosophy.[14] Another neo-Platonist, Plotinus, would provide one of the first formulations of which we have a record, which clearly defines astrology as being based on a symbolic, analogical relationship between the movements of the stars and man:

> We must say that the movement of the stars exists for the preservation of the universe, but that they also carry out another service; this is that those who know how to read this type of writing can, looking at it as if it were letters, read the future in its patterns, discovering what is signified by the systematic use of analogy.[15]

Saint Augustine, in spite of his hostile attitude towards the forms of divination, is strongly influenced by Neo-Platonism, which becomes clear when we note, for example, that he takes the material, sensible world as a symbol which, 'in a vague and imperfect way, reflects something of the splendour and Glory of God'.[16] That influence

---

[12] Veyne, Les Grecs.

[13] Cf. Keith Thomas, Religion and the Decline of Magic: studies in beliefs in sixteenth and seventeenth century England (Harmondsworth: Penguin, 1973), p. 54.

[14] Mondolfo, O Pensamento Antigo II, pp. 179–80.

[15] Plotinus, cited by Long, 1982, p. 186 [sic]. [This is the only information given for this reference. One of the works by Professor Anthony A. Long is a possibility, although which one it might be is unknown.—Ed.]

[16] Alexandre Koyré, Estudos de História do Pensamento Científico (Rio de Janeiro: Forense Universitária, 1982), p. 33.

is also present in the occult tradition associated with an eclecticism characterised by the assimilation of religious traditions distinct from the Christian, such as the Hermetic and the Judaic, present in the Kabbala. We see that the notion of symbol arose in the West closely linked to the interpretation of divinatory systems and the search for an internal coherence to syncretic religious combinations.

The Neo-Platonic conceptions went into decline with the scientific revolution's geometrising and mathematising nature, whose qualitative aspect began to be obscured. In this sense it could be said that the shift from emphasis on 'analogy' to 'identity', to which Vickers refers in describing the decline of occult thought with the scientific revolution, constituted a weakening of the symbolic perspective in Western thinking.[17]

As I have already noted, and will illustrate in detail in the description that follows these introductory remarks, the informants picked out in astrology its capacity to rescue this [symbolic] thinking [which was] suppressed by the rationalism of modernity. In affirming this, they are merely repeating something evident in the analyses of astrological theorists and of modern esotericism. For René Guénon, the modern mentality demonstrates a hostility 'more or less explicit', in relation to symbolism, given that it is 'entirely the opposite of what suits rationalism' and 'the way which is best adapted to teaching truths of a higher order, religious and metaphysical'. From this perspective, Guénon affirms that 'if symbolism is not understood today, that is one more reason for us to insist on it'.[18]

In spite of the differences which distinguish the symbolic domain in the esotericism of traditional and humanistic astrology, their diagnosis of modernity is the same. Stephen Arroyo says that 'Western culture' already has 'no viable mythology' which shows 'the relationship of man to a larger more universal reality'. Astrological symbolism can fulfil this function since it can be seen 'as the most comprehensive mythological structure which has ever arisen in human culture'.[19]

If there is a basis of truth in the idea that modern society, in comparison to other historical periods, has granted a much lesser rôle to symbolism—something which can be trivially confirmed by the secondary position occupied by magic and mythology—this statement must be contextualised in response to the unexpected complexity and fragmentation this society presents. Not only does symbolic thought continue in

---

[17] Vickers, 'Analogy Versus Identity', pp. 95–163.

[18] Guénon, *Os Símbolos da Ciência Sagrada*, p. 7.

[19] Arroyo, *Astrologia*, p. 44.

modernity—given that it is an attribute of the 'human spirit' as Lévi-Strauss would say—there are also cultural movements, typical of its ideology, which come to its defence. As an example, Todorov's presentation of the aesthetic ideas of Romanticism can be cited which, as he shows, are built on giving a high value to the concept of the symbol.[20] This would be opposed to the notion of allegory and, summarising Todorov's rich description, this corresponds to oppositions existing between romantic and classical art; between production and imitation; between an art which claims to possess a value in itself and the kind which aims to be a representation of nature. This last feature shows us how Romanticism is perhaps the first aesthetic movement to emphasise the autonomy of art with respect to the other 'orders of the world'. For its representatives 'to write a poem is to construct a separate self-sufficient reality', as Octavio Paz points out. This idea finds its most complete expression in the opposition between 'art' and 'life'. It possesses a paradoxical effect since the modern tradition—which began, according to Paz, precisely in the Romantic period—'is a passionate negation of modernity' and of the society which produced it. Critical of a culture which chose criticism as its principle, 'modern literature denies itself, and in denying itself, affirms-confirms its modernity'.[21]

This tendency, set in motion by the Romantics, became sharper in the artistic movements which followed. The avant-garde, whose idea is taken up again (as we saw) by counter-cultural and alternative theorists is, as an artistic movement, an acceleration of the modern ruptures through which the same artists originate and renounce new languages, sometimes in the space of a few years, running along the new paths opened to them 'so fast that they don't slow down on getting to the end and run into a brick wall'.[22] So, what we call modernism in the arts is not just a style of the epoch, but a proliferation of styles, with a multiplication of schools and '-isms', motivated by the common idea of renewal of forms. This tendency is an expression of the criticism of the principle of form, which Simmel identifies in modern culture in his already-mentioned article on the crisis in the latter. He sees in the artists of the time in which he wrote the article, especially the Expressionists, the same 'widespread search for originality' characteristic of modern art.[23] However, in discussing this text I showed how Simmel

---

[20] Todorov, *Théories du Symbole*, p. 235.

[21] Octavio Paz, *Os Fílhos do Barro: do Romantismo à Vanguarda* (Rio de Janeiro: Nova Fronteira, 1974), p. 43.

[22] Paz, *Os Filhos do Barro*, p. 146.

[23] Simmel, *On Individuality and Social Forms*, p. 384.

saw this tendency in the most diverse sectors of modern culture, including the economy. Thus, although the development of economic life has demanded its rationalisation—which generated an acute antagonism between the bourgeois *entrepreneur* and the avant-garde artist—there is also a kinship between these two typical products of the modern world, as Daniel Bell points out.[24]

The paradigmatic character of the opposition between Classical formalism and Romantic symbolism within modern culture allowed it to be appropriated by other authors who applied it to areas not necessarily related to art. Thus Michel Serres, in a short article originally written in 1961, uses these two concepts to comment on Gaston Bachelard. Bachelard could, thanks to the distinction he makes between scientific concepts and poetic images, figure in the contrast we made at the beginning of this chapter. However, rather than a distinction between two types of object Bachelard actually cites two different methods, absolutely irreducible between themselves, each one composing with its own epistemology [respectively] the new scientific spirit and its aesthetics. For Serres, in the last analysis, these two approaches represent the culmination of the Classical and Romantic tendencies present in Western philosophy:

> (...) there is classicism where cultures are excluded in favour of reason, where meaning is neglected in preference to truth (...) romanticism is an attempt to elevate and promote cultural contents as such (...), to understand the pluralism of meanings and decode all languages which are not necessarily those of reason.[25]

So Serres believes that in the nineteenth century—following the eighteenth in which the scientific and rational revolutions were consolidated—thinkers like Hegel, Nietzsche and Freud developed the technique of symbolic analysis. In contrast to classical mathematised formalism, they would attempt to base their models on the choice of archetypes from mythical history, such as Apollo, Dionysus, Ariadne, Zarathustra, Electra, Oedipus, etc.

The complexity of this opposition can be seen through an attentive reading of Todorov's commentaries on post-Romantic theories of semiology: in other words, the theorists of what Serres called symbolic analysis. Todorov, to some extent, seems to agree with the criticisms of the esoteric theorists in affirming that the great pioneers of this method—such as Lévy-Bruhl, Piaget, Saussure and even Freud—represent a neo-

---

[24] Bell, *The Cultural Contradictions of Capitalism*, pp. 16–18.
[25] Michel Serres, 'Structure et Importation: des mathématiques aux mythes', in *Hermès I: la communication* (Paris: Seuil, 1969), p. 22.

Classical thinking [style].[26] In spite of the innumerable differences which distinguish their theories, these authors converge in their immense difficulty in recognising the reality of the symbol. Thus:

> ...since it is difficult to ignore the symbol completely, we declare that we—the normal adult men of the contemporary West—are freed of the weaknesses implied by symbolic thought, which only exists among the *others*: animals, children, women, the insane, poets—those harmless madmen—savages, the ancients—who consequently, only know this [way of] thinking.[27]

Intimately linked to these conceptions is the idea of the intrinsically irrational character of symbolic thought. For Todorov, the rehabilitation of the latter was to happen with Jakobson and the artistic avant-gardes of the twentieth century.[28] It is not by chance that modernist art will reinforce its transgressive character and its opposition to the society from which it was born. Neither is the frequent connection which emerges between occult and esoteric thinking and these artists coincidental. As Octavio Paz says:

> ...from Blake to Yeats and Pessoa the modern poetry of the West is connected with the history of hermetic and occult doctrines, from Swedenborg to Madame Blavatsky.[29]

On the other hand, not just poets like Paz, but sociologists like Daniel Bell recognise the exhaustion of the avant-garde impulse in the arts, also because its attitude becomes more and more banal, invading the mass media and fashion, no longer provoking the rejection [it experienced in] the past. It is interesting to note that the last decades—in which the avant-garde attitude of criticism of those social values seen as dominant becomes more general, escaping the restrictive limits of the arts (the period Bell identifies with Post-modernism)—should also be the period of the spread of astrology and other esoteric and alternative systems.

As can be understood from these brief remarks, the symbol occupies a privileged place in several areas, some formative of modern society, others normally identified with it. It would be present therefore in religion, philosophy, and modern art. The

---

[26] Todorov, *Théories du Symbole*, pp. 337–38.

[27] Todorov, *Théories du Symbole*, p. 262.

[28] Todorov, *Théories du Symbole*, p. 341

[29] Paz, *Os Filhos do Barro*, p. 123.

importance of the occult tradition itself should also be remembered which, despite a relative decline, remained alive even after the Scientific Revolution.

Despite its links with astrology, art does not figure in my interviews (with the exception of Cláudio, a musician). I know of astrologers who do make this connection; several informants enjoy and even dedicate themselves to different forms of artistic activity. But they don't seem to detect a direct connection between their two interests, reflecting an attitude which, despite exceptions, seems to be common in the world of astrology I observed in Rio de Janeiro. The conception of symbolism [held by] my informants permits an approximation via the astrological system to three domains present in modern Western culture which share its symbolic character, mentioned in the previous chapter: psychoanalysis, religion and esotericism. Next, therefore, I shall discuss these domains and the way they emerge in the interviews, attempting to spell out the conception of symbolism through which the informants define astrology. In this way astrology will be linked to other manifestations of modern Western culture.

ASTROLOGY AND PSYCHOANALYSIS

Before describing the relations and distinctions that the informants made between the astrological system and psychological theories, I would like to explain the use of the term *psychoanalysis* which I employed in this section's title. From a rigorous point of view, this concept has a precise meaning, defining the theories of Sigmund Freud and his disciples, his clinical practice and the methods inspired by these theories. The theories which I will approach from my informants' point of view certainly go beyond this restricted definition. So for example, when I asked the informants about their experience with psychoanalysis their replies frequently included in this topic their interests and contacts with Jungian theories. Now, as is known, Carl Gustav Jung had been, at the beginning of his career, one of Freud's most important disciples; their relations broke off in 1911 when Jung moved on to develop his own theories and methods, called sometimes 'analytical psychology' or 'depth psychology'. On other occasions certain informants understood psychoanalysis to mean any psychological therapy that was used in regular sessions in which clients speak about their problems without their therapists following the rigid precepts suggested by Freud in their clinical practices, or in the relationship between the analyst and the analysand.

This term could perhaps be substituted by *psychology* which, because of its generality, would save me from such initial explanations. But evoking this larger discipline in which psychoanalysis is just one current would be too generalised, ignoring a detail which seems to explain this loose use [by my informants] of the term coined by Freud to denote the science which he founded. For example, when psychology was talked about in the interviews it had nothing to do with Behaviourism or the Gestalt theory of knowledge. My informants referred to a type of theory which is based on the use of symbolic interpretation in the search for [personal] development by a single individual: themes which are not exclusive to Freud, but whose introduction into 'behavioural science' is due, to a large extent, to him. So when they referred to psychoanalysis to designate another psychological theory, they were re-emphasising something which Freudian psychology embodies more than any other segment of psychology. In the last analysis, this wider (and to some extent, imprecise) use of the term is due to the fact that I am not interested in discussing exclusively the work of Freud and his followers, but rather to include its derivatives [which are] not necessarily related to the intellectual world. I refer to the 'culture of psychoanalysis'.

This latter concept, proposed by Sérvulo Figueira can be, in general terms, linked to the concept of the social world, such as it comes to be applied to astrology.[30] Figueira refers thus to a 'psychologism', which 'spreads centrifugally, contributing to the establishment of a psychoanalytic culture'; this, in turn, is not recognised or is denied by professional psychoanalysts who experience, without realising it, the reciprocal action of this psychologism on their practices.[31] So, even those social groups that have not yet experienced analysis feel the influence, to greater or lesser degrees, of the psychological '*eidos*', '*ethos*' and 'dialect'.[32] The definition of a culture of psychoanalysis does not stop us from recognising the internal conflicts of the psychoanalytic field which are reflected, in one way or another, in the most peripheral segments of this culture.

Given the great penetration that this culture has made in modern societies, Brazil among them, its influence is not limited to the Societies of Psychoanalysts and their members. We saw how Dwight MacDonald identified the 'vulgarisation' of psychoanalysis as one of the manifestations of 'midcult'. So, in the same widely circulated magazines where we find horoscopes, the culture of psychoanalysis is transmitted through articles which use its terminology and expound its principles, very often in a simplistic form.

From the point of view of symbolism, Freud's work has great importance within modern culture if we bear in mind that his first book, *The Interpretation of Dreams*, took

---

[30] Figueira, 'Introdução'.
[31] Figueira, 'Introdução', p. 9.
[32] Figueira, 'Introdução', p. 10.

up (claiming now a scientific authority) an inclination of the ancient hermeneutic tradition. From there, the Freudian theory of symbols unfolds a pathway to include myths, fairy tales, and especially the behaviour of the individual. This last feature, for example, is markedly present in the culture of psychoanalysis with the vulgarisation of the theory of 'Freudian Slips', through which the belief in an unconscious drive capable of producing and feeding desires and impulses greatly expands the dimensions of the areas of each individual's life over which he could have some control. The analytic situation itself, as Figueira points out, presents a determinism in relation to the behaviour of the analysand, which 'repeats, through expelling chance, the security of the hyper-determinism of magical thought'.[33] In this sense, we can also recall the famous articles in which Lévi-Strauss attributes to psychoanalysis the use of shamanistic logics of 'symbolic efficacy', no longer using mythology of the collective, but of the individual.[34]

Although the symbolism of psychoanalysis has as its focus, without doubt, the individual unconscious, it does not neglect to pay attention to collective manifestations like myths and fairy tales. Like Romanticism it recovers, via the notion of the symbol, the value of mythology.[35] Through interpretation, myths gain a relative truth value, something which astrology achieves more radically. But the author who went furthest in this direction is certainly Jung, with the formulation of his hypothesis of the collective unconscious. For him, individual symbolism finds itself directly linked to the collective since both express, in their most different manifestations, the same content, which he called archetypes. It is not by chance therefore, that this development of psychological theory has succeeded in influencing—more than just psychoanalysis itself—principally astrology, which Jung had seriously studied, although without always showing the same enthusiasm for it that is attributed to him by some astrologers.[36]

Beyond the simple use of astrological symbolism for establishing personality types, the association of astrology and psychoanalytic culture generally consists in the valuing

---

[33] Figueira, *O Contexto Social da Psicanálise*, p. 184.

[34] Lévi-Strauss, *Antropologia Estrutural*, Vol. 1, ch. 9 & 10.

[35] Cf. Todorov, *Théories du Symbole*, p. 247.

[36] In a text written in 1950, he went as far as to say that 'if with rare exceptions, astrologers had dedicated themselves more to statistics and examined scientifically the legitimacy of their astrological interpretation, they would have found out a long time ago that their claims rest on very fragile foundations'; Jung, *Sincronicidade*, p. 49. Later however he turned back to nourish hopes for the demonstration of its efficacy; Jung, *Sincronicidade*, p. 90.

of self-knowledge as a tool of self-improvement. In this way, the predictive aspect of the astrological system is taken as a secondary element in comparison to the possibilities which the individual has for intervening in the management of planetary influences that he receives. Following this direction, the symbolic character of astrology is emphasised, given that it allows the nature of these same influences to be defined in the most flexible way.

We can join to this the criticism from the interviews of the purely pragmatic use of astrology. This is not present solely among the astrologers interviewed and the members of the groups I studied. Such an attitude can also be found in other students of astrology who were not connected to these groups, such as Carla:

(…) the thing about prediction in astrology I don't accept, no. That thing: 'is going to happen'; I don't accept. I think that astrology is more a form of self-knowledge, more a psychology (…). So, I use that way and not predictions, fatalistic things (…). I don't like, I think that it's destructive and doesn't bring (you) anything.

Among the clients, the situation was more varied, apart from the fact that they felt less comfortable theorising about the astrological system. Bárbara, however, managed to distinguish between the astrologers she had frequented, some of more psychological inclination and others more deterministic; the first was more concerned to talk about her personality, the second to establish facts which had occurred or would occur in her life. She said she preferred the latter, in which she differed from Renato and Francisco. The attitudes among them [the interviewees] are also distinguished in other ways. Bárbara is not interested in understanding the astrological system, nor its methods, valuing astrology for its 'magical' and 'unknown' qualities. Renato and Francisco had already tried to understand some rudiments of the system, although they were never interested in deepening their knowledge, claiming a lack of time. I commented earlier on how Francisco, as a psychoanalyst, took the Sun sign or the Ascendant of an analysand as an interesting reference point for understanding their personality, although he only did so if the client happened to mention it. Haroldo, on the other hand, developed a great [degree of] pluralism, where he sought information for his self-knowledge among the most diverse divinatory systems, with which he had had contact in different parts of the world. This distanced relationship which he maintained with all these systems, without adhering to or learning about any of them in depth, made him give only a relative importance to the elements provided by each one. Astrology, in his opinion, would show him 'certain tendencies, certain possibilities' about his life and personality, many of which were useful for his self-knowledge. However, he recognised that he would never cancel a trip which he had already booked, for example, if an astrologer recommended that he do so. He always saw a sphere of free choice, despite the efficacy that these systems might have, remembering the warning of an old friend, the first to read his chart: 'man can do more than those determinations say'.

Greater involvement with astrology does not lead the students to develop a deterministic interpretation of their chart and its 'transiting planets'. The concept of astrological symbolism permits them to coherently defend the opposite thesis: precisely through better mastery of the astrological system it becomes possible to escape from this determinism. They accept the idea of free choice, which is conceived in terms of a greater awareness of their limitations, rather than a simple exercising of their desires and caprices. In this way Helen states that 'the more your self-awareness is developed, the more you have control over the energies of the stars'. I mentioned in Chapter 1 that the language of energy is used alternately with a symbolic theory to express the relationship between man and the stars. As I tried to show there, this does not imply mechanistic thinking, since the logic of the system remains that of magical hyper-determinism.

The importance of the idea of symbolism for the notion that the informants develop about free choice is that it makes explicit the *in*-determinism [my italics] which marks, as I have been insisting, this same magical logic. This feature is viewed positively, as a reflection of the polysemy of astrological symbols. We can confirm this when Carla talks about the analysis of a friend's chart who had suffered an accident, where she understood that when this disaster took place Uranus was crossing his Ascendant:

> When Uranus was crossing, it is like a break that happens. It could be something bad or something wonderful; it will depend on how you are, how well you are in harmony. In his case, it was not well, there was a disaster, he was done for (…). For each individual the Ascendant with Uranus is going to produce something. There will be breaks, separations; there will be marvellous things, a journey you never expected (…). It will depend on the use you make of this potential.

The chart provides, therefore, potentials for each person. Not just in terms of their personality and their health, but also the favourable times for certain events, the phases through which it [the chart] passes, the periodic cycles represented by the orbital movement of the slowest planets.

Those who are unable to understand the nature of their own limitations, by means of astrology or some other system, will be a slave to them. Thus Carla commented on the charts of her daughters who, through their immaturity, reflected what they showed in the most automatic way. In a conference meeting on the theme of free choice and determinism, astrologer Carlos Alberto Botton talked about an investigation in which he had participated, in which the charts and transits of schizophrenics were studied.[37] It would be useful for the confirmation of astrology because it was believed that they would react mechanically to the influences that were indicated. As in psychoanalysis there is, in this kind of astrology, the search for 'something else', 'imprinted on the personal plane', that could explain the behaviour of individuals:[38] identified in the first case with the unconscious, and in the other with the astrological chart.[39] However in the psychological perspective of the informants, in coherence with what is claimed by both the Jungian and Freudian versions, a conscious effort takes first place in the search for the psychic equilibrium of the individual.

The interesting metaphor suggested by Figueira, according to which psychoanalysis would be able to provide a map of the individual in modern fragmented society, is applied literally to astrology:

> One of the first things that you hear when you begin to study astrology is: 'it's all in the chart', which means (...), all your problems, but also the solutions to your problems are there too. For a difficult aspect, of tension, you will always be able to look it over to seek the solution (Beatriz).

As an absolutely individualised diagram which provides a specific combination of universal elements—the astrological symbols—the natal chart becomes an ideal vehicle for the expression of the uniqueness of each person, creating a qualitative individualism. Figueira draws attention to the amount of practical use psychoanalysis possesses, although it might be perceived by its participants as the revelation of a repressed reality, by means of a process of 'political-personal liberation'.[40] Within certain limits the interpretation of an astrological chart and, when it happens, the subsequent identification of the client with their chart, shows some analogies to the analytic process. Obviously the latter is necessarily a long and intense process, which seeks to bring about profound changes in the individual analysed. But the relationship

---

[37] 1st Ciclo Mandala de Palestras, took place in IBAM–Rio de Janeiro, 27 and 28 July 1987.

[38] Figueira, 'Introdução', p. 8.

[39] An identification of the unconscious with the astrological chart was made by three informants: Teresa, Cláudio and Laura.

[40] For Figueira's view on the practical uses of psychoanalysis, see *O Contexto Social da Psicanálise*, p. 170; For the views of participants, see Figueira, 'Introdução', p. 8.

of an astrologer to a client is much more flexible. Although many variations of practice exist among the various currents and schools which make up the world of psychoanalysis, in astrology the heterogeneity is certainly greater; there is no common definition of the duration, frequency, or even the objective of the consultation. Even so, the interviews suggest to us three ways in which the astrological interpretation contributes to the person's individual development.

One of the biggest attractions that the reading of their chart seems to offer individuals initially is what we could call self-recognition. There is no doubt that even among the most die-hard critics of a pragmatic astrology a great impact is made by predictions, or rather by the ability of the astrologer to refer to past events of which the client was unaware or to future events. Sometimes these are invoked as examples which demonstrate the efficacy of the system. However, in their descriptions of their first experiences with the interpretation of their charts, the informants generally highlighted as the most important factor the description of personal, intimate aspects of themselves. Beatriz told how she began to become interested in astrology after Roberto read her chart for the first time:

> I identified completely with the things he told me. In spite of being my cousin, someone who already knew me, he talked about things that even he could not have known, you see? Things about me, feelings, those things. I was absolutely fascinated and began to study later.

The 'fascination' produced by the reading of a natal chart is due in part to the revelation of the interior life of each individual which, consistent with the individualist *ethos* that is also present in psychoanalytic culture, does not imply any kind of violation of something that should not be exposed; on the contrary it signifies, for the informants, access to a more authentic and spontaneous experience of the *self*. In some cases, this effect may not be immediate; Helen, for example, said that only two years after her first chart reading did she begin to identify with her chart. The verb used by many of them to express identification shows the impact that this revelation can assume: 'to strike'. Thus, it can be said that such-or-such feature of a chart 'struck' or 'didn't strike', or that the things that someone had read about their sign 'had struck' to a greater or lesser degree.

Although Marcos had taken part in group **b**, at the time of the interview he no longer studied astrology. He used another kind of slang to express the type of observations about their personalities that most clients sought: 'touch'. He stated that after the group broke up he had a consultation with A, which had given him several 'touches'—such as his negligence with timetables, the fact that he didn't take on his responsibilities at home—that were very useful for him, and which allowed him to reflect on these defects. For the clients I interviewed, these 'touches' are, in Renato's words, merely 'contributions': useful in the search for self-knowledge, but not possessing any special place in the process. They are added to other 'contributions' from other sources: homeopathy in the case of Marcos, psychoanalysis for Francisco, and other divinatory systems for Renato.

The efficacy of this mechanism of self-identification resides in the capacity it possesses to articulate the impressions that each of them has of their individuality, understood in a more or less precise way. By means of a connected system like astrology, these impressions are given a coherence and a cause: the planetary positions at the time of birth. Depending on their degree of commitment to astrology, it will happen through simple 'touches' or could even constitute something that Rosa called 'cosmic identity'. Her description of her first visit to an astrologer, D, gives us an expressive example of how this works:

> I was a very difficult person, very sensitive (…). I always compared myself to other people, that they did not get upset by that, with that pain, that anxiety. So I felt that I had a mark, a sign (…). What was it? Upbringing, nature, temperament, what was it? It didn't have a name. When I drew my chart, I said: that's it, it's Neptune in the 12th house, it's the ascendant in Cancer.

In the constitution of this 'cosmic identity', astrology presents some particular features which make it especially effective in fragmented modern society. As Steve Kemper has already pointed out, one of its characteristics is that of 'allowing the person to develop, becoming aware of their multiple identities'.[41] Thus each of the different Sun and Ascendant signs might occupy any one of the twelve houses determining, with the planets that might also occupy them, ways of behaving specific to each of the areas of the individual's life: domestic (4th House), professional (6th and 10th Houses), conjugal (7th House). Rather than breaking 'each individual into many parts', as Kemper underlines, the interviews show us that an astrological chart can allow its subject to articulate two or more apparently contradictory principles in their chart, in the case that it has contrasting Sun and Ascendant signs. This is the case with Marcos, a Virgo [Sun] with a Pisces Ascendant, who relates his indecisive and 'difficult' character to the coexistence of these two signs which occupy opposite positions in the zodiac.

---

[41] Kemper, 'Time, Person and Gender', p. 753.

Renato, who also has the same feature in his chart, describes how this is expressed in his general personality, and especially in his art, in the following way:

> Astrologers in general say that I am somebody who is split between one very pragmatic side, very organised, and another with a lot of imagination and excitement. These things are very marked, so much so that they are part of my painting. Because painting, art in general, is something imaginative. And for me to express my imagination I express it in a geometrical style. So I paint in an extremely rigorous geometrical style.

These two examples are from informants that I classed as clients and, understandably, they make use of more general references, such as the Sun and Ascendant signs, due to their lesser 'astrological literacy'. So, the students and the astrologers, knowing their charts in greater detail, mastering their meanings, are able to describe the fragmentation of their personalities through more specific traits, such as the conjunction of a planet with the Ascendant, which might counterbalance the sign occupying that position.

> Since I have Uranus right on the cusp of the first house, in Taurus, I am a very practical person, I mean very practical, but on the other hand, I'm always wanting to do something different (Teresa).

> Because of my Virgo ascendant, I'm always trying to do things according to a method, in a sequence, but at the same time, I don't like methodical things. That is a contradiction, maybe my Neptune in conjunction there confuses things a bit (José).

As the reader must be noticing, independent of the flexibility which the symbolic concept attributes to astrological determinism, the form in which the system itself works implies that free choice has limits. These are given by the chart itself, which can be expressed by the individual in different ways, but from which they can never escape.

Obviously this idea is not visible to the clients of astrology, who look at it as just a source of information on their personalities and their lives, without giving up other sources. But the students know their charts in depth and are guided by them to a large extent in their search for self-improvement. The astrologers, then, are more incisive on this question. Rosa says that the first step for those who begin to make use of astrology is to 'take on their chart'; from that point, as she says, they can just make 'finishing touches', 'polishing', etc. Regina acknowledges that this is one of the most important problems that the astrologer has to keep in mind in dealing with their clients:

There comes a time when the astrologer asks himself: 'What am I going to do with this person whose chart shows a hardness, that they are a rigid, cold, hard and implacable person?' It's like that. It's no use you going to them and saying: 'Ah no, don't stay like that, no'. So, what you have to do is try to draw the most benefit from the nature of the person. Stone is hard, water is soft. Now, the stone being rigid has something important in the fact of being like that. So they have to canalise that energy, work with that energy.

Beyond self-identification, a second mechanism by which astrology makes its charting individual is by self-observation. According to Figueira, this mechanism is also found in psychoanalysis, defined by him as a 'process of harvesting idiosyncracies'.[42] The major difference resides in the fact that, in astrology, this harvest is obviously not guided by the 'psychoanalytic interpretation'. Among the clients, it can originate from the observations of astrologers which were not immediately identified: in other words, from 'touches' that don't 'strike' at the time of the consultation. The possibility of retaining these observations is made easier by the common practice among many astrologers of recording a consultation on a cassette tape, allowing the client to listen to it as many times as they wish. In other cases, as in one recounted by Renato, the astrologer can provide an interpretation that is retained in memory because of the surprise it provoked. So, **C** had talked about an aggressiveness in the way Renato treated his friends. He, who had always considered himself a docile and sociable person, commented on this remark with some old friends who, to his surprise, admitted that when they first met him they had felt this aggressiveness.

But astrological self-observation can be much more profound for students and astrologers who have their charts and are able to interpret them. Following the transits of the planets to their positions in their [birth] charts, studying and acquiring more knowledge about certain patterns in them, its subjects begin to see in them more and more intelligibility. As I tried to sketch out in Chapter 1, the existence of different symbols in astrology which can, in a birth chart, be combined in different ways, transforms an exhaustive interpretation into an almost endless task:

> There are trillions of things in my chart which I still have not the slightest idea about, there are things I see in my chart and I can already manage to say: 'it is really true, I am totally Moon opposition Sun'. I mean, things that I can already understand about my life and my attitudes. And there are things that I still don't know how I am going to manage to understand (...). And each day something different turns up: 'look, I've got

---

[42] Figueira, *O Contexto Social da Psicanálise*, p. 182.

such and such a point, the Part of Fortune, point of affinities, that is calculated like this, and so on'; and then I go and see how it is in my chart. (...) I mean, there are trillions of techniques, it's really unending! (Beatriz).

I really study my chart, this one here, half torn, done by my astrologer, (...). I carry on making all the connections possible: let's suppose that today I had an argument with my mother, a bit later on I go there in my chart and I'm going to check my relation with the Moon, with the 4th House, etc., altogether I'm going to have a look and try to understand the mechanisms in there that move, what kind of obligation I have to my mother that can make me be so upset by an argument. There I stay like that, looking for data in the chart (Cláudio).

Although many times focused on the individual themselves, the observations provided by astrology can also appropriate other objects. In this sense we have to remember how the symbolic language of astrology is also able to classify objects, activities, works of art, etc. On the other hand it is also a resource for the understanding and knowledge of the Other. The women that belonged to Group **c**, more than the rest of the informants, were concerned with studying the charts of relations and friends with whom they were experiencing particular problems. Given that hardly anyone was working, the mastery of astrology strengthened their rôle of 'housewife' within the family. Thus, Vánia mentioned that this mastery brought her a lot of respect from her husband, who consulted her when he had problems in business; Helen said that astrology allowed her to understand her relations much better and accept, for example, the 'longing for freedom' experienced by her Aquarian granddaughter.

If we take all these examples into account, both through self-identification and self-observation, astrology contributed to the individuation of each informant, without having the productive rôle attributed by Figueira to psychoanalysis. From the first to the second process there is a growing participation of the astrological system in this individuation: initially it articulates a growing awareness of the client's individuality that they already possess; in the latter, it guides the discovery of new dimensions of this individuality. But in both cases, this individuality exists prior to the introduction of astrology. Otherwise, the posture of [individual] autonomy in relation to astrology adopted by the students and clients I interviewed shows us that they have already absorbed individualist representations of the world to a considerable extent. This posture would be absent in certain characters, cited by the interviewees, with whom I had no contact: those who took the astrologer for a 'guru', or else remained tied to [only] one consultant and system.

It is difficult to know the characteristics of this type of person, who is almost always described with some exaggeration by the informants, since their function is to create the contrastive opposition which helps in the construction of the informants' identities. Examples of such types are rare, even among the astrologers interviewed; they disapprove, at least in theory, of this attitude, in line with their own creator-oriented conception of their work. Rosa referred to some clients who, however, may have approached her. With one of them she recognised that there existed an 'extra-astrological' relationship. He was always looking for her to vent his frustrations, talk about his problems, calling her at least once a day. According to Rosa, 'sometimes he didn't even want me to look at his chart, he just wanted to talk'. The astrologer said she tried to draw his attention to what was happening in his chart, but without much success, feeling that the client was clinging to her as a person. Although unhappy with the situation, she didn't manage to reject him, allowing herself to become involved with him, and trying to solve his problems since Rosa saw herself as 'extremely Cancerian'.

She also talked about other clients, of whom she was proud that they consulted her over a long period. I would like to reproduce her description of one of them in summary form:

> One was someone who came here, he was forty, very closed in his ways, brusque, tough (…). He sat there and for two and a half hours he never took his coat off. And his chart was simply of a completely crazy person, of an artist, of an extremely sensitive person. And I said: 'You must forgive me, but your story is not like that. You are a very creative person, an artist, Aquarian, you have Aquarius and Uranus everywhere, the 5th House completely full, what are you doing here?' I didn't say it quite like that, because you don't have the right to interfere in that way, but basically I was showing him something. Well, two months later, he gave up everything he was doing and became an artist, a decorator (…), took up Shiatsu,[43] turned over completely to the other side. That was someone I met.

Obviously it would be dangerous to try to draw too many conclusions from this process, of which we only have the viewpoint of the interviewee. However it is still useful. In the first place, this description corresponds (even if that wasn't what happened in this particular case) to what the process of transformation must permit,

---

[43] A body therapy similar to acupuncture, which instead of using needles is carried out through massage with the fingers.

ideally imagined by the informants as the self-knowledge provided by astrology or other systems. It shows us the way in which the individual would 'take on their chart', displaying some similarities with the self-representations which surround the analytic process. The realisation of this 'self-liberation' of uniqueness represents the third level in the creation of the qualitative individual. The configuration presented by the chart appears as a repressed reality of the individual, and he succeeds in adopting it to the extent that he frees himself from repressive social and family constraints. Individuation means, in this case, a personal independence which leads the individual to act in accord with his own nature. It is not by chance that Rosa ended her story saying that her client at that time was doing an 'alternative therapy', besides mentioning later that he had also begun to study astrology. It is important to make clear that this production of individuality never appears as such to the informants, who internalise the premises of the individualist ideology, believing in the existence of this uniqueness before contact with astrology as shown in the natal chart. Rosa ended her account [by] referring to her client as:

> Someone who was in a shell, he was in another place, and maybe would have remained there a very long time. Then suddenly, that chart revealed for him something which certainly he already knew but had not taken seriously, until the chart confirmed it.

As I said, for the majority of my informants this idea of individual independence and freedom with respect to therapeutic and esoteric systems existed prior to their contact with astrology, since as the contact moved forward they were already putting it into practice. They appear to believe that even when astrology plays the role of liberator (as in the case of Rosa's client) or is the primary influence (as in the case of several students), this does not imply exclusivity. Although this search for personal liberation through the awareness of their uniqueness may be present in psychoanalysis—since the latter has a privileged role in the dissemination of this value in Brazilian society—it [this need] is sometimes used to criticise psychoanalysis itself. Obviously this therapy does not imply an absolute control and determination in the client's life. But it exercises it to an intolerable extent for many informants.

With the exception of Francisco, a professional psychoanalyst, all of them made some criticisms of psychoanalysis during their interviews, pointing out the disadvantages it has compared to astrology. These were voiced even by those who were in an analytical process at the time of the interview. I raised the topic in all the interviews given that, from the beginning, I understood its importance and thus mentioned it even to those who did not refer to it spontaneously.

There were two main types of criticism; one of them is closely related to the incompatibility of the *ethos* of independence with psychoanalytic systems and the excessive attachment that the informants believe they see in the psychoanalytic relationship. I mentioned in the last chapter how Ruth, in spite of thinking that psychoanalysis is closer to astrology than is religion, criticised the former. Although the objective of self-knowledge might be a common feature, the friends that she knows 'go to an analyst (…) and spend ten, twenty years in a terrible suffering'. This suffering is related to the intense character of this treatment, and especially to the supposed possibility of the client developing a dependent relationship with the analyst, which makes any interruption of the treatment highly traumatic. Contrary to what normally happens with the informants, who move from one astrologer to another and compare different interpretations as well as making their own—given that they study astrology—the relationship with an analyst presents an exclusivity which is open to criticism for many interviewees.

But this generic criticism, which can always be contested by the argument that it only applies to the bad use of psychoanalysis, is followed by another more decisive. Among the symbolic manifestations associated with astrology, psychoanalysis is usually judged to be the one most incorporated into the values of modernity. That permits its distinction from the astrological system to be realised through its exclusion from the deviant identity attributed by the informants to various esoteric and alternative beliefs. Thus Ruth said that those who look to analysis for self-knowledge are 'the people most tied to Western culture', who end up following a path 'which is more difficult more complicated'.

If so far I have been citing only Ruth's criticisms of psychoanalysis, it is because she seemingly summarises several elements of this theme which reappear in other interviews. The idea of the greater simplicity of astrology is quite common and synthesises the main two criticisms [of psychoanalysis]. On one hand it can refer to the more superficial relationship between the astrologer and client, which provides more freedom for the latter. This opinion is expressed by various students and principally the clients, for whom astrology itself does not occupy a central place in the process of self-knowledge. For Renato, for example, psychoanalysis by its intensity involves great risk:

Let me use a metaphor to explain better what I think: it's as if I had a wound in my leg: the person can treat it but they can also take off the whole leg. Not that I'm afraid but I'm not going to run the risk of that.

In this way he believes that psychoanalysis would be a 'more tortuous, more complicated' method, exposing the client 'to enormous losses of equilibrium', contrary to what happens in astrology, in his opinion. For Bárbara the simplicity of astrology, like that of Tarot (which she also uses) resides in the fact that in both of them you don't go on working things out too much: 'things are said because they are in the chart, they are more immediate responses'. She accepts that, depending on the preferred approach of the consultant, the interpretations can demand intense reflections and discussions, but there remains for her 'a crucial difference': always 'it's a consultation, I mean, it's an hour and a half and not seven years'. But the search for a simpler language is also, according to Ruth, the search for something different, marginal:

> I try to know myself, like everyone else, but not the method that is there on show in the window. I look for something else. Maybe it's the wish to be different, I don't know (…) All my generation, all my friends, they all go to the psychoanalyst.

But if clients are also capable of valuing the 'marginal' character of astrology to the detriment of psychoanalysis, there are students of astrology, with their more theoretical viewpoints, who want to deepen this idea. The excessive elaboration of psychoanalysis—which Bárbara counterpoises to the idea that in astrology the 'determinations' are outside the client—is attributed by the students to its limited symbolism, which explains its acceptance by 'Western culture'. The criticism of this restricted use of symbolism can go in two directions. The first is related to the 'tortuous' nature of analytic practice, censuring it for excessive rationalisation. Contrary to symbolic systems, which are intuitive ways of knowing, psychoanalysis would possess a type of discursiveness typical of the Western mentality.[44] Claudio explains his preference for astrology as his means of self-knowledge through this type of argument:

> Astrology is closer to experience itself, the living experience of things, and not to the elaboration of theories like in psychology, with all that elaboration.

---

[44] It is well to remember, however, that the idea that symbolic knowledge is by nature intuitive and sensitive is already admitted by Romanticism, having first been formulated by Kant; see Todorov, *Théories du Symbole*, p. 236.

For most of the informants, the symbolism of psychoanalysis, enclosed by four walls, would make it inferior in comparison to that of astrology, which talks of elements, of daily life, with its language of the concrete.

The second criticism of psychoanalytic symbolism is not aimed at its form, but at its interpretive assumptions. For Freud, all symbolic activity is produced by the unconscious of the individual; if it involves objects and other individuals, these symbols only exist insofar as they are projections of that same [individual] unconscious. In consequence it will be exercised basically over that which is found near to the latter [the individual's unconscious]. In this way Beatriz, who was in analysis at the time of the interview, recognised the merits of psychoanalysis, but affirmed that 'astrology is much more inclusive'. She demonstrated this by referring to the sequence of astrological houses which start from an individualistic first house and move gradually through levels which become progressively more distant from the individual, reaching twelve; linked to the spiritual domain, the Twelfth is known by reincarnationist astrologers as the house of Karma, the one which determines the place of the individual in the totality. Psychoanalysis lacks, according to Beatriz, any reference to the spiritual while astrology tries to make a linkage with a totality, using a synchronistic language:

> Psychoanalysis is completely based on the cause-and-effect relationship. This restricts you a lot: you are the product of the family in which you live (...), the product of father and mother. As much as you go there to free yourself from father and mother, you see, you find yourself in a bit of a complete shambles (...) I do analysis and I thinks it's the best, for me it's super-good, but I think [it's] limited, it isn't only that. It doesn't help me to come out super-confident in myself, ready to face people, my relationships; I think it would be missing something, like an idea of this type (...), of a greater awareness of the world, of a whole, you understand?

From what can be understood from Beatriz' words, the pluralism that the informants value does not mean an adherence to a radical individualism. It is very common besides, that the latter adjective [radical] is used pejoratively to describe psychoanalysis. The fact that they recognise the differences of style among astrologers and students—explained by each one's chart itself and the diverse interpretations that each chart can have, based on the conception of symbolism that I have described— leads us to justify the multiplication of viewpoints without, however, abandoning the idea of an inclusive, universal level. On the contrary, the two levels complement each other; each microcosm is particular only to the extent to which it reflects the macrocosm. In this way Teresa went to three different astrologers and made, during her interview, criticisms of each one, but agreed that the reports that they drew of her personality were all correct: concentrating on her, each one from a different angle. For her part, Alice said that anyone who wants to learn astrology must take part in all the courses and conferences and read all the books possible, in order to formulate their own opinion on the subject, 'without running away from the truth of astrology'.

If it is believed, as is the case for my informants, that the natal chart really reveals the truth of the individual to whom it belongs, the multiplication of astrological consultations and references to it are not simply a random accumulation of opinions, but an attempt to find the nature of a common point among them, which is the chart itself. In psychoanalysis, where this common point doesn't exist and visiting many therapists is less viable, the informants tend to think it very likely that the analysands allow themselves to become involved in the personal vision of the analyst.[45] This can be illustrated through the statement of Laura who, before deciding to study astrology, was a regular client of astrologers with a pragmatic and deterministic approach. With her training in psychology, she had already experienced analysis at the time of the interview; however, in that earlier period, she used to go to a Kleinian analyst, whom she now criticises. For her, the function of astrology and other divinatory systems would be

> To enter into contact with your unconscious (…) not to want to fight with who you are, not to want to create a character which is incompatible with your tendencies. If the astrological chart gives you this possibility it's excellent; if it's psychoanalysis, if it's the Tarot, if it's the priest that does it, I think it's irrelevant.

---

[45] I am recounting, obviously, only the opinions of the informants without intending to discuss Freudian theory in depth, whose validity it does not fall to me to judge. Even so, it is good to remember that Freud shared with the informants this valuing of individual independence. So, as Figueira points out, he recommended that the interpretation be provided according to a definite timing, by means of which it is offered only 'when the patient is already at the point of discovering it himself'. (Figueira, *O Contexto Social da Psicanálise*, p. 187). Apart from this, it can always be argued that this truth about the individual would be induced by the analyst, an accusation which could always be made against astrology or any other system with which we disagree. This question of timing would be comparable to the tact which Rosa displayed with her second client in relating the incompatibility between his attitudes and his chart, justified by the argument that 'one can't interfere like that'.

We see above an example of the pluralism which governs the esoteric and alternative world, and I will comment on it later. We see that this informant in particular—who, by her training was more tied to psychology—goes so far as to include psychoanalysis among the systems she accepts. However, this does not prevent there being a type of analysis that she criticises, and that she had already given up at that time. Many informants, less critical of psychoanalytic therapy, are accustomed to divide the latter into two camps: one orthodox, which remains more rigidly loyal to Freudian principles and intolerant of any magical system, another heterodox or alternative, more eclectic and 'open'. As happened with Rosa and Laura, therapists in the first group did not usually take their experiences with astrology seriously, which led Rosa and Laura to look for therapists of the second type. These are therefore accepted, while the orthodox are rejected, in order to remain on the side of the flexibility and tolerance that is present in the psychological approach of those groups. Thus Laura criticised, retrospectively, her first experience with psychoanalysis precisely because, for her, it did not allow her—in the way that astrology does—the contact with her unique individuality: present in her unconscious and/or in her astrological chart:

> My recollection of those five years of Kleinian analysis (…) was of a strait-jacket, was of something that had nothing to do with what I understand nowadays by the unconscious. It was something pedagogical, didactic: the analyst had some presuppositions about what he considered to be a healthy person and he tried to fit me into that frame.

So even when my informants criticise psychoanalysis or one of its forms, they do so to reaffirm aspects of their *ethos* which are also partially present in the 'psychoanalytic culture': the valuing of self-knowledge as an instrument of personal liberation and an expression of their uniqueness. In this way, some informants believe that astrology is capable of going further than what is promised by psychoanalytic theory. On the other hand, they are concerned with the question of symbolism, believing that it is not applicable only to the unconscious of each individual, a concern which causes them to move closer to the theories of Carl G. Jung. For Jung, astrology, alchemy, and other manifestations of occultism represented routes to the unconscious which were available even before the advent of psychiatry. Thus Jung is taken as a theorist of esotericism for providing explanations of the efficacy of such esoteric systems, as well as for other divination systems such as the I Ching—which he linked, respectively, to the archetypal nature of the collective unconscious and to the phenomenon of synchronicity. It is this coexistence of various forms of self-knowledge that I will deal with in the next section.

ASTROLOGY AND ESOTERICISM

The expansion of the concept of psychoanalysis, provoked by the use the informants made of it, is analogous to the broad use I have made of [the concept of] esotericism in this work. As we saw in the previous chapter, there is emerging scholarly literature in the social sciences which has attempted to treat it as a widespread 'culture' whose *eidos*, *ethos* and dialects would penetrate segments of modern culture. Not having theoretical or institutional contours as precise as those of psychoanalytic culture, the delineation of this field has presented some difficulties. If we leave aside the term 'alternative' used by Ferreira—which even in a vague and imprecise way would denote a wide-ranging lifestyle, affecting many areas such as eating, politics, etc.—and try to give a rough idea of what characterises esotericism as an intellectual movement, we could define it as an effort to bring together the most varied religions, assuming them to have a common nucleus. This wide acceptance of religions which are different one from another produces, in esoteric thought, the distinction between a literal aspect of each one—the 'exoteric'—and their properly esoteric meaning, in which their true connections emerge. The linking together of esotericism with symbolism would belong here because this second dimension would reveal the 'profound symbolic significance' of the literal principles which characterise the exotericism of each religion.

Such a conception can be encountered as much in initiatory and secret societies like the Rosicrucians or Freemasons as among Neo-Platonic and occultist thinkers. However, from this *a priori* acceptance of diverse religious forms there develops an effort to re-establish the grounds for their reconciliation. It is on this plane that the divergences between the different currents of the 'esoteric movement' arise. So in the same way as with the category 'alternative', that of 'esoteric' can also become a mechanism for the creation of boundaries which define legitimate ways by which the contents of religious systems should be interpreted and, similarly, for the divinatory and therapeutic systems associated with them. Thus a delimitation of the esoteric world in any particular place has to start from the definitions of the members themselves, being attentive to the negotiations and conflicts which they reflect. Here my objectives are a good deal more modest: attempting to describe and analyse my informants' references to esotericism and the practices and beliefs associated with it and their relationship to astrology.

First however, I will present some of the basic themes of esotericism, attempting to map this wide domain, guided by the suggestions of Antoine Faivre, head of '*History of esoteric and mystical movements in modern and contemporary Europe*' at the École Pratique des Hautes Études since 1979. It must be emphasised that, due to the rare position he occupies as an esotericist in academia, he represents an 'erudite' sector of esotericism which may distance itself very much, for example, from the esotericism of the 'New Gnosis' present in the media. Besides this, many users of esoteric systems can justify the combined use of multiple esoteric practices, based solely on the practical efficacy they attribute to them, without being concerned with the finer points of the debates among the esoteric *intelligentsia* on the theoretical coherence between these practices.

According to Faivre, the word *ésotéricisme* only appeared in Europe in the nineteenth century, having been invented by Éliphas Lévi. Until then this domain was usually described by such expressions as *'philosophia perennis'* or *'philosophia occulta'*. He associated this conceptual deprivation with the actual absence of a need to delimit a common terrain for its various manifestations ('theosophy, hermeticism, Cabala, alchemy, theurgy, astrology...'), since this combination 'was sufficiently well integrated with the surrounding [cultural] environment'.[46] Such a need was only felt with the gradual emergence of modern society and the relative marginality to which these ways of knowing were consigned.

The Greek etymology of esotericism (*eso-thodos*) would mean, according to Faivre, an internal path or method. In its restricted sense, therefore, it would correspond to 'an entering into oneself (...) which passes through a *gnose*—a knowing—in order to reach a form of individual illumination and salvation'.[47] Michel Mirabail offers another etymology, *esotéricos*, which he attributes to the words *escondidos, secreto* [hidden, secret]. The esoteric ways of knowing are thus opposed to the exoteric: in other words, those which are openly accessible.[48] This distinction is inspired not only by initiatory or secret societies (such as the Rosicrucians or Freemasons) which employ various notions of occultism, but also those of the ancient Greek philosophers such as Pythagoras. Faivre, however, insists on making explicit his disagreement with the idea that esotericism would necessarily be linked to the idea of secrecy. According to Faivre limiting it 'to this unique dimension is frequently the result of bad faith, of ignorance or even of intellectual prejudice'.[49] On the one hand there is an obvious argument which completely excludes the possibility of any close articulation between the idea of esotericism and this notion [of secrecy]; nowadays those who proclaim themselves

---

[46] Faivre, *Accès de l'ésotérisme Occidental*, p. 13.
[47] Faivre, *Accès de l'ésotérisme Occidental*, p. 14.
[48] Mirabail, *Dictionnaire de L'ésotérisme*, p. 88.
[49] Faivre, *Accès de l'ésotérisme Occidental*, pp. 31–32.

representatives of esoteric thought publish books and penetrate more and more into the mass media. On the other hand, the defence of such a linkage seems clear to any casual observer of this literature.

During his interview, one informant, Haroldo, reflected on this paradox and, in so doing offered some conclusions very similar to those of several esoteric writers on the subject. For him:

> These days, you don't need to join the Rosicrucians, or a Masonic society where you have to be initiated and the whole thing is secret (...), because the information is all there. Just search and you will find. And find fantastic things.

If the existence of this 'free market', as he describes it, presents some positive features it also implies dangers. The greatest risk would be represented by the misuse of the knowledge which, 'if used by each person in accord with their own personality', 'can do harm to many people, as has happened'. Such risks, as we saw, also led the informants to criticise the misuse of psychoanalysis. But for Haroldo, these are inevitable; they are risks that must be taken due to the crisis which he associates with modern society, as we saw at the beginning of Chapter 2. At a time in which the values of contemporary society are more and more precarious and its very survival is threatened by nuclear dangers, he considers that this 'opening' is the only way to accelerate the social changes which are part of the Age of Aquarius and the subsequent overcoming of the crisis.

In this way, since the term esotericism was first coined, it has been linked with the notion of secrecy, even including systems which experienced extreme popularity, as much in the present as in various periods in the past—as is the case with astrology itself. Lévi, an abbott whose real name was Alphonse-Louis Constant (1810–1875), was responsible not only for the revival of interest in some of these systems like the Tarot and the Kabbalah, but also for a certain diffusion of esoteric and occultist thought, exercising its influence in the intellectual milieu of Paris of his time and read, for example, by Victor Hugo.[50] The popularity of this kind of thought in France increased even more thanks to the influence of Papus, *alias* Gérard Encausse (1865–1916). When he was a student of medicine, unhappy with the evolutionist teaching he received, he discovered in the National Library ancient Hermetic works which taught him, in his own words, 'to work with this marvellous analogical method, so little known to modern philosophers that allowed all the sciences to be grouped together in a

---

[50] Cf. Alexandrian, *Histoire de la Philosophie Occulte* (Paris: Seghers, 1983), pp. 96–101.

common synthesis'.[51] His preoccupation with popularising esotericism is reflected in his founding in 1887 of the *School of Hermetic Sciences* and in the publication of various manuals on the subject, one of which was prefaced by Anatole France.[52] On the other hand, although having numerous students the school also prepared candidates for an initiatory organisation linked to Papus: the *Martinistic Order*, 'which claimed to have its origin in the regular transmission of the ancient Order of the Elect of Cohens, founded in the nineteenth century, by Martinès de Pasqually'.[53]

In the Anglo-Saxon world one of the most important figures of this esoteric revival at the end of the last century was Helena Petrovna Blavatsky (1831–1891), who also adopted the ambiguous position associating esotericism simultaneously with publicity and secrecy. A Russian by birth, Madame Blavatsky (as she was known) founded the *Theosophical Society* in 1875. This was an important organisation for the history of astrology because one of its members, William F. Allan, or simply [by pseudonym] Alan Leo (1860–1917), is considered responsible for the modern rebirth of astrology.[54] For Blavatsky one objective of this society, which still exists today, is that of 'reconciling all religions, sects and nations under a common system of eternal truths'.[55] The novelty introduced by Blavatsky into the syncretism which characterises esoteric thinking was to associate Neo-Platonism with oriental religions, such as Buddhism, which, until then, had not experienced the influences of this philosophy [Neo-Platonism]. However, due to the incompatibility which existed between this religion and the theories of the occultist tradition, Blavatsky accepted the hypothesis that Buddha had transmitted esoteric knowledge to certain disciples who had kept it secret, although there is no record of this.[56] As we saw for Blavatsky, as well as for a number of occult theorists, all religions present a visible side (the exoteric) aimed at satisfying the ritualistic and dogmatic needs of the masses, and an esoteric wisdom in which doctrinaire differences dissolve. For Blavatsky, Theosophy would constitute the synthesis and the revelation of this latter dimension.

According to its founder, the choice of name for the society was absolutely natural; she believed that the path remained unchanged since it was first formulated by the

---

[51] Cited in Alexandrian, *Historie de la Philosophie Occulte*, p. 261.

[52] Papus, *O Ocultísmo* (Lisbon: Edições 70, 1986).

[53] Antônio Carlos Carvalho, 'Prefácio', in René Guénon, *A Crise do Mundo Moderno*, (Libon: Veja, 1977), p. 10.

[54] Hone, *The Modern Textbook*, p. 295.

[55] Helena P. Blavatsky, *A Chave da Teosophia* (Lisbon: Edições 70, 1978), p. 18.

[56] Cf. Blavatsky, *A Chave da Teosophia*, pp. 25–26.

Neo-Platonic philosophers of Alexandria, and that there would be a complete continuity between the theories of these first occultists and hers. Faivre, more concerned to establish precise conceptions, makes a careful survey of the use of this name, especially since the Renaissance. At the end of his description of its history Faivre puts forward [both] a restricted and a more general meaning [of theosophy], condemning the confusion provoked by the 'very syncretic teachings' of Madame Blavatsky.[57] The first meaning is more closely tied to its etymology (*theos-sophia*, wisdom of God) and its initial use by the Church Fathers, referring to the study of a divine nature, of the 'occult mysteries of the divinity'.[58] In his wider definition he situates theosophy as a basic element of esotericism. The latter is distinguished by not having the subjective element usually associated with the traditional idea of mysticism. Contact with God is simply mediated by nature, given that it reflects His glory. Founded on this idea of universal correspondences, theosophy is applied to time, through the identification of atemporal archetypes in the 'mythological symbolism'; and to space, seeking the natural reflection of the divine nature in the 'occult structures of the universe'.[59]

As Faivre emphasises, theosophical thought has a tendency to privilege aspects of myth which are often neglected by the established churches. Thus the distance between the esoteric and the common vision is always related to the ability of the latter, to a greater or lesser degree, to move away from literal interpretation of myths and rites and, with its adaptability in relation to its dogmatic aspects, in the direction of greater pluralism. The relationship with myth, for example, takes on a particular quality, no longer including an adherence to the religion to which it belongs, but offering the possibility of the interpretation of mythology, which would have a cognitive function. This can be observed when homeopaths involved with astrology employ the biblical story of Genesis, no longer as a narrative to explain the origin of the world, coming into contradiction with scientific theories on the subject, but as a symbolic account of the fall of man. Without removing from the latter the theological consequences of Catholicism, one author relates it to the emergence of pain, suffering, and illness: in other words, to the loss of harmony between man and the cosmos, which

---

[57] Faivre, *Accès de l'ésotérisme Occidental*, p. 22.

[58] Faivre, *Accès de l'ésotérisme Occidental*, p. 50.

[59] Faivre, *Accès de l'ésotérisme Occidental*, pp. 27–28.

homeopathy claims to re-establish.[60] In this, as in the majority of cases, the literal interpretation doesn't entirely contradict the symbolic. Another example would be [found in] the use of Greek myths in astrology courses for the explication of the meaning of astrological symbols, which attributes to the former the representation of universal principles.[61]

Faivre attributes a special place to the divinatory, therapeutic or magical systems of esotericism, representing its practical side.[62] This would be occultism,[63] the domain that would be dedicated to 'applying' the knowledge of analogical correspondences about which theosophy theorises.[64] Although theoretically linked to these theories, the practice of occultism can receive a pejorative meaning when it is not accompanied by an adequate theoretical explication. However, it is very difficult to define the presence of the latter unambiguously without taking the side of one of the tendencies within esotericism. Thus, the concept is sometimes used as a type of accusation, to condemn certain varieties of esotericism without failing to recognise that they have some practical value. Faivre, especially, uses the term to criticise the vulgarisation of esotericism, stating that the definition of occultism he uses arose in the nineteenth century, coinciding 'with the appearance of a trivial form of esotericism'.[65]

---

[60] Luiz Henrique Fontes de Carvalho, 'Associação de Netuno com Urano ou homeopatia e Astrología', in Ana Maria Costa Ribeiro, et al., *Astrología Hoje; Métodos e Propostas* (Rio de Janeiro: Massao Ohno, 1985).

[61] I only gave examples of what Faivre calls 'temporal theosophy'. A good example of spatial theosophy can be found in the description which I made of the symbolic analysis employed by Olavo de Carvalho, which attempted to find in the structure of the solar system the relationship between intelligence which would be symbolized by the Sun, and thinking which would correspond to the Moon.

[62] The association of homeopathy with esotericism is not as common as in the case of astrology, also because it was elaborated only in the eighteenth century. Within the homeopathic camp itself there exist different tendencies, espousing different opinions on the subject. The most 'esoteric' try to show how much its founder Hahnemann owed to traditional Hippocratic and Galenic medicines.

[63] Faivre recognises that this concept is sometimes used as a synonym for esotericism; see Faivre, *Accès de l'ésotérisme Occidental*, p. 30. It was in this form that I already employed it, following various esotericists and researchers of the history of the esoteric world. Thus employing a strategy followed several times by Faivre himself, I will utilise his definition [given here] as the 'restricted sense' of the term, while the other would be the 'larger sense'.

[64] Faivre, *Accès de l'ésotérisme Occidental*, pp. 28–29.

[65] Faivre, *Accès de l'ésotérisme Occidental*, p. 6.

Integrating theosophy and occultism, esotericism would be, for Faivre, a search for 'salvation and individual illumination'. These would correspond roughly to the ideas of 'self-improvement' and 'harmony' encountered in the discourse of my informants. They would be attained, according to Faivre, by means of a form of knowledge defined as 'gnosis', of which the gnostic movement of the first centuries CE is just one particular example. Faivre prefers to use the word because its Greek root does not disconnect it from the wisdom of mystical and religious experience. Gnosis can therefore bring about a transformation and individual liberation.[66] Illumination and Gnosis, although related, constitute two poles of a continuum, with mysticism being closer to the first pole. The astrological practice of the majority of my informants is found at the extreme opposite end, probably along with the majority of divinatory systems, although some informants took part in other more mystical sectors of the esoteric world—such as the meditation already practiced by Haroldo—and some explicitly religious practices, as we shall see in the next section.

So it can be said that the conflicting etymologies of esotericism—one linked to the idea of the 'internal', the other to the 'secret' and 'occult'—still converge when they are thought of in the context of an 'individual gnosis'. In this, the knowledge sought would be obtained slowly, not even being secret since, in reality, it would go beyond the 'appearances' in which 'common knowledge' of the real remains, unveiling their profound symbolic connections. On the other hand its acquisition would transform the individual internally, not being therefore a 'disinterested knowledge'. Detached from a literal conception of the secret, the idea of the 'occult' comes close to the notion of interiority present in the psychoanalytic concept of the Unconscious, as can be seen in several interviews; this shows us once again the possibilities of the likening of psychoanalysis to esotericism.

I showed in the previous chapter that several students of astrology also had great curiosity about other divinatory systems, mythology, oriental religions, alternative therapies, etc. Haroldo—who became interested in astrology through being a homeopathic doctor—in talking about his youthful interest in oriental religions, yoga, macrobiotics, etc., used the expression 'one thing pulls the other'. Some students made their first contacts with astrology in other areas of esotericism. Teresa and Sônia heard it mentioned for the first time in their yoga schools. The astrologer Regina only began to study astrology after having studied not only Jungian psychology, but also divinatory systems (such as graphology, numerology and palmistry), 'Indian philosophy', and

---

[66] Faivre, *Accès de l'ésotérisme Occidental*, pp. 15–16.

'Taoist poetry' which, according to her, are 'things that the official culture denies'. However, the majority of [my] informants made their entry into the esoteric world through astrology since, among the systems that comprise it, astrology is the one with the greatest penetration into the mass media. Therefore, it is very common for someone to arrive at other sectors of the esoteric world after an initial contact with astrology.

In spite of the great plurality expressed by the informants they also set limits on it. José expressed approval for a declaration by the writer Millôr Fernandes, according to which he tried to read absolutely everything: from 'advanced studies' to cake recipes, small ads and funeral notices, 'where very pleasant news can be had', he said ironically. For this informant, astrology teaches us to 'know God and people', not allowing us to remain 'limited, restricted, prejudiced'. Although the majority of astrologers and students accept, as Beatriz said, that 'astrology is just one of the languages for attaining self-knowledge', they admit that they cannot know all of them and it is necessary to make choices.

The same level of complaint with which the students and astrologers that I interviewed charge the media and their clients—that they limit themselves to a superficial view of astrology—rebounds on themselves, serving to justify the fact that they don't practice other esoteric systems; 'in the end', in the words of Regina, 'everything can't be studied in depth'. Even in cases like that of Haroldo, who had contact with several sectors, he had chosen just a few, astrology and homeopathy, from criteria based on exactly this requirement.

> In essence, all these things are interesting, but few go really deep (…). I believe really that the majority of things that exist in this market are just cosmetic and not paths to transformation. I was opting for the ways that transform most profoundly through being less simplistic.

Homeopathy and astrology, insofar as they are 'languages for transformation', would be difficult languages to learn, like 'German or Chinese'. He recognises that there are courses in which, 'in two months you come out drawing charts or prescribing medicines', but in his opinion, 'this is charlatanism'.

Unlike Haroldo, the majority of 'students' did not make great criticisms of other esoteric systems in their interviews. One or another perhaps mentioned negative experiences but they could not be generalised to all the students of that particular system. Generally, it can be said that there is an *a priori* belief in the efficacy of all the ancient esoteric systems; once they make contact with one of them, in theoretical or practical terms, the criticisms that might perhaps arise will be directed towards their inadequate utilisation.[67] This is because, having accepted the validity of the symbolic and analogical logic of astrology, it becomes possible to admit the existence of other systems which employ it. These are, as we saw, closed systems, which cannot be verified or refuted experimentally. My informants' theory of symbolism is a conscious elaboration of this feature. As I showed in Chapter I, the closed character of astrology implies its stability. Its development, for most informants, is lost in times immemorial:

> Because astrology comes from four thousand years before Christ, and the peoples of that time were already guided by the stars (Alice).

> What appeals in astrology (…) is to search by means of symbolism, that has been there, I don't know how many thousand years, to try to see how you are linked to all that history (Cláudio).

> Astrology is an ancient heritage, you have to take this into account. It isn't like psychoanalysis, which was born inside the present capitalist system. It is a much older heritage (…) which can be applied in the present day world (Sônia).

> Astrology is a sacred science. Sacred in what sense? In the sense that it was a science that read symbols, a knowledge of symbols which take man back to his original source (Rosa).

This emphasis on the antiquity of astrology, frequently exaggerated compared to the data available, is similar to what we found in the theorists of esotericism about the origins of their doctrines. This is an ancient attitude. The philosophers of the first centuries CE tried to create a hierarchy of the wisdom of oriental peoples in accordance with their antiquity and believed, very often, that the classical Greek philosophers were instructed by the 'barbarian wisdom'.[68] The Egyptians were almost always the ones chosen and the god Thoth, associated later with Hermes Trismegistus, was considered

---

[67] It is important to re-emphasize that even within esotericism, there is a strong current, in which Blavatsky and Papus are included, which tries to make it scientific. On the other hand there are astrologers who dedicate themselves to explaining the efficacy of astrology by means of statistical surveys and the establishment of electro-magnetic influences between the planets. Although this is a fascinating topic, it did not arise in the majority of my interviews, which leads me not to discuss it here, in order not to over-extend myself.
[68] Festugière, *La Révélation*, pp. 20–23.

the father of all science. Yates in turn tells us that in the Renaissance Ficino established Trismegistus *'como fons et origo* ['as source and origin'] of a tradition of wisdom that followed an unbroken line to Plato', and which also included (for example) Zoroastro, Orpheus and Pythagoras.[69] The modern representatives of esotericism proceed in a similar way, Papus declaring his ideas were linked to 'the teachings in Egyptian temples from 2600 years BC', while Blavatsky affirmed that her doctrine 'is much earlier than all the philosophers of Alexandria', having been preserved by the 'initiates of all countries'.[70]

However, in relation to the esoteric theories of the last century and the beginning of the present one [the twentieth], the students and astrologers that I interviewed placed less emphasis on the secret character of esotericism. For them the most important thing is the more 'profound' understanding which the latter possesses of religious and occult phenomena. Within their symbolic view, they define it by its capacity to transcend literal and pragmatic conceptions. They converge here with Faivre, who argues that the true meaning of 'secret' in esotericism resides in the fact that:

> The mysteries of religion (…), the hidden forces of cosmic order (…), cannot lend themselves to a literal comprehension, nor to a didactic or unambiguous explication, but must be the object of a progressive penetration, on several levels, by each man seeking knowledge.[71]

As I have been insisting, astrology presents a double aspect. Its mastery is the product of study and is obtained through knowledge. Parallel to this 'rational' aspect it has a symbolic, intuitive side. If the students and astrologers define themselves by their possession, to a greater or lesser degree, of this mastery which allows them to better understand their potentialities, they value ancient knowledge as an escape from scientific rationalism. The world of the ancients as much as the orientals, 'is more symbolic', as Cláudio points out. Those closest to the psychological approach would say that they find themselves closer to the Unconscious. They possess, according to Sônia, a knowledge which is more 'intuitive and closer to the sensory'. Some go so far as to state that, outside of the rationalised world of the great urban centres, the need for divinatory systems like astrology would be less:

---

[69] Yates, *Giordano Bruno*, p. 15.
[70] Papus, *O Ocultismo*, p. 17; Blavatsky, *A Chave da Teosophia*, pp. 21–22.
[71] Faivre, *Accès de l'ésotérisme Occidental*, p. 32.

The man of the countryside doesn't need a horoscope to decide what to do in his life, because he knows the laws of nature. But the city dweller, having lost his direction, needs a compass (Regina).

This conception of astrology means that they develop a critical posture on the limitations of scientific thought. Speaking for the astrologers, Rosa affirms that 'for us, we are not interested in the status of a science' for astrology. Carla, who is a physicist, says it would be 'absurd to try to turn astrology into a science' because 'astrology is another type of knowledge', incapable of presenting the experimental repeatability demanded for the acquisition of scientific status. It is true that some informants allow the possibility that, in the future, science could be able to take account of the phenomena investigated by esoteric systems but that, in its present form, it is not capable of doing so.

It is necessary now to specify the limitations of this description, which must be restricted to students and astrologers because the attitude of clients is different. José and Renato, while attributing a 'magical' character to astrology, recognise a greater 'scientific basis' than in the other divinatory systems. Among them, Renato sets up a scale of trustworthiness, affirming that astrology is situated in a better position than, for example, Tarot or reading coffee grounds. In this way the clients, who are less interested in knowing the principles of the astrological system either don't take an interest in the question of its scientific credibility or allow themselves to be impressed by its technical features.

On the other hand, the view of astrology that I have been describing is not common to all the students. Their symbolic conception is just one of the possibilities of erudite astrology, linked to some of its theoretical currents. Although my experience in the field leads me to suggest that it could be a form typical of the recent *boom* in astrology in Rio, even today there exist other views. One of them, as I stated earlier, was apparent in the interview with Eliana, the only one to distance herself significantly from the symbolic conception and its corollaries in affirming the scientific character of astrology. Summarising her opinions, it can be said that she interprets astrology in a more deterministic way, comparing it to the 'meteorological service' which informs her 'if there is going to be good or bad weather'. In the second case, the only thing she can do is 'grab my hat and umbrella'. Beyond this, Eliana does not share the pluralist vision that I have been describing:

Astrology is something very concrete, you understand? It has numbers. Exact time etc. (...) So, it isn't something done like Tarot or I Ching, you know, which is something vague, poetic (…). They don't have five percent of the precision of astrology, which is something 'absolutely certain'.

It is curious to see that other divinatory systems are described by her as 'poetic': in other words, more symbolic than 'concrete'.

I have tried to refine the picture of pluralism which at first sight appears to the observer of the esoteric world. In this world, the existence of a closed symbolic logic in its various manifestations leads to the acceptance of the efficacy of other similar systems. The search for coherence among them is facilitated by the classificatory character which they almost always possess. Attempts at inclusion of distinct sectors are common in the esoteric world. Some are already associated from the start, as in the case of the symbolism of the metals in alchemy which are related to the planets. Sometimes attempts are made to reconcile distinct systems which converge in particular ways, as in the case of association of the planetary spheres with the 'names of God' or *Sephiroths* of the Jewish Kabbalah, proposed by Pico della Mirandola.[72] Earlier these spheres had already been linked with the seven principal prophets of the Islamic tradition by Muhyaddin Ibn Arabi (1165–1240), one of the most important representatives of Sufism, an Arabic esoteric movement.[73] New kinds of inclusions are always possible and are always being suggested. Thus, the *Jornal do Brasil* (8 March 1986) published a report about an astrologer, Ana Graziela Prodan, who associated the twelve zodiac signs with the twelve Orishas [gods in West African religion that form part of Candomblé].

These associations are not always possible due to the structural differences between the systems, in addition to the fact that they can always be disputed. For the purist homeopath, for example, each individual has their own unique remedy which would be

---

[72] Cf. Yates, *Giordano Bruno*, pp. 99–101.

[73] This association is made by means of the description of a spiritual ascent, similar to that in the Divine Comedy, in which the pilgrim encounters one of the prophets in each sphere, and which is described in the Book of Lights (Risalat al-anwar). For this book and that of Ibn Arabi see Michel Chodokiewicz, *Le Sceau dês Saints: prophétie et sainteté dans la doctrine d'Ibn Arabi* (Paris: Gallimard, 1986). The descriptions of the planetary heavens are very similar to the astrological symbolism which remains to this day, such as Mars, where 'terror, fear and affliction' are found, and is Aaron (in Arabic Hârûn, general of Moses); or that of Venus, 'the world of form, of ornament and beauty', where José (Yusuf) resides, 'who is *par excellence* the interpreter of dreams, the one who deciphers forms'. (Chodokiewicz, *Le Sceau des Saints*, pp. 203, 201).

capable of dealing with their specific disequilibrium and which manifests itself in the multiple symptoms presented. To carry out this homeopathic classification of his clients we saw Haroldo make use of astrology, although he accepted that there was no unique correspondence between one system and the other:

> To say that 'such and such trine here always turns up in patients with pulsatila and then when they have it, I am always going to give them pulsatila' is madness. (…) things are not mathematical, Cartesian.

In this way he believes that analysis of the chart only gives a few general indications to the therapist, assisting them with their questions in trying to find the patient's problem. But despite this failure he has to accept that the rich symbolism of astrology, with its four elements, twelve signs and houses, ten planets (or at least seven visible), makes it able to realise various syntheses. Regina, who, like Haroldo, had access to different systems of the esoteric world justified her choice of astrology for its capacity for not allowing dispersion. 'Astrology' she states 'links everything, colours, stones, metals, etc.'

As Mirabail reminds us, this apparently infinite hermeneutics does not exhaust its limits in its structural feasibility; 'the criteria and the degree' by which it is carried out 'are those of the Tradition'.[74] The possibility of conceiving some compatibility between the different systems derives from their common traditional character. The African traditional magical systems mentioned by Haraldo draw the legitimacy for their closed character from a mythical past which is of a different type from [that of] the present. The cyclic temporality of these societies depends on the fact that this past is not only prior to the present but is also its foundation. The societies in which astrology and other esoteric systems flourish not only have a more profound temporal perspective, but several such perspectives. The challenge of esotericism is precisely that of reconciling distinct traditions, a number of which did not originate in the societies into which they are now incorporated.

As I stated in Chapter 1, the more complex a society becomes the more difficult it is to determine the true nature of traditional knowledge. The word *tradition* is related to the idea of transmission; it implies therefore that a group preserve their original knowledge by allowing access to it. It is this that Renaissance Hermeticism wanted to establish with its line which began with Hermes and Zoroastro, ending with Plato.

---

[74] Mirabail, *Dictionnaire de L'ésotérisme*, p. 89.

Even using hypotheses about the secret transmission of doctrines, which many esoteric writers do not hesitate to use, such authors can only obtain recognition of the value of their theories through persuasion. In spite of making reference to tradition the legitimacy, whether of astrology or [other] esoteric theory, is something rational. The existence of a plurality of churches and sects claiming a traditional authority moves the debate on the validity of each one of them onto the theoretical field which, today, is that of esotericism.

The focus of debate in this field is therefore the nature of the coherence of doctrines and symbols in the different traditions. According to Faivre there would be three ways of investigating tradition. The first, classified as purist, is that of Guénon and his disciples.[75] It takes all traditions from the start as being true. However, each one forms a consistent whole, more or less closed, so that each of its parts only makes complete sense in that context. [In] the principle of traditions the divine is singular; but in order for it to appear on the plane of manifestation it becomes multiple because we find ourselves in the kingdom of multiplicity. Each religion presents itself exoterically as exclusive, and esoterically as one of the possibilities, but only makes sense through integrating these two dimensions. Through manifesting itself, this principle gradually degrades, and 'the crisis of the modern world' corresponds to the end of the Age of Iron of Homer or of the Kali Yuga in the Hindu tradition. An authentic religiosity becomes more and more difficult in the West, where Christianity has lost its esoteric character, degenerating into sentimentalism while an 'occultism' stripped, according to Guénon, of any traditional character continues to grow.[76]

Guénon's theories are not only widely disseminated in the world I studied, they also represent a limiting case of the demands which thinking about esotericism places on students of astrology. For its supporters this practice, like all esoteric systems, is only really valid when associated with the practice of one of the traditional religions which incorporate it into their esoteric dimension: Christianity and Islam. At big astrological events, where they make contact with listeners who are less familiar with its theories, traditional astrologers criticise, for example, the use of yoga outside of Hinduism or of acupuncture without Taoism. In one article Olavo de Carvalho criticises macrobiotics, a naturalist diet which classifies foods according to the Taoist opposition of Yin/Yang. Showing how in Chinese tradition it is applied not only to food, but to other planes

---

[75] Faivre, *Accès de l'ésotérisme Occidental*, p. 34.
[76] Guénon, *A Crise do Mundo Moderno*; Guénon, *Os Símbolos da Ciência Sagrada*.

such as time and space, etc., Carvalho argues that, with only simple tables of foods, the macrobioticist will never be able to use the system correctly.[77]

Faivre calls the second path the historical way. It could be summarised by noting the multiplicity of traditions and combining them syncretically in the style of Madame Blavatsky. He speaks ironically of this approach, saying that its representatives 'remain generally and happily "shopping around"'.[78] Rather than a classification of two segments of modern esotericism, Faivre offers us two poles of a continuum in which there is a variation in the degree of rigour with which the tradition is treated. If the Theosophists are very often branded as syncretists, Mirabail (for example) attributes a 'sectarian intransigence' to Guénon.[79] Faivre is not so critical of the latter, but puts forward a 'third way'. It is difficult to say to what extent this represents an important sector of esotericism or just a means for Faivre to expound his personal vision which attempts to simultaneously defend erudition and dialogue [along] with science and modernity.[80] He cites other authors who are little known in Brazilian esotericism who follow this path, which can be related to his ambiguous position as an esotericist in a university.

The debate on the compatibility between esoteric systems is not just concerned with deciding which type of use is valid; it also refers, in the last analysis, to the nature of its efficacy. So each esoteric theory seeks to elaborate a cosmology that guides the use of the system. In his workshop at the First International Congress of Astrology, Luiz Roberto B. Oliveira tried to provide a framework for this debate in the context of astrological practice with his lecture *Prologomena for an Epistemology of Astrology*. After some introductory remarks on the nature of epistemological investigation, he described the three currents which in his opinion made up the intellectual field of astrology in Brazil. First, he commented on the influence of Theosophy among the number of students of the German Emmy de Mascheville who settled in Brazil after World War Two. After this he described the humanistic theories as a second important source.

---

[77] 'It is only the vulgar stupidity of our "mass culture" which imagines it is able to express cosmological concepts in pictures and dietetic tables of correspondencies which are flat, linear and in addition purely fictitious'. (Carvalho, *Astros e Símbolos*, p. 31).

[78] Faivre, *Accès de l'ésotérisme Occidental*, p. 36.

[79] Mirabail, *Dictionnaire de L'ésotérisme*, p. 247.

[80] Faivre, *Accès de l'ésotérisme Occidental*, pp. 40–48.

Oliveira identified himself with traditional astrology, the third tendency which he examined. From these pre-suppositions he criticised the two previous approaches for syncretism in the first case and, in the second, for its willingness to compromise with paradigms allied to modern science like psychoanalysis. Obviously the hypotheses of Oliveira do not present a complete description of the astrological world of Rio de Janeiro, because concern with the theoretical fundamentals of its practice—with esotericism—is not homogeneous. The rigour that the traditional theorists demand of their own practice and the restrictive conditions in which it should be used is not present throughout the world of astrology in Rio; but it explains the fact that they have featured more strongly in my description of esoteric questions in astrology. More than for any other group, the foundation of astrology is found, according to them, in religion. However, even for the humanists, for whom (as I showed in Chapter 1) valuation of tradition is more moderated, the basis of astrological efficacy—in this case the archetypes—are 'transcendentals in themselves (that is, they are much too subtle or immaterial to be immediately understood)'.[81] There would be in the fundamentals of the astrological system a non-rational, mysterious factor which legitimates the untestable postulates which sustain it, comparable to the mythical origin of traditional African beliefs.

I have tried, in this section, to offer a description of the worldviews and meanings associated with esotericism which appeared in my interviews, which I complemented with some basic pointers about the esoteric debate. Through being, as in the case of psychoanalysis, more interested in the repercussions of these theories in the world [of astrology] I investigated than in the theories themselves, I ran the risk of being simplistic in my summary descriptions. I tried to show, at least, how they constitute a rich collection of discussions about tradition, otherness, and religion, offering interesting material for anthropology and the social sciences in general, and deserving to escape from the [academic] ghetto in which they find themselves trapped.

ASTROLOGY AND RELIGION

Unlike the two previous topics connected with the astrological practices of my informants, religion is not an object of recent interest on the part of the social sciences; there is a solid, longstanding tradition of studies on this theme which, however, until today seems to have reached no consensus on the nature of the object of their studies.

---

[81] Arroyo, *Astrologia*, pp. 48–49.

For example, a competent evaluation of the theories that the social sciences produced on this theme, carried out by Evans-Pritchard—after pointing out the errors which characterised the theories of the evolutionists who had dominated the debate until the 1920s—recognised that, apart from those theories, religion has received only vague definitions, such as those in which it was related to 'a-logical' or 'irrational' spheres of social life.[82] Such ways of reasoning can lead us to attribute a religious character to a multiplicity of phenomena which also possess these traits.

This type of solution departs from, while transcending, an old debate in evolutionist anthropology which sought to define the phenomenon of religion through its contrast to magical practices. One of its best-known versions was the famous evolutionist hypothesis of James Frazer, according to which magic was an attempt to control nature through the use of 'laws' of similarity and contiguity: 'merely two mistaken applications of the association of ideas'.[83] By contrast religious thought would abandon the ingenuous belief in the omnipotence of man, judging that he finds himself submitted to the oppression of divine beings with whom a reconciliation is necessary.

For Frazer it seemed obvious that religious reasoning, although pre-scientific, was superior to magic. This led him to postulate the chronological priority of magic; humanity would have lived through a stage in which, despite the presence of magical thinking, it did not possess any form of religion.[84] At the same time he admits that the 'radical conflict of principles' which exists between religion and magic would have become clear 'relatively late in the history of religion'. Frazer appears to be leaving it implicit that Christianity, particularly its Protestant version, would represent a superior phase in the evolution of religion, in which magic would have been completely eliminated.

Frazer seems to have had a great influence on the historians of astrology. At the beginning of the century, the Belgian Franz Cumont identified as the great enigma offered by the study of this divinatory system the motive of the 'alliance, which at first sight seems monstrous (...) formed by mathematics and superstition'.[85] This prevents

---

[82] E.E. Evans-Pritchard, *Antropologia Social da Religião* (Rio de Janeiro: Campus, 1978), pp. 157–63.

[83] Sir James Frazer, *The Golden Bough: a Study in Magic and Religion*, Vol. 1 (London: Macmillan, 1980), p. 53.

[84] Frazer, *The Golden Bough*, p. 226.

[85] Cumont, *Astrology and Religion*, p. xiii.

him from accepting that such a rational system as astrology could have an essentially magical foundation, preferring to present it as an

> (...) erudite theology, which, including the whole world in its speculations, would eliminate narrower beliefs and, altering the character of ancient idolatry, would prepare in different ways the advent of Christianity.[86]

We saw in Chapter 1 how Lévi-Strauss criticised this kind of evolutionist formulation. When he refers to religion and magic he does not set up any logical or chronological pre-eminence between the two forms:

> There is no religion without magic, anymore than there is magic that does not contain at least a grain of religion. The notion of a supernature only exists for a humanity that attributes to itself supernatural powers, and which lends nature in exchange the powers of its super-humanity.[87]

Lévi-Strauss suggests an alternative solution which does not distinguish magic and religion in a hierarchical manner; instead, he attributes to each a specific type of symbolism. While religion, illustrated by rituals of sacrifice, would always try to establish relations of contiguity between the divinity and humanity, magic would suppose a relation of homology between the two levels—as happens in the example of totemism—between natural species and social groups.[88]

Although it presents in its symbolism metonymic elements which, according to Lévi-Strauss, are typical of religion, the astrological system is dominated by metaphorical principles. In this way we could say that it is an example of a magical system, in spite of its high level of rationalisation in the Weberian sense. This might explain the fact that, for the majority of my informants, religious practice is rather easy-going. The need for religion arises for them when they begin to reflect on the fundamentals of the efficacy of astrology which provides them with a highly intellectual type of religion. Therefore, it is in terms of astrology that the religious theme appears—or sometimes does not appear—in the interviews. Thus rather than try to respond to the investigations which this topic still stimulates in the immense tradition

---

[86] Cumont, *Astrology and Religion*, p. xvi.

[87] Lévi-Strauss, *La Pensée Sauvage*, p. 293.

[88] Lévi-Strauss, *La Pensée Sauvage*, pp. 291–302.

of religious studies already produced by the social sciences, I will try to present religion such as it is understood by the informants.

A counter-example which seems to confirm an initial hypothesis that religion arises as a result of speculation about the fundamentals of astrological efficacy can be found in the position taken by users of astrology who don't fit into the category of 'astrological students'. The three informants who never studied astrology in depth (Bárbara, Haroldo and José), do not relate in the same way to any kind of religious explanation, the last two being declared atheists. Due to the small size of the sample this data does not necessarily indicate any reliable statistic on the subject; however, it demonstrates the possibility of the regular use of astrology without any accompanying religious implication. On the other hand, almost all my informants recognised that the study of astrology drew their attention to religious questions in the larger sense. Even Eliana, the only student interviewed who insisted on affirming that astrology is a science, related that her study led her to develop a religious involvement. It does not seem to be by chance that such questions are posed precisely for those who are concerned to know the foundations of the astrological system. Rosa stated that after having learned the techniques by which astrology makes predictions, 'a bigger question' arose: 'where does this come from?' From then on, according to her, a 'second leap' becomes necessary which places the question on 'another level', 'archetypal, transcendental, metaphysical'. Thus Rosa justifies, after a number of years as a professional, her growing interest in esotericism, particularly the way it is treated in the context of the Tradition.

Although the question of the foundation of astrological efficacy is posed, one way or another, by almost every student of astrology, some do not have the time, ability or desire to go deeper into the subject: to dedicate themselves to reading esoteric authors until they find an explanation which they judge to be consistent. For Beatriz it was enough to take on the symbolic and synchronistic conception of astrology for her to turn back to the idea of God, recovering something that she had earlier lost:

> This pulsation together of all things, of the All and its parts, I think it was that which I used to call God (...). With astrology, that idea comes in a much more digestible language, it is much more attractive for me and much richer.

The path for Beatriz, of separation and later return to religion through the medium of astrology, is repeated to a greater or lesser degree in the majority of students and astrologers. The principle exceptions were Alice and Helen who remained Catholics and had still, at that time, not reconciled their faith with the idea of astrological determinism. However it is natural that, in the case of the other informants, this path does not simply re-establish lost beliefs. They may be the subjects of a re-evaluation, and past attitudes that the person had come to consider absurd come to be recovered and seen in a positive light once they return to having concerns of a religious nature. On the other hand the distancing and the return take place to very different degrees, although they are repeated among the majority of informants. Another common trait is that the [informants'] new religiosity is almost always reached via the intermediary of esotericism, which had not played any part in their religious education. Some people, such as Sônia, hardly received this type of education from their parents; having only slight contact with religion thanks to their school and more distant relatives, it did not leave a great impact. However, even having recently come to know astrology, Sônia seemed to be one of those most interested in 'mystical matters': in her case, oriental philosophy and spiritism.[89]

The contact with religion that esotericism offers the informants does not imply, in most cases, belonging to a specific religious group. It would be an intellectual and individual religiosity, based on the study of certain religious traditions and their manifestations and, in the search for self-improvement, following the teachings which each person finds useful during their studies. But there is, as we saw, one type of esotericism with great influence in the astrology world in Rio; it affirms the importance that astrological self-knowledge takes place within a specific religion associated with the theory of Tradition. This does not mean that its adepts are not interested in other traditions. Guénon himself studied with Papus and belonged to different initiatory organisations at the beginning of the [twentieth] century. Later, convinced that the

---

[89] Spiritism occupies an intermediate position in the esoteric world, not being condemned as much as other 'exoterised' religions. The ideas of Alain Kardec arose in the context of French occultism and this is reflected in its syncretic association with the doctrine of Karma as well as the Christian tradition, even in its scientist discourse, which was common in the esotericism of the previous century (Mirabail, *Dictionnaire de L'ésotérisme*, p. 242). But, because its teachings had taken the form of a coded message revealed to Kardec by the spirits themselves, spiritism is rejected by a large number of esoteric theorists (Maria Laura V. de C. Cavalcanti, *O Mundo Invisível: cosmologia, sistema ritual e noção de pessoa no Espiritismo* [Rio de Janeiro: Jorge Zahar Editora, 1983], pp. 20–23); Mirabail accepts it with limitations (*Dictionnaire de L'ésotérisme*, pp. 241–47). There are several criticisms, but the principal objection appears to be that it is not so much a comment about religions, but rather claims to be one of them, and superior to the others. This does not stop some members of the esoteric world from moving towards it, however not always committing to it completely.

West had entirely lost its traditional character, he moved to Egypt, where he converted to Islam. However, that did not stop him from writing several books about his theories, analysing various traditions.[90]

For the informants who adhere to his ideas, they appear as a safe haven after living through an intense period of syncretism. Roberto, who at the time of the interview had still not been convinced to follow them, admitted to me that he always saw astrology from a religious point of view, but at that time he was attracted by Candomblé, saying that he wanted to compensate for the inclination he had hitherto felt towards oriental religion. For her part, Rosa revealed that she had begun to give up the psychological orientation which infused her consultations in favour of an emphasis closer to Guénon's philosophy, seeking the 'second leap', to which I have already referred. Before contact with astrology, however, she had 'a very strong affiliation with Buddhism, with yoga' and moved on 'to Macumba, Umbanda, spiritual centres', etc. On the other hand, according to Guénon's perspective, religion intervenes in esoteric practice in order to articulate it coherently, not permitting the accumulation of disconnected experiences. Rosa states that:

> The word religion (...) means 'religar', to join something to what it was once joined to but is now disconnected from. Astrology is a religion is this sense, in the sense that it has a symbolism, it has a language capable of joining man to something cosmic, something much more inclusive than himself (...)

In a posture typical of what I have been calling erudite astrology, traditional astrologers suggest that its symbolism should not be taken for what it may indicate through its divinatory use, but for what it is in itself. Paula talked about her first encounter with these theories, describing a workshop with H. in an astrology congress:

> He put in the workshop (...) that astrology is an illustration of a principle, of a principle of order in the universe; and put it together with something else that he called God, with religion.

---

[90] Obviously Guénon and his disciples would never agree that they speak of *their* theories. The theories he presents are part of the Tradition: in other words, of the transmission of esoteric and metaphysical knowledge which always existed—although, before the modern [period of] confusion, they had remained occult and known only to an elite.

For one author of this approach astrology cannot be understood unless we take into account that it forms a group with three mother sciences which explain its foundation—metaphysics, cosmology, theology—and six sister sciences, which apply the same symbolism to different domains of reality, and are identified with the esoteric vision in the so-called liberal arts.[91] Religion would provide not only a foundation but also the rituals which are able to allow an appropriate spiritual development, given that they also possess the same symbolism. The only use of esoteric systems acceptable to these theorists is one accompanied by all the elements which make up a tradition, which necessarily possess a complete consistency.[92] Thus, over a long period of time the astrologers of this following experienced a paradoxical situation, given that, for them, the West had already almost entirely lost its traditional links. To some extent Rosa experienced this impasse, aware of the limitations of her professional practice, but without knowing how to introduce her reflections into it. Olavo de Carvalho, for example, repeating the response of Guénon, converted to Islam.

In the same impasse, a different solution to the problem was open to the students of H, among them Roberto, Paula and Luísa. This astrologer [H] went to Portugal and was ordained a priest in a branch of the Greek Orthodox Church which claims a traditional character. He founded churches in Recife, João Pessoa, and Rio de Janeiro (in Recreio dos Bandeirantes). Gradually several of his students who had assimilated Guénon's ideas through his courses were joining it, being baptised and taking part in the services. Among the informants mentioned above, only the last remained outside the church, although she said that several of her friends took part. Roberto took me one day to a Dominical mass in which a group of about twenty people took part, mostly young. The service lasted about two and a half hours, presenting—contrary to what can be found in contemporary Catholicism—a methodical ritualisation. From what I was able to understand, talking later with the priest, the mass followed faithfully the form established by St. John Chrisostom in the fourth century. This priest was no longer H, who had moved away from the church after some internal conflicts. This astrologer [H] had arrived at the conclusion that it did not have the traditional character which he had originally supposed. However, a large part of the group that he

---

[91] Carvalho, *Astros e Símbolos*, p. 20.

[92] 'And what is most surprising, in the science of these civilisations, is their degree of synthesis, of unity. In a traditional civilisation, there is practically no expression of culture which is not organically linked to the body of founding principles which sustain these civilisations'. (Carvalho, *Astros e Símbolos*, p. 23).

had brought to the church remained. I found out later through the last interview of this study with Luísa that Cláudio had been baptised.

Although these informants were certainly convinced that they had found the true foundation of the astrological system, there exist—as I have been insisting throughout this study—different ways of appropriating it. Even among the students, it would not necessarily be in theoretical discussions on esotericism that they would determine their astrological practice. As far as religion is concerned, even among those I mentioned earlier, a basic dilemma can be summarised. They seem to be divided between the experience of religious education received from their parents or the schools—which appeared to them to be repressive and an obstacle to their highly-valued individual autonomy—and the image they were offered by esotericism. In the case of the latter, it seemed to re-acquire the attraction it had lost, invested now with a liberating image linked to their opposition to 'official culture'.

Among the students, Marcos, who at the time of the interview had already moved away from the study of astrology, was one of those who referred the least to religion. On the one hand he was not very interested in the subject; at the same time he had 'the feeling that religion exists as something profound, serious, with that business of re-connecting'. It is possible to recognise some of Guénon's theories that he had come to read and with which he had contact through his old friends from the study group. However he appeared not to have [either] mastered the subject or to be interested in it, and ended by saying that he didn't think he knew exactly what religion was. The only contact that he had kept with astrology since then had been perhaps to go to two astrologers (A and F) in the almost two years since the group broke up.

This shows that there is no set pattern in the paths followed by the informants. After the dissolution of the group Roberto and Cláudio moved closer to religion via astrology; Marcos and Luísa left the latter more to one side and began to guide their 'self-knowledge' by a different system: homeopathy. Luísa also attended the courses which led to the formation of the branch of the Orthodox Church, but preferred not to enter it. In order to understand such choices we must attempt to understand the meaning which religion takes on in the symbolic conception which, not being uniform, displays certain tensions that run through the interviews and play a part in these choices.

I tried to show at the start of this chapter how, through certain authors, we can identify a symbolic leaning in Western thought which is opposed to its classical and formalist tendencies. This debate would take the form of a confrontation between pluralist and universalist conceptions, both of which are typical of the modern age. Todorov identifies, within his own symbolic analyses, neo-Classical and neo-Romantic tendencies which repeat this confrontation. In the same way, two poles can be found in the symbolism attributed by the informants to astrology. I showed how, when they approach the topic of psychology the interviews reveal astrology as an instrument of identity confirmation and the production of personal uniqueness. But the latter is only possible by expressing, in each individual chart, a particular arrangement of cosmological symbols which confer order on the universe. Religion, as I have been pointing out, is cited in these interviews as a source of this order, corresponding to the most comprehensive example in the discourse of the interviewees. I hope to have showed in the previous section how esotericism seeks to reconcile the demands of both particularism and universalism, being able to distribute each of its varieties according to the positions they occupy between these extremes.

If traditional astrologers are used to explaining the nature of religion in a clear and articulate manner, supported by a rigorous theory, other informants, [who are] less influenced by the esoteric debate, like Marcos, exhibit difficulties. But always, whenever they recognise in astrology a path of access to God or religion, they do so from the argument that it permits them to know a cosmic force, something universal, an order:

> The word *God* defines all this unavoidable force, of everything, of the universe (...) I went to the College of St. Ignatius and took that Catholic training (...), I was obliged to go to mass, but I never went out of conviction. There, I never understood this greater force. And in astrology, suddenly, we begin to understand, to comprehend this greater force which moves us (José).

The conception of this totality does not have to be obtained, according to the informants, only through astrology. Other esoteric systems which have self-improvement as their objective can also awaken it:

> Through yoga, I cured myself of a series of things, which for years I had been treating with [the help of] doctors (...). So, that made me investigate yoga more and more. (...) Through that I moved on to natural food (...), and I went through all that and astrology as well, succeeding more and more, to go on following the paths of self-development. Then this path was only leading to a greater one which would be God (Teresa).

This greater whole, according to Teresa, could not be limited to just one religion. After losing 'all enchantment for the Catholic religion', in which she had grown up, she said she had given up being a religious person. Curiously, her new attitude after her contact with esoteric systems is no longer described by her as 'religious', but rather as 'spiritualist'.[93] She said that before 'there was only the Catholic religion', but now she accepts 'any religion'. Teresa says that spiritualism means accepting 'any form of spiritual expression, but within certain limits'. So she says she does not accept Jehovah's Witnesses, probably shocked by the fanaticism attributed to this sect by the media for not permitting blood transfusions in any circumstances. Therefore, for Teresa, religion is the domain of obligation, of fanaticism, as compared to spiritualism; as she says on another occasion 'the true religion is that you achieve a better life (...), for you, for others, as a form of self-development'.

As happens in some casual uses of Durkheim's definition of religion as a system of 'sacred' values, the term *religion* can receive a negative connotation. Despite believing that astrology leads to the understanding of God, José, when asked about the relationship between the astrological system and religion, responded: 'this word *religion* should be used very carefully'. The reason for his attitude does not appear to be a prejudice against the idea of religion in the larger sense in which I have been using it, but against certain particular religions. For a number of esoteric authors, Guénon included, religious diversity—which for them happens exclusively on the exoteric plane—is due to specific circumstances, the psychology of different peoples, the period of history, etc. The informants, without making detailed analyses of esotericism, recognise this, thinking that the 'true religion' cannot be in the domain of the particular.

> All religions have their positive and negative points, but they all have their limitations, for historical or geographical reasons, or social problems. But then all that is [due to] the constitution of that people, that race (...). I think that astrology transcends all these things (...), these limitations. Because, within holism, the philosophy that makes a comparison between the micro- and macrocosm, there is an understanding of something bigger that is called God (José).

It is necessary to interpret José's words carefully, given that transcendence does not belong to astrology itself, but to the philosophy underlying it: in this case, holism or the correspondence between the macrocosm and microcosm. We have here the same paradox we met in discussing astrological pluralism and psychoanalysis. Astrology, as

---

[93] This term is common in esoteric circles, and Kardec stated that spiritism was one of the phases of spiritualism, which he defined in a more general sense. For him, 'everyone who believes that they have something non-material inside them is spiritualist'. (cited in Cavalcanti, *O Mundo Invisivel*, p. 15).

Beatriz points out, is a sacred science; in other words it has a basis of truth which must be unveiled by religion. This does not impede her from accepting that the system is practiced by 'people who study and research'; this is an advantage since it allows her to disagree and debate with them. In her adolescence Beatriz was, in her own words, 'a super Catholic'; she belonged to youth movements, 'often went to the church to pray', etc. With time, however, she began to see that the Church, which was said to be 'so sacred and powerful' was 'something completely ordinary, the priests were human beings as ridiculous as anyone else'. So she rejected this Catholic education and today prefers astrology because it has 'a more familiar language', not presenting itself 'as a bible but as a form of study'.

The religious crisis of informants in Beatriz's generation is closely linked with the information they obtain in school and university environments. Beatriz, Paula and Luísa were explicit on this point and showed how this movement away from their earlier religiosity was due in part to the manner in which their lecturers in history and the faculties of human sciences where they studied contributed to making them see economic, political and sociological motivations, etc., behind religions. Laura, the daughter of an important politician, also came into contact with such motivations in practice. Reminding herself of the masses which accompanied the inaugurations of building works, the great ceremonies in Candelária, she stated that the Catholic religion in which she was educated was linked with 'the rituals of power', with 'the control of the spectacle (...), with what has to be done to attain certain goals'. This, for her, had nothing to do with the 'spirituality' she saw in her relationship to astrology and other divinatory systems.

Thus this wide-ranging religiosity predominated, [one] which articulated the freedom of individuals in relation to their beliefs with an idea of God represented by a cosmic order or 'the harmony of the forces of nature', as Carla said. The fact that the religiosity of these interviewees did not fit into any specific religion is due to their presentation of an extremely abstract and universalising idea of this cosmic order. This does not imply however, that they neglected to see the value of religion; this can be demonstrated by their interest in different religious manifestations which had, on the other hand, to be viewed esoterically. Self-knowledge and the perception of a whole are two extremes of astrological symbolism which interrelate at the same time as they are opposed. As Helen says, the study of a chart is not the mere statement of the individuality of each person, but also allows them to see their 'tiny rôle in the gigantic universe'. One can emphasise either the 'tiny rôle' or the 'gigantic universe', but both are always present. So as modernity represses symbolic thinking, it would cause man to lose the notions of the 'sacred and divine' which, according to Beatriz, are inherent in being human. For the informants, the idea of symbolism thus includes the notion of harmony, of the interdependence of the parts which make up the universe.

It is from this opposition between the religious and psychological perspectives of astrology that we can better understand the options open to each informant when building their own specific pathways. Although almost always trying to reconcile the universalising and particularising tendencies of the two poles, they end up occupying different positions between them. Cláudio, for example, well before entering the Orthodox Church, already said in his interview that in astrology 'it is impossible for you to understand yourself alone'; for this it is necessary to 'become part of the whole'. Both he and Paula had been disappointed with 'established religions' when they were younger. The latter stated that from age fourteen 'you began to see the social implications of things', creating a 'disgust with everything that was institutionalised'. She, who had always been very religious, stopped believing in God and, according to her, was only able to return when she saw her astrological chart interpreted for the first time. Before coming to Orthodoxy she had an interesting religious experience whose description will help us to understand her subsequent choices. For about a year she followed the doctrine known as *Daime*, a syncretic religion which brings together elements of Christianity, Spiritism and Indigenous religion. As in Spiritism, it involves trance which is obtained through the consumption of a hallucinogenic plant known as Daime; this allows its users to have visions, known as '*mirações*', during which they enter into contact with 'the spirits'. This plant is also known as Ayahuasca. Once restricted to the inhabitants of Amazonia, this religion began to attract attention through its entry into the urban middle classes during the 1980s, associated with a certain 'naturalism'.[94]

Looking back, Paula criticises the syncretism as well as a series of doctrinal features of Daime. But her principal objection concerns the way that trance is used, which is guided by hymns and people 'who are more or less spiritual guides', but 'at the same

---

[94] One of the things which marked this urban penetration was the involvement of Alex Polari de Alverga, a poet and ex-political prisoner, who recently published a description of his experiences with Daime (Alex P. Alverga, *O Livro dos Mirações: viagem ao Santo Daime* [Rio de Janeiro: Rocco, 1984]). His book exemplifies the introduction of certain traits of esoteric thought, such as [those] I have been describing. So Alverga tells how he came to the conclusion after these experiences, that 'the so-called "irrational" pathways maintain a notable coherence and density, which challenge the passage of time. (...) And that in spite of all sorts of silliness and sentimentality which the institutionalized versions make of these religions, they all possess a kind of common source that must be respected'. (p. 17).

time it is very free'. At the end of each 'journey' each person has had completely different experiences, constructed (according to her) 'within the Unconscious of each person'. Using the contrast between subconscious and superconscious which Guénon employs to distinguish 'traditional psychology' she affirms that, while Daime works at the former level, Orthodoxy develops the second.[95] The latter basically uses prayer, which 'works through an annulment of individuality'. The choice of Orthodoxy therefore, is of a unity in preference to a multiplicity:

> Daime makes you carry on working with millions of entities and stay in the multiplicity, when in reality I know that God is a unity above everything, which works through stopping the mind, not having images, not having forms. God is beyond that: neither man nor woman, neither round nor square, neither one colour nor another.

We see that this group's extremely abstract definition of divinity, as with the majority of esoteric currents, makes it difficult to associate religion with anthropomorphism, which we find in my earlier quotation from Lévi-Strauss. Perhaps the category of totality, which Durkheim chooses as the product *par excellence* of the religious experience—stripped of Durkheim's sociologism—would be closer to the conception of my informants; as we can see in the interview above, this is not the only one to be found in the esoteric world.[96]

Returning to the informants, it is odd that Paula classifies the doctrine of Daime, whose ritual she considers very 'psychotherapeutic, as a Lunar doctrine since it works with reflection, the unconscious', while 'the superconscious, revelation, is Solar'. José, one of the astrologers interviewed who manifested a vision more influenced by psychology, used astrological symbolism in a similar way, but to state the opposite. His conception of religion should include 'our Solar side, symbolising reason, the lighter part', as well as the Lunar side 'the part which is completely hidden, intuitive'. Again, Regina states that she cannot practice an 'esoteric astrology' because she doesn't believe it is possible to separate 'the mundane world from the spiritual'. She believes that the 'positive and the negative, the feminine and masculine must be worked on together'. As we can see—thanks to its emphasis on the expression of unconscious and emotional aspects of individual behaviour with the goal of developing individuality— the psychological approach to astrology tends to move away from setting up hierarchical relationships between the areas of the psyche. In the same way,

---

[95] Cf. Guénon, *Os Símbolos da Ciência Sagrada*, p. 36.
[96] Emile Durkheim, *Les Formes Élémentaires de la Vie Religieuse* (Paris: PUF, 1979), p. 629.

psychoanalyst Roberto Sicuteri, on examining the different manifestations of the archetype of Lilith—labelled as demoniacal by many religions—commends modern astrology for understanding it, no longer as a 'totally destructive energy', but as 'a dark force to be understood and integrated'.[97]

We have seen, therefore, that the tension between universalism and particularism—which (according to Todorov and Serres) characterises the presence of symbolic thinking in modern society and can be described as individualist and rationalist at the same time—is also present in the way the notion of symbolism is employed by my informants. This notion does not merely allow them to articulate the convergences and divergences present in their discourse; it also serves as a bridge between astrology and the three areas of the surrounding society which I have been considering. This happens mainly in esotericism, where the symbolic logic which governs its elements permits the interpretation of each one in terms of the others and the establishment of 'correspondences' between their different classificatory systems. But this mechanism is also present in the relation of astrology with other domains. Rosa affirmed that the clients she likes best—those most interested in the study of the logic underlying astrology and its possibilities of transformation—are those 'linked to the symbolic world in psychoanalysis'. Meanwhile, Alice based her position—according to which there would be no incompatibility between her Catholic faith and astrology, despite the warnings of the Pope—precisely on the fact that her religion is full of symbolism:

> You see, the parables of Christ: what was he talking about? About symbols. Our rituals are all made of what? They are based on symbols.

Being a point of communication, symbolism does not merely imply a closer approach to astrology. Among the choices that make up the paths of each of my informants many, after a while, moved away from this system. I briefly described the case of Paula earlier. Her contact with astrology facilitated her access to different esoteric debates which she was able to follow in the courses she initially attended. However, more than specific information, it offered her a symbolic way of seeing the world which allowed her to return to the search for spiritual development. But slowly she moved away from astrology to the extent that it seemed to her to be limited in relation to this development. Even after re-connecting with her colleagues of the astrology course, after leaving Daime and entering the Orthodox Church, Paula confessed she did not

---

[97] Roberto Sicuteri, *Lilith: a lua negra* (Rio de Janeiro: Paz e Terra, 1985), p. 150.

have time to take up her astrological studies again; her new interests, linked to religion and theology, did not leave her any spare time.

Luísa completed the whole training process of this church but, up to the time of the interview, had shown no desire to join it. Although in practice she had not seemed to completely follow the theories of traditional astrology it is interesting that she valued that approach, continuing to attend courses (not specifically on astrology but more on philosophy) with teachers who were linked to this branch. For Luísa the search for an original source of astrology permitted access to its 'most complete, most true' form, purified of the personal influences of each professional. Curiously, she referred to this same point when she justified her 'step backwards' towards religion as a reason for not joining Orthodoxy. She referred equally to the internal personal conflicts which happened in this group and the criticisms that other astrologers of this following made about its supposedly traditional character, illustrating the power struggles which she expects to find in religions.

On the other hand, both Luísa and Marcos, after the dissolution of the study groups to which they had belonged, also gradually moved away from astrology. They became more interested in another symbolic system: homeopathy. Again, personal reasons were invoked for this choice, which was not justified by any devaluation of astrology. Both argued in general terms that homeopathy offered a concern with the physical dimension of their existence which was absent in the approaches to astrology with which they had contact. Thus, despite the 'alternative' character which its students often claimed for astrology, we see how effective it is in dealing with the fragmentation of modern society. The 're-mapping' that it achieves can define it as a nucleus capable of articulating, through its symbolism, beliefs and values which are apparently heterogeneous. But it can also then allow, through this approximation between different systems, that the different systems begin to assume a greater importance than astrology itself in the fragmented daily life of modern individuals.

CONCLUSIONS

At the beginning of this work I stated that its main investment of effort would be made in Chapters 1 and 4, which correspond to the most general and most particular poles, respectively, of my research. In this way I attempted to supply an interpretation of the structure and mechanisms by which the astrological system worked, in order to describe its practice in particular sectors of the urban middle classes in Rio de Janeiro, employing a number of studies that have been concerned with these sectors in recent years. In the intervening chapters I have tried to build a bridge between these two subjects, being forced to give only a brief treatment of such topics as modernity and the world of esotericism, of which much more remains to be said. Having taken this route in approaching my subjects, I hope not only to have furnished descriptive data on areas little explored by the social sciences thus far, but also to have shown the fertility of applying theories developed in anthropology to the various debates that were raised in this work; the conclusions here have the purpose of reviewing them and attempting to show their articulations.

Astrology, an erudite magico-classificatory system that demands the possession of advanced astronomical and mathematical knowledge for its practice, ends by being taken as an object of study principally in historiography. The particularist tradition of historiography accounts for the fact that the social sciences have never offered a global analysis of astrology. Faced with this, I have tried to take advantage of some suggestions of authors who, although mainly concerned with the analysis of primitive societies or discussions of larger methodological issues, have understood astrology as an example of a classification system. Developing this hypothesis, I hope to have shown that the stability that astrology seems to present throughout its historical trajectory— and which is valued by its practitioners—is related to the internal logic of these [types of] systems. The theories of Lévi-Strauss are particularly valuable here because they offer the possibility of questioning evolutionist approaches that refuse to recognise in astrology a system and coherence similar to that presented by scientific knowledge.

For Lévi-Strauss, classificatory systems are characterised by an 'attentive and meticulous observation entirely directed towards the concrete'; they encounter in symbolism 'at the same time their principle and their realisation'.[1] Within the various

---

[1] Lévi-Strauss, *La Pensée Sauvage*, p. 294.

appropriations that astrology has experienced—and still does—what we find in the groups that I have investigated is justifiably based on the emphasis on its symbolic character. Lévi-Strauss has previously emphasised the importance of conscious models for structural analysis.[2] In the case of my research, as often happens in the study of complex societies, its importance grows more significant due to the fact that the reflections of its practitioners on its representations of the world are often made using reference points held in common with the researcher. In the case of symbolism, for example, we saw how Dan Sperber tried to contextualise the 'semiological illusion' present in various theories on the phenomenon in the West—including those of astrologers themselves—besides pointing out residues of these concepts in the interpretation that Lévi-Strauss gives of his own work. On the other hand the groups studied occupy a particular place in the world of astrology; I therefore tried to contextualise the vision that they possess of the system in relation to those of others. For this I referred to considerations on cultural consumption, whose analogy with the consumption of astrology I explored, to show that the specificity of the position of my informants was similar to the abstract view of 'high culture' defined by Gans as a 'creator-oriented' viewpoint.

One of the values of Lévi-Strauss's theory is that it permits the postulation of the stability of the astrological system without preventing us from recognising, theoretically, the modifications astrology presents in each of its appropriations. Contrary to Jung's hypothesis of the Collective Unconscious, it does not attribute fixed symbolic contents; it tries, on the contrary, to explain the regularity of the system through the *relations between the component elements* [translator's italics]. More than a vocabulary of signs and planets, it is the relations between these terms that constitute the stable element of astrology, [thus] conferring meaning on each part. From this constant structure, different interpretations can be elaborated, in the same way that they can be appropriated by different worldviews. Even new elements that have been incorporated into the system tend to reproduce the existing structure.

The difference between science and magico-classificatory systems does not reside in the greater elaboration or complexity of the former, but in the raw materials used by each for its organisation. Astrology works, not with concepts but with signs or, to use Bachelard's terminology, images. Bachelard's work, which went through several changes of position, at times can lead us to believe that the Four Elements of Empedocles—my principal example in the analysis of this part of the astrological

---

[2] Lévi-Strauss, *Antropologia Estrutural*, Vol. 1, p. 319.

system—would be, by themselves, privileged objects for systematisation at the concrete level. Such an assumption would agree with the opinions of my informants on their archetypal and universal character. Against this type of hypothesis, it is necessary to re-affirm the contextual character of symbolic meaning. It would thus be interesting to refer to the uses made of the symbolic representations in relation to the physical-ethical alterations of [the meanings of] 'iron' [ferro] and 'phosphorus' [fosforo] among the Brazilian working class, where we can understand their transformation, in Lévi-Strauss's terms, from concepts into signs. These two elements, which in Mendeleev's Periodic Table have an abstract and mathematised conceptual meaning, acquire, according to the description of these representations by Luiz Fernando Duarte, a new symbolic meaning. Thus 'phosphorus', through sharing—in the Portuguese language—the same meaning attributed to 'objects that are routinely involved with obtaining fire', is allowed to overlap with ideas of 'heat' and 'light'.[3]

There is no doubt that the presence of astrological concepts, which are opposed to the logic of scientific thought in modern society, illustrates the fragmentation which characterises this society. Going beyond this statement, it could still be asked what the meaning of their presence is, and to what extent it allows us to reflect on the nature of modernity. Among the many implications that can be drawn from this question, I will focus on just a few.

This can begin by commenting on a fairly common response, formulated by observers of the growth of astrology, such as historian and orientalist Georges Contenau; like the astronomer R.R. de Freitas Mourão, he relies on the hypothesis that astrology would offer an element of security and coherence in the midst of an uncertain world. This response is not completely mistaken but it risks being simplistic. Every system of values and/or representations furnishes its users with certain reference points or, as Figueira puts it, a map. On the other hand all maps imply, to a greater or lesser extent, some tolerance of fragmentation and difference.

This type of hypothesis expresses in the most direct way a supposition implicit in the analyses presented in Chapter 3, which attributes a deviant character to the practice of astrology in modern societies. In their various biases these analyses can be summarised according to Philippe Defrance, a member of Morin's group, according to whom 'the spread of and attraction to astrology are a measure of contemporary uncertainties and confusions'.[4] The sectors that are characterised by this practice are,

---

[3] Duarte, *Da Vida Nervosa*, p. 148.
[4] Morin et al., *O Retorno dos Astrologos*, pp. 109–10.

as concluded in *The Return of the Astrologers,* 'areas of no culture', that possess 'fewer or weaker antibodies against astrology', or sectors which present a situation of 'deprivation' as identified by the North American authors listed by Jorgensen.[5] Astrology would thus be a mere reaction to modern values and their crisis, although—as I have already said—Simmel established that crisis is [the single factor] which most clearly characterises modern culture.

In the last analysis, the weakness of the hypothesis that attributes the growth of astrology merely to a desperate search for a safe haven from the fragmentation of modern life resides in the fact that this system does not possess a unique group of values to guide its use, or even a cosmological foundation for its efficacy. We have seen that it can be applied to a multiplicity of objects and that different parts of the astrological world hold different opinions on the legitimacy of each of its uses. Thus astrology, based on its potentials, associates itself with the worldviews of the groups that ally themselves to it. The difficulty of making a definite 'diagnosis' on [reasons for] its growth as Morin and his team have tried to do lies exactly in the polymorphism of this system.

So, abandoning excessive ambitions the researcher, when furnished with an analysis of the properties of the astrological system, must investigate how it is related to the worldview of each group. Duarte, while recognising that he relies on a limited bibliography, shows how it converges with the holistic conceptions that he wishes to identify in the Brazilian working class.[6]

The world of astrology presents great heterogeneity and, when I attempted to map it, I made clear that I was privileging the sector with which I had the most contact, which I called (following Morin) erudite astrology. We can understand that in Rio de Janeiro, as an example of what happens in other large modern cities, [astrology] is organised like a market in which the circulation of symbolic goods is formally free, constituting a network based on 'choices' and 'affinities', and where the main limits imposed on individuals who take part are determined by the 'symbolic capital' of each person. Beyond the worldview that each individual or group incorporates into their astrological practice, that practice is equally influenced by their degree of belonging to this world; this is in turn determined by their level of absorption of the astrological discourse. This belonging may be superficial or reach the point at which the language of astrology colours all the areas that make up the fragmented social life of big city

---

[5] Morin, et al., *O retorno dos Astrologos,* p. 132; Jorgensen, 'The Esoteric Community', p. 403.
[6] Duarte, *Da Vida Nervosa,* pp. 208–09.

dwellers. This same fragmentation produces, as we saw, a specific form of belief defined by Jean Pouillon of which the world of astrology, to the extent it is illustrated by the area studied here, is a privileged example.

Although I tried to diversify the types of interviewees the majority, by choice, were students of the subject: in other words, typical consumers of erudite astrology, the form which occupies a central position in this world, which is typically taken up by members of the educated urban middle classes. Gilberto Velho defined the middle classes as those who live *par excellence* the experience of modernisation in Brazilian society. It is characteristic of the non-'traditional' pole of these classes according to Tania Salem to take part in this type of network, as defined above, in which family and locality are only secondary determinants of its constitution. This adaptation is not only due to their specific values, but also to sociological factors. The great majority of informants were studying, or had completed a course of higher education, mostly in the human sciences. As I showed, education—together with free time—is one of the most important determinants of 'taste-culture', in Gans's terminology. Contrary to the conclusions Morin's team appeared to show, the group I studied (as can be verified in Appendix 1) shows a fairly high level of culture compared to the standards of their society, and are also influenced by psychoanalytic ideas. In the last analysis, a certain perseverance of reading and study is a necessary quality for a student of astrology. The participation of someone in the world of astrology shows the presence of a degree of cosmopolitanism in the lifestyle, reflected in reading foreign books or, in Haroldo's case, meeting astrologers outside Brazil.

The responses that this study can provide regarding the growth of astrology therefore mostly concern these classes. Although we cannot suppose that my data provide a global portrait of astrological practice among these groups, we see that the discourse of informants shows a tension between a particularising and a universalising pole, which is characteristic of modernity itself, and which [the informants] seem, in part, to represent. On the one hand the system permits them to express a qualitative individualism; on the other they seek, through the speculations that surround it, to express a religious diversity. Thus we can see how the speech of informants presents questions that can be found in other analyses of the middle classes.

Velho, for example, suggested recently that an interesting element of Simmel's theory on modernity is his hypothesis, according to which there will be an unevenness between what he calls a subjective and an objective culture.[7] In this situation the development of qualitative individualism—through self-cultivation, technical progress and the heterogeneity of modern social life—allows cultural life to gain a relative autonomy in relation to the person, who does not succeed in accompanying it. Velho suggests that 'for certain social groups'—referring to members of the middle classes analysed in this book—'the development of subjective cultures, which attempt to reduce this unevenness of levels, can be associated with their exercise of social activities'.[8] I would like to close these final observations by showing how astrology can become, as it is in the group studied here, another possibility for this development.

Cultural heterogeneity has often been associated with historical periods in which astrology and esotericism were present. The former, as we saw, was born in a clearly syncretic environment, while the latter is really a response to the diversity of religions which attempts to reveal their common inner identity. Taking up the commentary I developed on the idea of second-degree mapping proposed by Figueira, we can say that this process takes, as a reference point, not just the individual (as does psychoanalysis) but also the surrounding totality. The symbols which constitute the astrological system would be present in both the microcosm and the macrocosm, each one connected by the two opposing poles that I identified in the discourse of my informants.

On the other hand, not only is the starting point important, but also the form in which the re-mapping of astrology is carried out [if we are] to understand its nature. According to Simmel the rationality and impersonality that characterise urban life 'tend to take away the real personal qualities [of individuals] and the incompatibilities [between them]'.[9] To preserve his singular self in harmony with the principles of qualitative individualism, modern man would sometimes be obliged to exaggerate his 'distinguishing features so as to remain visible [*audivel* in the original text] even to himself'. As we have seen, astrological self-cultivation provides another alternative. Through its language of classification the individual is able to regain the qualitative aspect of reality and symbolically relate to it. It is in this sense that we can understand the emphasis placed by informants on sensitivity and intuition in understanding astrological language. An extreme example of this tendency can be found in a writer

---

[7] Simmel contrasts subjective and objective culture, meaning by the first the wishes and beliefs of people in a society, as opposed to the technical means of communication and institutional social structures (Simmel, *The Sociology*).—Trans.

[8] Velho, *Subjetividade e Sociedade*, p. 16.

[9] Simmel, *The Sociology*, p. 422.

cited by Arroyo: Huston Smith, who states that, after the mechanical conception of nature which prevailed from the seventeenth to nineteenth centuries, and the biological conception of the twentieth, we are moving towards a psychological vision, 'with less determinism and more freedom'.[10]

Even while privileging the particular and the individual over the totality, informants utilised symbolism as a fundamental ingredient. In doing so, without doubt they move away from the principles which orient scientific thinking. The historical account offered by Koyré shows how the emergence of scientific thinking resulted from a renunciation of a global understanding of the meaning of the structure of the cosmos in an attempt, as Lévi-Strauss put it, to control the inequality between the signifier and the signified, which characterises human thought.[11] But this attempt is always limited, since that inequality is the 'guarantee of all art, all poetry and all mythic and aesthetic invention', which makes possible the hope that 'the relation between symbolism and knowledge conserves common characteristics in both industrial societies and our own'.[12] Thus astrology, as practised by my informants, does not merely reveal an [anachronistic] survival nor an activity which is deviant and marginal. The emphasis on its antagonism to scientific values, which is part of the means used by the interviewees to construct an identity, does not prevent them, as we saw in the previous chapter, from relating to modern values where symbolism persists in various domains. Contrary to the theoreticians of occultism, it can be seen how astrology truly becomes a vehicle that expresses and problematises the tensions of these values themselves, even while apparently denying them.

---

[10] Huston Smith, Editorial in *The* Cooperator, vol. 1 (1971): pp. 1–4, cited in Arroyo, *Astrologia*, p. 21.

[11] Koyré, 1985, p. 240 [*sic*]. [It is unclear which work of Koyré's serves as the source of this reference since its date does not match the publication dates of either *Estudos de História* or *Do Mundo Fechado*.—Ed.]

[12] Lévi-Strauss, *Antropologia Estrutural*, vol. 1, p. 34. [When Lévi-Strauss talks of the 'inequality of signifier and signified' as being 'the guarantee of all art' he adopts a term from Saussurean structural linguistics to say that when a word (the signifier) is used to express a signified (mental image) it always runs away from the writer, calling up unknown associations in the mind of the reader, (and reflexively in the writer too), escaping all attempts to pin down stable meanings. In the post-structuralist period (which began in the 1960s) this became the central focus of hermeneutic criticism.—Trans.]

APPENDIX 1:
THE INTERVIEWEES

Along with some basic details about the informants, whose enumeration could be tiresome to list, I give here, with the list of the interviewees, a brief description of each person's relationship to astrology. Although some details can be found distributed through the last three chapters, I try here to offer the reader a reference source which will help them to avoid getting lost among all the names. Unless otherwise indicated, the data refer to the time at which each interview was conducted; they began in July 1985 and were completed two years later. The order of their enumeration is chronological. The astrologers with whom the informants had contact are indicated by means of the initials used in Chapters 3 and 4.

1) ALICE (aged about 48), housewife, trained in library management without ever having worked in that profession, but having been employed in the past. Married with children, residing in a flat near Copacabana beach, mother of Roberto and aunt to Beatriz. She first had contact with astrology thanks to the interest of her son and a sister who lived outside the city, but hesitated to get involved with the system due to the death of one of her brothers, which had been predicted astrologically. After the trauma had passed she had by then been organising the study group **c** in her house, having studied for more than two years.

2) BEATRIZ (aged 19), student of psychology, single, living with her father in Copacabana. She had been very interested in astrology since her cousin, Roberto, had read her chart. She decided then to organise group **b**, with him which, at the time of the interview, had been running for some months. She viewed astrology mainly as a form of self-knowledge.

3) CLÁUDIO (aged 22), musician, giving private singing lessons, single, lives with his parents in a flat in Ipanema. A woman friend, whom he met while taking part in a musical, drew his chart for the first time. From then on, she began to give him his first information about astrology, which he tried to extend through reading books. He had been taking part in group **a** for a few weeks.

4) VÁNIA (aged 35), housewife, trained in economics, without ever making a career, married with two children. Daughter-in-law of Alice, she only knew of astrology through the media, decided to join the group organised by her mother-in-law, motivated by curiosity.

5) HELEN (aged about 55), married, housewife, with children and grandchildren, North American of Irish descent, settled in Brazil for some years. Connected her interest in magical things with her family heritage and while in the USA had had her chart read. In Brazil she consulted other astrologers and joined group c. She says that her interest in astrology is in understanding her individuality and the "tiny role" she could have 'in this immense universe'.

6) RUTH (aged 39), separated, trained in library management, resident in Laranjeiras, was not working (although she had practised her profession). She defined her interest in astrology through the curiosity she felt to know more about what 'was offered by Oriental culture'. After several readings and courses she joined group c, saying that she studied astrology in order to understand herself and others better.

7) SÔNIA (aged 22), single, lived with her parents in Copacabana and had qualified shortly before in economics, not yet working. She was interested in astrology as a result of talking to friends and had her first chart done by an astrologer she met in a fair, who recommended the course run by A, where I met her. She was very enthused by these first studies since she believed that astrology provided her with a 'symbolic language' for knowing herself and her friends better.

8) TERESA (aged 48), married with one child, resident of Copacabana, trained in law, employed part-time in the Ministry of Justice. Having heard about astrology in regular attendance at a Yoga academy, she decided to have her chart drawn by B. Despite not having agreed completely with his interpretation, she took her first courses with him. Later consulted she G and then A, with whom she decided to take classes. Because astrologer A considered her very advanced he introduced her to group c.

9) JAIME (aged 19), single, studying industrial design, living with his parents in a three-room flat in Copacabana. He stated that he had been interested by the 'mystical side of things', without ever having gone into any particular topic in depth. On returning to Brazil after a period abroad, he was surprised that astrology was so much 'in vogue',

which affected his friends, among them Paula and a member of group **a**, who invited him to join.

10) ROBERTO (aged 26), astrologer, single, son of Alice, with a studio in Leblon. Without having finished any of the various university courses he had begun, he decided to set himself up in a studio after studying for three years, which gave him financial independence. Always interested in esotericism, he says he always had the inclination to 'believe in everything'. After the interview he became interested by the theories of the Tradition, joined the Orthodox Church run by H and became a member of a centre of astrological studies which put on courses and workshops.

11) BÁRBARA (aged 37), married with children, lives in a penthouse in Leblon, and completed her post-graduate studies in a branch of the social sciences. States that she feels a strong interest in divinatory systems—in her words, 'these systems that I can't explain'—having already consulted three astrologers (D, E and F) and a Tarot reader. Despite this, says that the predictions and indications of astrology do not alter very much the way she looks at things.

12) LAURA (aged about 47), trained in psychology, works in a social science research institute, divorced with children, lives in a house in Jardim Botânico. She always felt a great fascination for magic and various forms of divination. After some time regularly consulting D and disagreeing with one of his interpretations, she decided to study astrology. She read various books, many of which she bought abroad, began to take private classes, but hardly ever frequents the world of astrology, as she says she 'doesn't do well in collective things'. That study, she believes, taught her to accept her way of being, not trying to be someone different.

13) RENATO (aged 41), married with children, trained in the social sciences (without ever practising his profession), businessman and plastic artist. For many years he had a high-level post in a state-run company which allowed him to live abroad, where he made contact with different types of divinatory systems in various parts of the world. Although he shows an equal interest in all of them he considers astrology, of which he has only a superficial knowledge, to be the most trustworthy.

14) ROSA (aged 34), astrologer, single, trained in communication to post-graduate level, worked initially in publicity. Always interested by 'esoteric matters', was very impressed by the reading of her chart which D made, which showed her things about

her personality that she had spent years discovering in her analysis. After studying for some years with this astrologer, she began charging the people who were constantly asking her to read their charts, eventually being convinced of the viability of this work as a profession. Today she has a studio in Leblon, gives courses in chart reading and is moving closer to the theories of traditional astrology.

15) REGINA (aged about 45), astrologer, single, one of the pioneers of astrology in Rio. Trained in law, she gave up this profession, interested in the study of 'borderline sciences' and the plastic arts. Made her first studies of astrology (about which she knew nothing previously) in Europe at the beginning of the 1970s. Returned to Brazil in 1973 and from then on gave consultations and courses. Her approach is basically inspired by Jung.

16) FRANCISCO (aged 48), psychoanalyst and psychiatrist, married, resident in Laranjeiras. His first contact with astrology was thanks to a musician friend with whom he shared accommodation, who did his chart at the end of the 1950s and who is also a friend of Renato. In recent years he has watched the growth of astrology with interest, having already been to six different astrologers. Despite finding it very useful for self-knowledge, his curiosity never led him to study it in depth, which led him not to explore systematically the references that his clients make to their zodiac signs during psychoanalytic sessions.

17) ELIANA (aged about 45), journalist, divorced, one daughter, resident of Ipanema. She began studying astrology by herself in 1972 after a consultation with G, which impressed her with its precision. She believes that this quality cannot be found in any other divinatory system, and does not usually participate in events of the world of astrology.

18) CARLA (aged 42), married with children, resident of the Barra da Tijuca, post-graduate studies in Physics. In spite of her training, she stated that she has always been interested in the 'less well made sides of science' since her time as a student. Busy with her training and with bringing up her children, she only began to study astrology in 1979, organising a study group. She is interested in antigymnastics [antiginástica],[1] says

---

[1] Antiginástica is a generic word in Portuguese for all kinds of alternative bodywork and therapies, including Yoga, Chi-Kung, Alexander Technique and Feldenkrais's Method.—Trans.

that she only treats herself with homeopathy and insists on making clear its links with humanistic astrology. She thinks that these systems deal with 'subtle energies' which contemporary science still cannot identify, being pre-occupied with repeatability and precision in its experimental researches.

19) HAROLDO (aged 31), homeopathic doctor with a studio in Ipanema, married a month after the interview. Told how, in university he entered into a 'crisis with medicine', which led him to seek information about 'alternative therapies' (macrobiotics, acupuncture and eventually homeopathy). Convinced of its complexity, says he has moved closer to astrology 'bit by bit', taking courses with E and F, who also interpreted his chart. He has been investigating the possibility of using it in diagnosis and coordinates a study group on homeopathy which Carla also takes part in.

20) JOSÉ (aged 46), astrologer, also working with music, in which he trained, and photography. Married ('not officially' as he wants to make clear), he has a three-room flat in Ipanema, where he gives consultations. He has been studying astrology for ten years, attended courses and workshops, but records that his training was basically autodidactic. He follows a psychological line, affirming that he tries to make his clients more aware of themselves by means of astrology.

21) PAULA (aged 21), single, student of psychology, living with her parents in a flat in Leblon. She remained curious, after astrology was mentioned by a teacher who studied it. He read her chart, which made such an impression that she was immediately convinced of the efficacy of the system. She took several courses with H, which led her to approach the ideas of Guénon and to join the Orthodox Church. Before that, however, she adhered for a year to the doctrine of Daime.

22) MARCOS (aged 24), lives in a three-room apartment in Ipanema with his mother and sister and works with video and photography. His first contact with astrology was due to knowing Luísa and Beatriz. He took part in group **a** and Roberto did her chart. He thinks astrology is an instrument for self-knowledge, having been to two more astrologers (A and F) since the breakup of the group. However, he has not studied much more, since he considers the weekly consultations that he makes with his purist homeopath would be more effective for this process of self-knowledge because [the homeopath] values the psychological dimension as well as the physical.

23) LUÍSA (aged 23), single, lives with her mother in a three-room apartment in Leblon and studies medicine. She entered group **b**, made up of old friends of hers, after having taken a sabbatical year from her university studies. Later she took part in the courses of H, where she familiarised herself with the theories of the Tradition and of esotericism in general. She, who had already treated herself by homeopathy for some time, decided to take the entrance exam for medicine so that she could study this branch later.

APPENDIX 2:
GLOSSARY

ASCENDANT – The point in which the zodiac cuts the horizon at its eastern extremity at the moment for which the chart is made. The ascendant is the beginning of the 1st House.

ASPECTS – The relation between planets placed at certain (numerical) distances apart in an astrological chart, which requires that the properties of these planets have to be combined in the interpretation. The most important are the conjunction, opposition, trine and square.

ASTROLOGICAL CHART – A diagram in which the planetary positions are shown along with the houses and other points (such as Lilith, the Part of Fortune, etc.) in relation to the zodiac at a given time and place.

ASTROLOGICAL HOUSES – The division of the (astrological) chart into twelve parts that represents the daily rotation of the earth, and which causes the ascendant (the cusp of the 1st House) to make a complete turn every twenty-four hours.

CARDINAL – That which refers to an axis. In astrology, specifically, the signs which are counted from the two (seasonal) axes of the chart, beginning the four seasons into which they divide it.

CONJUNCTION – The aspect formed by two or more planets that are separated by a distance of up to eight degrees, characterising a convergence in their actions.

CUSP – A sharp edge; the line which represents the beginning of each astrological house in the chart.

DESCENDANT OR WEST POINT – The point opposite the Ascendant, where the 7th House begins.

ECLIPTIC – A circular line which marks the path traced out by the sun in its imaginary movement around the earth.

ELEMENTS – Each of the four 'substances' (fire, earth, air, water) named in antiquity and the Middle Ages as material components of the sublunary world. In astrology, each sign is associated with one of them, whose properties are described at length in Chapter 1.

EPHEMERIS – A table which provides the position of a planet in the zodiac at regular intervals of time. Used in the preparation of astrological charts.

FIXED – Each of the four signs which occupy the middle of each season, following the cardinals.

HOROSCOPE – The original meaning was 'hour of birth', and it is used by Ptolemy to refer to the ascendant. Nowadays it has been appropriated by the press to refer to the daily, weekly or monthly astrological predictions for the natives of each sign; in practice the term is only used with this meaning.

LIGHTS – The names attributed to the sun and moon to distinguish them from the rest of the planets.

LILITH – The point in an astrological chart which indicates the diameter of the lunar apogee or perigee. It takes this name from a character in Jewish mythology, and in interpretation of a chart the position it occupies is associated with sexuality.

MIDHEAVEN OR MC – The point in which the ecliptic intercepts the upper meridian, and the beginning of the 10th House.

MUTABLE – The four signs which occupy the final period of each season.

NATIVES – Those who have a given zodiac (Sun) sign, for example natives of Aries, who have the Sun in this sign, and so on. The term is most common in media astrology.

NODES OF THE MOON – Two points in a chart which show the intersection of the ecliptic with the Lunar orbit. They are always 180 degrees apart and are known as the Head and Tail of the Dragon. Both affect 'relationships' and 'traditional attitudes'.[1]

OPPOSITION – Aspect formed by two or more planets that are close to 180 degrees apart in the zodiac, characterising a tension between them.

PART OF FORTUNE – The best known of the 'Arabic Parts'. Its position is calculated by adding the position of the Ascendant in degrees (counting from the beginning of Aries) to that of the Moon, then subtracting the result from the (zodiacal) position of the Sun (counting from the beginning of Aries). This point would provide information on the 'projection of the personality, (…) riches and fortune'.[2] Other Parts include that of Commerce (Ascendant plus Mercury minus Sun), or of Love (Ascendant plus Venus minus Sun), etc.[3]

PLANETS – In antiquity they were the 'wanderers'; as seen from the earth they move in relation to the fixed stars. In astrology the Sun and Moon continue to be planets, a classification which they do not possess in Copernican cosmology (which does not take our planet as a fixed reference point).

QUALITIES OR QUADRUPLICITIES (MODALITIES) – Describes a 'behavioural type' characteristic of each sign.[4] According to this classification they may be cardinal, fixed or mutable.

SIGN – Each of the twelve subdivisions of the zodiac to which are attributed properties which interact with the elements that are found there in an astrological chart. The word is also used commonly to designate the Sun sign.

SQUARE – An aspect formed by two or more planets which are separated by about 90 degrees, implying a conflictual relation between their respective actions.

---

[1] Ribeiro, *O Conhecimento da Astrologia*, p. 368.
[2] Ribeiro, *O Conhecimento da Astrologia*, p. 196.
[3] Freeman, *How to Interpret a Birthchart*, p. 118.
[4] Ribeiro, *O Conhecimento da Astrologia*, p. 44.

SUN SIGN – The sign in which the Sun is situated in the (astrological) chart of an individual.

TABLE OF HOUSES – A table which allows the house cusps to be located in the zodiac at a given time for any latitude required.

TRANSITS – Aspects which may form between the positions of planets in an individual (astrological) chart and their positions at another specific time. Their interpretation allows the person to know their astrological tendencies during the specified period.

TRINE – An aspect formed by two or more planets separated by a distance of about 120 degrees, describing a harmonious combination of their respective actions.

VERNAL POINT – The intersection of the ecliptic with the equator, in which the Sun is situated at the start of spring.

ZODIAC – The belt eight degrees in width projected onto the celestial vault, where the planets are situated in their apparent movement around the earth. It is divided into twelve signs of 30 degrees each, with Aries the first, starting from the vernal point.

BIBLIOGRAPHY

Adler, Oskar. *La Astrologie como Ciencia Oculta: el testamento de la astrologia*. Buenos Aires: Kier, 1984.

Alexandrian, Sarane. *Histoire de la philosophie occulte*. Paris: Seghers, 1983.

Alverga, Alex P. *O Livro dos Mirações: viagen ao Santo Daime*. Rio de Janeiro: Rocco, 1984.

Arroyo, Stephen. *Astrologia, Karma e Transformação*. Nem Martins: Europa-America, 1979.

———. *Astrologia, Psicologia e os Quatro Elementos; uma abordagem astrologica ao nível de energia e seu uso nas artes de aconselhar e orientar*. São Paulo: Pensamento, 1985.

Bachelard, Gaston. *L'air et les Songes. essai sur l'imagination du mouvement*. Paris: José Corti, 1943.

———. *La Formation de l'esprit scientifique: Contribution à une psychanalyse de la connaisance objective*, 7th ed. Paris: PUF, 1970.

———. *La Philosophie du non: Essai d'une philosophie du nouvel esprit scientifique*. Paris: PUF, 1960.

———. *La poétique de la rêverie*. Paris: PUF, 1961.

———. *La poétique de l'espace*. Paris: PUF, 1957.

———. *La Psychanalyse du feu*. Paris: Gallimard, 1985.

Barbosa, Dom Marcos. 'Astrologia', *Jornal do Brasil*, 29 Dec. 1987 2, Caderno B.

Becker, Howard S. *Art Worlds*. Berkeley: University of California Press, 1982.

———. 'Arte como Ação Coletiva'. In *Uma Teoria da Ação Coletiva*, edited by Howard S. Becker, Marcia Bandeira de Mello Leite Nunes and Gilberto Velho. Rio de Janeiro: Jorge Zahar Editora, 1977.

Bell, Daniel. *The Cultural Contradictions of Capitalism*. New York: Basic Books, 1976.

Bellah, Robert. 'The Historical Background of Unbelief'. In *The Culture of Unbelief*, edited by Rocco Caporale. Berkeley: University of California Press, 1971.

Blavatsky, Helena P. *A Chave da Teosophia*. Lisbon: Edições 70, 1978.

Bloch, Maurice. 'Astrology and Writing in Madagascar'. In *Literacy in Traditional Societies*, edited by Jack Goody. Cambridge: Cambridge University Press, 1968.

Bourdieu, Pierre. *Algeria 1960: The Disenchantment of the World: The Sense of Honour. The Kabyle House or the World Reversed: Essays*. Cambridge: Cambridge University Press, 1979.

———. *La Distinction: critique sociale du jugement du goût*. Paris: Editions de Minuit, 1979.

———. 'O mercado do bens simbólicos'. In *A Economia das Trocas Simbólicas*. Sao Paulo: Perspectiva, 1982.

———. *Le sens pratique*. Paris: Editions de Minuit, 1980.

Bratcher, Robert G. and Eugene A. Nida. *A Handbook on the Gospel of Mark*. United Bible Societies, 1961.

Carvalho, Antônio Carlos. 'Prefácio' in *A Crise do Mundo Moderno*, by René Guénon. Lisbon: Veja, 1977.

Carvalho, Luiz Henrique F. De. 'Associação de Netuno com Urano ou homeopatia e Astrologia'. In *Astrologia Hoje: Métodos e Propostas*, edited by Ana Maria Costa Ribeiro, et al. Rio de Janeiro: Massao Ohno, 1985.

Carvalho, Olavo de. *Astros e Símbolos*. São Paulo: Nova Stella, 1986.

Cavalcanti, Maria Laura V. de C. *O Mundo Invisível: cosmologia, sistema ritual e noção de pessoa no Espiritismo*. Rio de Janeiro: Jorge Zahar Editora, 1983.

Chodokiewicz, Michel. *Le Sceau dês Saints: prophétie et sainteté dans la doctrine d'Ibn Arabi*. Paris: Gallimard, 1986.

Courdec, Paul. *L'Astrologie*. Paris: PUF, 1978.

Cumont, Franz. *Astrology and Religion among the Greeks and Romans*. New York: Dover, 1960.

Curry, Patrick, ed. *Astrology, Science and Society*. London: Boydell, 1977.

Delumeau, Jean. *La Civilisation de la Renaissance*. Paris: Fayard, 1967.

Dodds, E.R. *The Greeks and the Irrational*. Berkeley: University of California Press, 1951.

Duarte, Luiz Fernando Dias. *Da Vida Nervosa nas Classes Trabalhadoras Urbanas*. Rio de Janeiro: Jorge Zahar Editora; Brasilia: CNPq, 1986.

Dumont, Louis. *Homo Hierarchicus: An Essay on the Caste System*. Chicago: University of Chicago Press, 1970.

———. *O Individualismo: uma perspectiva antropológica da ideologia moderna*. Rio de Janeiro: Rocco, 1985.

———. 'Religion, Politics and Society in the Individualistic Universe'. *Proceedings of the Royal Anthropological Institute of Great Britain and Ireland*, no. 1970 (1970): pp. 31–41.

———. 'Vers unec Théorie de la Hierarchie'. In *Homo Hierarchicus: le système des castes et ses implications*. Paris: Gallimard, 1979.

Durkheim, Émile. *Les Formes Élémentaires de la Vie Religieuse*. Paris: PUF, 1979.

Durkheim, Émile and Marcel Mauss. 'Algumas Formas Primitivas de Classificação'. In *Ensaios de Sociologia* , edited by Marcel Mauss. São Paulo: Perspectiva, 1981.

Eco, Umberto. *Apocalípticos e Integrados*. São Paulo: Perspectiva, 1970.

Eglin, Trent. 'Introduction to a Hermeneutics of the Occult'. In *On the margin of the visible: sociology, the esoteric, and the occult*, edited by Edward Tiryakian. New York: Wiley, 1974.

Evans-Pritchard, E. E. *Antropologia Social da Religião*. Rio de Janeiro: Campus, 1978.

———. *Bruxaria, Oráculos e Magia entre os Azande*. Rio de Janeiro: Jorge Zahar Editora, 1978.

———. *Nuer Religion*. Oxford: Clarendon Press, 1956.

———. *Os Nuer: uma descrição do modo de subsistência e das instituções políticas de um povo nilota*. São Paulo: Perspectiva, 1978.

Faivre, Antoine. *Accès de l'ésotérisme Occidental*. Paris: Gallimard, 1986.

Ferreira, Aurelio Buarque de Holanda. *Novo Dicionario da Lingua Portuguesa*. Rio de Janeiro: Nova Fronteira, 1986.

Ferreira Neto, José Fonseca. 'A Ciência dos Mitos e O Mito da Ciência'. Master's Dissertation, Brasília: UnB, 1984.

Festugière, André J. *La Révélation d'Hermès Trismegistre I: l'astrologie et les sciences occultes*. Paris: Les Belles Lettres, 1981.

Figueira, Sérvulo A. 'Introdução: psicologismo, psicanálise e ciências sociais na "cultura psicanalítica"; Modernização, família e desorientação: uma das raízes do psicologismo no Brasil'. In *A Cultura da Psicanálise*. São Paulo: Brasiliense, 1985.

———. *O Contexto Social da Psicanálise*. Rio de Janeiro: Francisco Alves, 1981.

Frazer, Sir James. *The Golden Bough: a Study in Magic and Religion*, Vol. 1. London: Macmillan, 1980.

Freeman, Martin. *How to Interpret a Birthchart*. Wellingborough: The Aquarian Press, 1980.

Gans, Herbert. *Popular Culture and High Culture: An Analysis and Evaluation of Taste*. New York: Basic Books, 1974.

Goody, Jack. *The Domestication of the Savage Mind*. Cambridge: Cambridge University Press, 1977.

———. Introduction to *Literacy in Traditional Societies*. Cambridge: Cambridge University Press, 1968.

Goody, Jack and Ian Watt. 'The Consequences of Literacy'. In *Literacy in Traditional Societies*, edited by Jack Goody. Cambridge: Cambridge University Press, 1968.

Granet, Marcel. *La Pensée Chinoise*. Paris: Albin Michel, 1981.

Guénon, René. *A Crise do Mundo Moderno*. Lisbon: Veja, 1977.

———. *Os Símbolos da Ciência Sagrada*. São Paulo: Pensamento, 1984.

Hartner, Willy. 'Mediaeval Views on Cosmic Dimensions and Ptolemy's "Kitāb al-Manshūrāt"'. In *L'Aventure de l'esprit: Mélanges Alexandre Koyré*. Vol. I. Paris: Hermann, 1964.

Hone, Margaret. *The Modern Textbook of Astrology*. Essex: L.N. Fowler, 1980.

Horton, Robin. 'African Traditional Thought'. In *Witchcraft and Sorcery*, edited by Max Marwick. Harmondsworth: Penguin, 1970.

Hubert, Henri and Marcel Mauss. 'Esboço de uma Teoria General de Magia'. In *Sociologia e Antropologia*, Vol. 1, edited by Marcel Mauss. São Paulo: EPU e Edusp, 1974.

Jorgensen, Danny L. 'The Esoteric Community: An Ethnographic Investigation of the Cultic Milieu'. *Urban Life* 10, no. 4 (Jan. 1982): pp. 382–408.

Jung, C. G.. *Fundamentos de Psicologia Analítica: as conferências de Tavistock*. Petrópolis: Vozes, 1972.

———, *Sincronicidade, Obras Completas* Vol. 8/3. Trans. by Padre Dom Mateus Ramalho Rocha, OSB. Petrópolis: Vozes, 1984.

Kant, Immanuel. *Crítica da Razão Prática*. Lisbon: Edicões 70, 1984.

Kemper, Steven. 'Time, Person, and Gender in Singhalese Astrology'. *American Ethnologist* 7, No. 4 (Nov. 1980): pp. 744–58.

Koyré, Alexandre. *Estudos de História do Pensamento Científico*. Rio de Janeiro: Forense Universitária, Brasília: UnB, 1982.
———. *Do Mundo Fechado ao Universo Infinito*. Rio de Janeiro: Forense Universitária, 1986.
Leo, Alan. *Astrología para Todos*. Barcelona: Teorema, 1980.
Lévi-Strauss, Claude. *Anthropologie Structurale*. Paris: Plon, 1958.
———. *Antropologia Estrutural*, Vol. 1. Rio de Janeiro: Tempo Brasileiro, 1974.
———. *Antropologia Estrutural*, Vol. 2. Rio de Janeiro: Tempo Brasileiro, 1976.
———. 'Introdução à Obra de Marcel Mauss'. *Sociologia e Antropologia* , edited by Marcel Mauss. São Paulo: EPU e Edusp, 1974.
———. *La Pensée Sauvage*. Paris: Plon, 1962.
———. *A Noção de Estrutura em Etnologia: Raça e História; Totemismo Hoje*. São Paulo: Abril Cultural, 1980.
MacDonald, Dwight. 'Uma Teoria da Cultura de Massa'. In *Cultura de Massa: as artes populares nos Estados Unidos*, edited by Bernard Rosenberg and David M. White. Sao Paulo: Cultrix, 1973.
Malinowski, Bronislaw. 'Magic, Science and Religion'. In *Magic, Science and Religion and Other Essays*. Garden City: Anchor Books, 1954.
Manilius, Marcus. *Os Astrológicos: ou a ciência sagrado céu – introdução e notas de René Alleou*. Rio de Janeiro: Artenova, 1974.
Mirabail, Michel. *Dictionaire d'Ésotérisme*. Paris: Marabout, 1981.
Mondolfo, Rodolfo. *O Pensamento Antigo II: desde Aristóteles aos neo-Platônicos*. São Paulo: Mestre Lou, 1973.
Morin, Edgar. *Cultura de Massas no Século XX: o espírito do tempo I, nevrose*. Rio de Janeiro: Forense Universitária, 1977.
———. *Cultura de Massas no Século XX: o espírito do tempo II: necrose*. Rio de Janeiro: Forense Universitária, 1986.
Morin, Edgar, Philippe Defrance, Claude Fischler, and Lena Petrossian. *O Retorno dos Astrologos: diagnostic sociológico*. Lisbon: Moraes, 1972.
Mourão, Ronaldo R. de F. 'Importáncia Histórica da Astrología'. *Jornal do Brasil*, 31 Dec 1986 2, Caderno B.
Murray, Alexander. *Reason and Society in the Middle Ages*. Oxford: Clarendon Press, 1978.
Needham, Rodney. *Belief, Language and Experience*. Oxford: Basil Blackwell, 1972.
Neugebauer, Otto. *The Exact Sciences in Antiquity*. New York: Harper Torchbooks, 1962.
Oliveira, Cid de. 'Plotino e as funções fundamentais da astrologia'. In *Astrología Hoje: métodos e propostas*, edited by Ana Maria Costa Ribeiro, et al. Rio de Janeiro: Massao Ohno, 1985.
Papus. *O Ocultísmo*. Lisbon: Edições 70, 1986.
Paz, Octavio. *Os Fílhos do Barro: do Romantismo à Vanguarda*. Rio de Janeiro: Nova Fronteira, 1974.
Pouillon, Jean. 'Remarques sur le Verbe "Croire"'. In *La Fonction Symbolique: essais d'Anthropologie* edited by Michel Izard and Pierre Smith. Paris: Gallimard, 1979.

Ptolemy, Claudius. *Tetrabiblos*. Translated and edited by F.E. Robbins. Loeb Classical Library. Cambridge, MA: Harvard University Press, 1980.

Ribeiro, Ana Maria Costa. *O Conhecimento da Astrología*. Rio de Janeiro: Hipocampo, 1986.

Rosenberg, Bernard. 'A Cultura de Massa nos Estados Unidos'. In *Cultura de Massa: as artes populares nos Estados Unidos*, edited by Bernard Rosenberg and David M. White. São Paulo: Cultrix, 1973.

Rouanet, Sergio Paulo. 'A Verdade e a Ilusão do Pós-Moderno'. In *As Razões do Iluminismo*. São Paulo: Companhia das Letras, 1973.

Salem, Tania. 'Família em Camadas Médias: uma revisão da Bibliografia'. *Boletim do Museu Nacional*, no. 54 (Outubro, 1985): pp. 1–29.

———. 'A Trajetória do "casal grávido": da sua constituição à revisão do seu projeto'. In *A Cultura da Psicanálise* edited by Sérvulo A. Figueira. São Paulo: Brasiliense, 1985.

Schütz, Alfred. *Collected Papers I: the problem of social reality*. The Hague: Martinus Nijhoff, 1971.

Serres, Michel. 'Structure et Importation: des mathématiques aux mythes'. In *Hermès I: la communication*. Paris: Seuil, 1969.

Sicuteri, Roberto. *Lilith: a lua negra*. Rio de Janeiro: Paz e Terra, 1985.

Simmel, Georg. *On Individuality and Social Forms*. Chicago: University of Chicago Press, 1971.

———. *The Sociology of Georg Simmel*. New York: The Free Press, 1954.

Smith, Pierre. *Le Fonction Symbolique: essais de anthropologie*. Paris: Gallimard, 1979.

Sperber, Dan. *Le Symbolisme en Général*. Paris: Hermann, 1974.

Tester, S. J. *A History of Western Astrology*. London: Boydell, 1987.

Thomas, Keith. *Religion and the Decline of Magic: studies in beliefs in sixteenth and seventeenth century England*. Harmondsworth: Penguin, 1973.

Todorov, Tzvetan. *Les Théories du Symbole*. Paris: Éditions du Seuil, 1977.

Truzzi, Marcelo. 'Definition and dimension of the Occult: towards a sociological perspective'. In *On the Margins of the Visible: sociology, the esoteric and the occult*, edited by Edward Tiryakian. New York: Willes, 1974.

Tucker, William. *L'Astrologie de Ptolomée*. Paris: Payot, 1981.

Tiryakian, Edward, ed. 'Preliminary Consideration: toward the sociology of esoteric culture'. In *On the Margins of the Visible: sociology, the esoteric and the occult*. New York: Willes, 1974.

Velho, Gilberto. *Desvio e Divergência: uma crítica da patologia social*. 5th ed. Rio de Janeiro: Jorge Zahar Editora, 1985.

———. *Individualismo e Cultura: notas para uma antropologia da sociedade contemporânea*. 2nd ed. Rio de Janeiro: Jorge Zahar Editora, 1987.

———. *Nobres e Anjos: um estudo de tóxicos e hierarchia*. São Paulo: USP. Tese de Doutorado, 1975.

———. *Subjetividade e Sociedade: uma experiência de geração*. Rio de Janeiro: Jorge Zahar Editora, 1986.

Veyne, Paul. *Les Grecs, Ont-ils Crus à Leur Mythes? essai sur l'imagination constituante.* Paris: Seuil, 1983.

Vickers, Brian. 'Introduction: Analogy versus Identity; the Rejection of Occult Symbolism'. In *Occult and Scientific Mentalities in the Renaissance.* Cambridge: Cambridge University Press, 1984.

Weber, Max. *A Ética Protestante e o Espirito do Capitalismo.* São Paulo: Pioneira, Brasília: UnB, 1981.

———. 'Rejeições religiosas e suas direções'. In *Ensaios de Sociologia.* 4th edition. Rio de Janeiro: Jorge Zahar Editora, 1979.

White, David M. 'A Cultura de Massa nos estados Unidos: outro ponto de vista'. In *Cultura de Massa: as artes populares nos Estados Unidos,* edited by Bernard Rosenberg and David M. White. São Paulo: Cultrix, 1973.

Yates, Frances A. *Giordano Bruno and the Hermetical Tradition.* London: Routledge and Kegan Paul; Chicago: The University of Chicago Press, 1964.

INDEX

acupuncture, 110, 143, 163
Adler, Oskar, 43–44
aesthetics, 28
African societies, 58, 79
Age of Aquarius, 18, 152
Age of Iron, 163
Age of Pisces, 18
AIDS, 60
alchemy, xv, 29, 149, 151, 161
allegory/-ies, 77, 129
Allen, Woody, 104
Amazonia, 176
analogy, 36, 45, 54, 56–57, 152
anthropology, xi, 14, 64, 68, 75, 94, 111, 123,
     166, 181
antiquity, 5–6, 15, 125–26
Apollo, 130
Appadurai, Arjun, xviii
Aquinas, St. Thomas, 85
Arab civilization, 6
Arabic Parts, 18
arbitrary/-iness, xv, 45, 124
archetype/-al, 41, 130, 134, 149, 154, 183
Argentina, xxii–xxiii
Ariadne, 130
Aries, (see zodiac signs)
Aristotle, 26–27, 41, 47, 48
Arroyo, Stephen, 13, 30, 33, 41, 44, 48, 55–
     56, 61, 113, 119, 128, 187
art, 69, 81–82, 97–98, 100–102, 109, 129–
     31, 143, 187
Asia, 53
Ascendant, the, (see natal chart)
aspect/-s (planetary), 21, 25, 51, 54
     conjunction, 21, 51; opposition, 21, 51
     orb, 21; sextile, 21, 51; square, 21, 51, 63
     trine, 21, 51
asteroids, 62
     Ceres, 62; Pallas, 62

astrology
     and science, 12
     as a language, xiv, xviii, xx–xxi, xxv, xxvi, 4,
         55, 102, 104, 106, 111, 121, 127, 142, 157,
         175, 182, 184
     authority, 9, 59, 83
     consumption of, 99–100, 105, 110–11,
         120
     courses, 1, 2, 54, 106–8, 110, 112–13, 117,
         120, 148, 171
     decline of, 12, 66, 70
     definition of, 5, 10, 99, 116–18
     historiography, 3
     history of, xiii, xv, 1, 5–6, 66
     Humanistic, 13, 113
     Jungian, xiv, xxiv
     mundane, 54
     practice of, xxi–xxii, 3–4, 8–9, 55, 87. 106–
         7, 137–49, 165, 168, 184
astronomy/-ers, 35, 45–46, 62
Aquarius, (see zodiac signs)
atheism, 168
atom/-ic energy, 27, 62
Australia/-n society, 24, 40
Augustine, St., 85, 125, 127
authority, 59, 82, 163
Ayahuasca, 176
Azande, 55, 80
Babylon/-ian astrology, 5–6, 17, 53
Bachelard, Gaston, xv, xxvi, 28–30, 41, 130,
     182
baptism, 171–72
Bauhaus, 89
Becker, Howard S., xx, 97–98, 100–3
belief/-s, xxi, xxiv, 1, 23, 76–86, 96, 114, 124,
     157, 165, 169
Bell, Daniel, 65, 130–31
Bellah, Robert, 80–82
Bible, the, 80–81, 126, 154

occultism, xxiv, 2, 69, 75, 78, 82, 91–92, 94,
123, 128, 131–32, 149–56, 159, 163, 169,
187
Oedipus, 130
Oliveira, Luiz Roberto B., 164–65
oracle/-s, 10
of Delphi, 126
Order of the Elect of Cohens, 153
Orishas, 161
Orpheus, 159
pagan, 10, 127
Pai-de-santo, 84
Pallas, (see asteroids)
palmistry (see also chiromancy), 156
Papus (Gérard Encausse), 152–53, 158–59,
169
Paris, 152
Paris Observatory, 85
pathology, xix
Paz, Octavio, 129, 131
Pennsylvania, xxiii
pensée sauvage, xiii, 23–24
Periodic Table (of the Elements), 29, 183
persona, 47
pessimism, 63
Pessoa, Ferdinand, 131
Petrossian, Lena, 84–85, 90
phenomenology, xvii
Phillipson, Garry, xii
Philo of Alexandria, 127
phosphorus, 183
physics, 15, 26–27, 41
Piaget, Jean, 130
Pico della Mirandola, 161
Pisces, (see zodiac signs)
Placidus, 19
Planet X, 62
planets, 15, 17, 19–21, 35, 40, 44–46, 48–51,
52, 54–55, 59–64, 104, 140, 162, 182
earth, 5, 15, 19, 46, 49, 50
Jupiter, xv, 19, 21, 46, 50, 51, 61, 62, 63
Mars, xxi, 19, 21, 46, 49, 51, 55, 62, 63, 161
Mercury, 19, 21, 46, 49, 50, 59, 62

Moon, the, 16, 18, 19, 21, 45, 46, 47, 48,
49, 50, 51, 55, 59, 62, 104, 141, 155
Neptune, 18, 19, 45, 61, 139, 140
planets, (con't),
outer, xiii, 45, 59–61
Pluto, 18, 19, 45, 60–62, 119
Saturn, xv, xxi, 19, 46, 50, 51, 61, 63, 104
Sun, the, 15, 16, 18, 19, 31, 39, 45, 46, 47,
48, 49, 50, 55, 59, 62, 63, 127, 139, 141,
155
Uranus, 18, 19, 45, 61, 136, 140, 143
Venus, xv, 19, 46, 49, 50, 51, 55, 62, 63,
161
Vulcan, 62
planetary cycles, 18, 47
Plato, 77, 80–81, 159, 162
Plotinus, 127
Plutarch, 126
Pluto, (see planets)
polysemy, xxi, 44, 124, 136
polytheism, xvii
Pope, the, 115, 178
Popper, Karl, 58
Portugal, 171
positivism, 56
postmodernism, xviii, xxi, 88, 131
Pouillon, Jean, 78–81, 86
prediction, xviii–xix, xxii, 83, 107, 114, 121,
135, 168
prestige, 105
primitive knowledge, 7–8, 22, 34
primitive societies, 53, 58, 79–80, 111
privilege, 96, 185
Protestant/-ism, 166
psychoanalysis, xv, xviii, xxii, xxiv, 62, 73, 89,
114–17, 124–25, 132–50, 152, 156, 158,
165, 174, 178, 186
Kleinian, 148–49
psychology (see also Jungian psychology),
13, 114, 123, 132, 146, 177, 187
psychotherapy, xix, xxii, 13, 115
Ptolemy, Claudius, 5, 46, 48–50, 59, 62, 64
Purple Rose of Cairo, The, 104

Sophia Centre Press

http://www.sophiacentrepress.com/

The Sophia Centre Press is a spin-out company from the University of Wales Trinity Saint David. It specialises in studies in cosmology and culture. It publishes in association with the Sophia Centre for the Study of Cosmology in Culture:

http://www.uwtsd.ac.uk/sophia/

www.ingramcontent.com/pod-product-compliance
Lightning Source LLC
Chambersburg PA
CBHW072103020426
42334CB00017B/1618